CLACTON PIER

The first 150 years

THE PIER THEATRE
BATHING DANCING FISHING
SKEEBALL
AMERICAN SODA FOUNTAINS
BLUE LAGOON LOUNGE
COFFEE SPECIALISTS
HEALTHY HAPPINESS

DEVELOPING PRINTING
MURRAYS PHOTOGRAPHS
FILMS CAMERAS POST-CARDS

DANCING
LYONS
ICE CREAM

CLACTON PIER
FREE ENTRY
FREE ENTRY
OSCARS
CHIPS

CLACTON PIER
FISH & CHIPS

CLACTON PIER

The first 150 years

Norman Jacobs

Clacton Pier Co. Ltd.

Published by Clacton Pier Co. Ltd.
No. 1 North Sea, Clacton-on-Sea, CO15 1QX United Kingdom
www.clactonpier.co.uk
www.Facebook.com/Clactonpier

This edition published 2022
Limited Hardback edition: 978-1-7391035-0-7
Paperback edition: 978-1-7391035-1-4

*Dedicated to the memory of my late son, Tom,
who spent many happy hours on Clacton Pier.*

British Library Cataloguing-in-Publication Data:

A catalogue record for this book is available from the British Library.

Designed and printed by Green Square (greensquare.me).

Contents

ACKNOWLEDGEMENTS

First and foremost, I would like to thank Billy and Elliot Ball for asking me to write this celebration of 150 years of Clacton Pier. I have thoroughly enjoyed researching and writing it and I have found out so much more about Clacton's iconic building in the process.

I would also like to thank other members of Clacton Pier staff for all their help and co-operation, in particular, Nigel Brown, my main contact and facilitator throughout all this, and Peter Watts, who has been an unbelievable mine of information, supplying not just his memories but also some amazing photos and plans from The Pier's own archives.

I am also indebted to former owners of The Pier and their families for all the magnificent support they have given, to Peter and Susan Kingsman for their memories, some amazing photos and other memorabilia from their father and grandparents' time; to Michael Goss also for his memories and for his equally amazing collection of photos, news cuttings and artifacts which he has donated to The Pier and which I got first go at! Also to John Threadwell and Ted Harrison for taking the time and trouble to talk to me about Clacton Pier under their ownership and to Pauline McGinty for the informative chat about the history of the Jolly Roger Café (as well as the free coffee!).

Much information on Teddy Dobbs and his band was kindly provided by his grandson, Andy Dobbs, along with permission to reproduce his photographs.

Outside The Pier, I would like to thank the Clacton & District Local History Society, especially George Hardwick and Roger Kennell, who have been more than happy to help me with their own research findings. I am also indebted to Clacton Museum, in particular the archive of local newspapers with its invaluable store of first hand reports on Pier events of the past.

Many Society members have also helped with their own memories and photos directly or via its Facebook page. I would also like to acknowledge Bernard Polley's exhaustive research into the Rambla Concert Party and the Ocean Theatre and his foresight in depositing his work with the Society.

Martin Allen has been an amazing source of information, especially on the Dolphinarium but also on other aspects of Pier History, both in personal conversation and also from his website, https://www.dolphin-art.co.uk/ Many of the photos in the section, "North Sea World" are from his collection and are reproduced with his permission along with Peter Bloom's.

Reg Young, who willingly handed over his folder of information on the history of Clacton entertainments which contained much information particularly on the Ocean Theatre as well as spending time with me recounting his own memories.

To Matt Zawadzki, archivist at the National Fairground and Circus collection, Sheffield University, for all his invaluable help and support.

To Newsquest for permission to reprint articles and photos from the Clacton Gazette.

Many individuals have contributed photos and memories. In particular I should like to mention, Robert Gunthorpe, Carole Star, Harry Francis, Jan Stedman, Suzette Mizen, Dave Humphrys, Paul Chandler, Dan Burrell as well as all those whose names are mentioned in the book itself.

The team at Green Square, Steve Green, Mick Smith and Kim Allen, for their invaluable advice and for making such a wonderful job of putting the book together in such a readable and attractive manner.

Cover photograph by Matthew Mallett.

Foreword

By Billy and Elliot Ball

It is hard to believe that it is now more than 13 years since we took over the ownership of Clacton Pier from the Harrison family.

On the other hand, a great deal of work and investment has taken place and we have achieved so much in what is a relatively short period of time in this iconic landmark's 150-year history.

[Photo: Kevin Jay]

Everyone involved in The Pier over the past decade or so – family, friends, staff, contractors, suppliers and tenants – have pulled together to help get us to where we find ourselves today. An amazing transformation has taken place which we believe makes us the number one attraction of our kind on the east coast.

We have created a truly 52-weeks a year attraction which employs more people and offers many more facilities for our visitors to enjoy.

It has been a steep learning curve and we continue to discover more each and every day. There have been many long days and sleepless nights; challenges to take on at every turn; meetings with all kinds of organisations from both the public and private sectors; new rides brought in; an array of projects both small and large undertaken, culminating in the biggest single investment in The Pier's history which started in 2017 and was completed in 2019.

One of the most recent projects is this book – a celebration of The Pier's first 150 years and of the families and businesses who have played their parts in keeping it afloat (in all senses of the word). It is an honour and privilege for the Balls to be the latest in the line to have done so – but it also comes with a great deal of responsibility.

All profits from the book will be put towards maintaining The Pier structure deck down. This means being used for its upkeep and helping to ensure it is here for at least another 150 years for future generations to enjoy and make happy memories.

Most of our visitors only really involve themselves with the deck up, but there is so much going on underneath which must support the rides, attractions and buildings on top. Without it, there would be no Pier.

We also need to raise awareness of the vulnerable buildings, such as the Jolly Roger, which require attention if they are to survive longer term. Included in this vision is attracting outside funding that is desperately needed to achieve our goals and provide valuable facilities for the community to use and enjoy.

Although The Pier has reached the 150-year milestone, it is far from the end of the story, and we have other major plans in the pipeline. The future is all about creating a destination attraction that the people of Clacton and the Tendring district as a whole can be truly proud of. We aspire to be a business that has its roots firmly in its community, and hope that our efforts to return The Pier to its former glory are a catalyst to seeing the rest of the town and its businesses prosper.

To mark the first century and a half we have published this book to chart The Pier's evolution and the many changes that have taken place over that time. We hope that you will enjoy looking back with us.

There are many people who have helped us along the way in our journey, both in writing this book and in improving and regenerating The Pier and we would especially like to thank.

Billy & Lynn Ball

None have energised and motivated us more than our late parents, Billy and Lynn Ball. They have both encouraged us throughout our lives and in everything we do. Without their support and guidance we would not have achieved our dream of taking over The Pier, nor would we have had the same kind of determination to make it what it is today. We owe them everything and their memory will always continue to inspire and drive us to be the best we can be.

The Harrision Family

Ted Harrison, along with his late father Ted Snr, gave us the exclusive opportunity to purchase The Pier back in 2008. Without their confidence and support we would have been unlikely to have achieved our goal and we will always be grateful for the chance they gave us.

Roy Ruffler

Roy has been a close friend of our family for many years and his guidance and support has been invaluable in our achievements.

Norman Jacobs

We would also like to thank Norman Jacobs for his hard work and dedication. He has done a wonderful job of writing this book and in collating the wider history of The Pier and separately our town.

Chapter One The Origins

The opening of the Royal Hotel in 1872. This is the first known photograph of both Clacton Pier and Clacton-on-Sea.

Although Clacton Pier was opened on 18 July 1871, its origins date back to 1865. At that time the area we now know as the centre of Clacton-on-Sea was simply known as Clacton Beach, named after the nearby village of Great Clacton. It was mostly farmland with just a few cottages scattered along a road then known as Rosemary Lane (now Rosemary Road) to house the coastguards who were stationed there to keep an eye out for the smuggling that used to go on off Clacton Beach during the 18th and early 19th centuries.

Much of the land that made up Clacton Beach belonged to a farm called Seaside House Farm, which was situated on the corner of what is now Station Road and Rosemary Road.

In October 1779, this farm was acquired by a St Osyth man called William Howard. When he died in 1809 he left the land in trust to his daughter, Elizabeth. One of the conditions of this Trust was that the land could not be sold during the lifetime of Elizabeth or her husband, William Watson. It was for this reason that, in the early and mid 19th century, just at the time when a visit to the seaside was beginning to become fashionable and entrepreneurs were looking to cash in on this new craze of sea bathing by buying up land on the coast to turn into seaside resorts, the area around Clacton Beach was safe from any such development.

Elizabeth Watson died in 1848 but her husband lived on until November 1864, and it was with his death that the Trust conditions at last expired and the farmland could now be put up for sale. The Watsons' son, Joseph Yelloby Watson (known generally as J Y Watson), lost no time in advertising the property for sale.

And so it was that just a few months later, in April 1865, the press carried an advertisement announcing that an auction was to be held in "*June or July next*" at which the "*valuable freehold building land*" known as Clacton Beach was to be sold off in lots. The advert went on to mention "*the fine sandy beach*", "*the purity of the air*" and the "*extraordinary healthiness of the place.*" At the bottom of the advert, Watson added that he was willing to discuss the possibility of selling the whole as one lot prior to the auction.

One man who was interested in buying the whole lot was Peter Bruff, who saw the opportunity to

GREAT CLACTON BEACH

To Building Societies, Builders, and others

VALUABLE FREEHOLD BUILDING LAND FOR SALE

Forming the Cliff portion of the late W. Watson, Esq.

The fine Sandy Beach at Great Clacton, the purity of the air, and the extraordinary healthiness of the Place, particularly for Children, has long rendered it a favourite resort for the searcher after health and quiet, notwithstanding the very limited accommodation afforded, and, but for the impossibility during the last 50 years of obtaining the Cliff for building purposes, Great Clacton would have become what it deserves to be, the principal watering place on the East Coast.

The Weeley Station of the Tendring Hundred Railway will shortly render the place more easy of access, and, as several applications have already been made for Building Land, the Executors of the late Mr. Watson have determined to offer for Sale (in Lots) in June or July next—unless previously disposed of by private treaty—about 50 acres near the Sea, and the only available Land to be had for Building.

Any one disposed to treat for the whole in one Lot may apply to Mr. J. Y. Watson, Roupell Park, Brixton, Surrey.

The auction announcement that appeared in the newspapers.

create and plan a brand new high-class seaside resort entirely to his own specifications exactly as he wanted. Originally from Portsmouth, but by now domiciled in East Anglia, with houses in both Ipswich and Walton-on-the-Naze, Bruff was a civil engineer and currently engineer in chief of the railway line being built from Colchester to Walton (the Tendring Hundred Railway).

He was a remarkable example of a Victorian entrepreneur. As well as overseeing the work on the Walton line, he was also involved with the development of both Walton and Felixstowe as seaside resorts and with civil engineering projects in Colchester, Harwich, Ipswich and Lowestoft. He had also been responsible for the London to Colchester, Colchester to Ipswich, Ipswich to Norwich and Norwich to Spalding railways. He had designed the Colne Valley Viaduct and was owner of the Clifton Baths, Walton. He was actively involved in Colchester politics and served on the Board of Improvement Commissioners for Walton, the forerunner of the Town Council. As if all that wasn't enough he also made time to found the Tendring Hundred Waterworks Company.

At the time Seaside House Farm came up for sale, as well as building the Walton railway, Bruff was investing a great deal of money in promoting Walton as a seaside resort. However, as soon as Clacton Beach came on to the market, Bruff dropped Walton overnight as Clacton appeared to be a much more attractive proposition and he saw the potential right away. Four factors attracted Bruff.

1. It was a virgin site with hardly any existing buildings and just the one road, Rosemary Lane, so he could plan it all out as he wished.
2. There was plenty of room for expansion both inland and along the coast whereas Walton was very restricted in its development potential due to its siting on a narrow headland bounded by the sea with marshes to the rear.
3. Clacton was not subject to coastal erosion to anything like the same extent as the more exposed site of Walton
4. It was near his current railway and he felt it would not take much effort to link Clacton to the line.

Consequently, Bruff bought the 50 acre site in 1865 for around £10,000. He knew that if he was to create a successful seaside resort, the first thing he had to do was to find a way to bring visitors to his new town. So he immediately sought Parliamentary powers to construct a railway from Thorpe-le-Soken to a point just 60 yards from the cliffs. In addition, he sought powers to build a 300 yard long pier to accommodate passenger ships as travelling by ship was a much more popular way of getting

Peter Bruff.

around in those days because travelling long distances by road in a horse drawn vehicle could be very uncomfortable not to say dangerous.

The Thorpe and Great Clacton Railway Act was passed in July 1866, giving Bruff permission to build the railway and pier, with the proviso that they had to be completed within five years otherwise the powers would lapse. The Act also laid down a scale of charges for landing goods at The Pier, this included 6d for a barrel of gunpowder, anchors 9d per cwt, chimney pots 3d each, 1d per cubic foot for musical instruments, 2/6d for turtles, 9d per pig and £1 for a corpse.

Even though Bruff was proposing a "*high-class*" resort, his proposals did not go down at all well amongst the village elders in the nearby ancient village of Great Clacton. They were most concerned about the effect this new town would have on their rural peace and calm. Consequently, at a village meeting just before Christmas 1865, they unanimously agreed to "*dissent from the company carrying on this scheme*". And just in case anyone was still not clear about how strongly they felt on the matter, they underlined the word "*dissent*" in the minutes - twice.

Unfortunately for Bruff, because of all his other projects, he was fast running out of money and nothing was done for several years and in 1868 his Tendring Hundred Railway Co. was forced to call in the receiver and so the railway never actually materialised under Bruff.

Still determined to go ahead with his resort however, he looked for outside finance to complete his pier and turned to the Woolwich Steam Packet Company. This company was successfully running steamers on the London to Margate route and was looking for a stopover point about the same distance north of the Thames as Margate was to the south as a way of increasing the trade on their Ipswich route. And so, in 1870, Bruff arranged to meet their chairman, William Parry Jackson, on the windswept and desolate beach at Clacton. According to Mr Jackson when later recalling the conversation they had, he said that they discussed

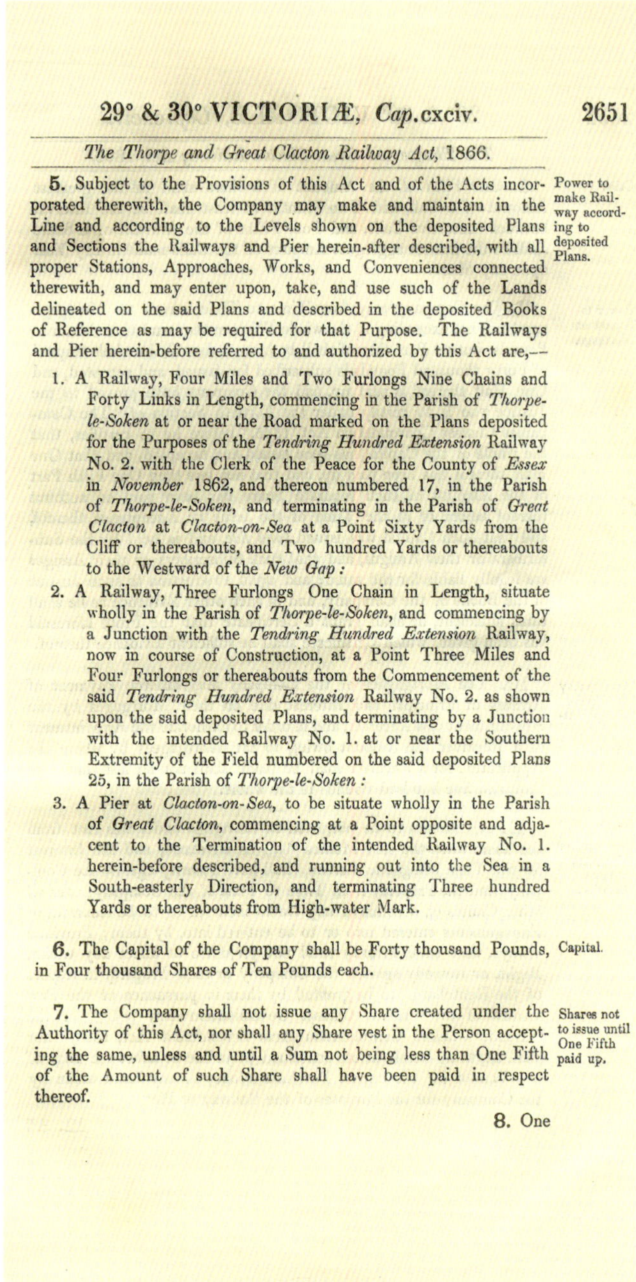

29° & 30° VICTORIÆ, *Cap.*cxciv. 2651

The Thorpe and Great Clacton Railway Act, 1866.

5. Subject to the Provisions of this Act and of the Acts incorporated therewith, the Company may make and maintain in the Line and according to the Levels shown on the deposited Plans and Sections the Railways and Pier herein-after described, with all proper Stations, Approaches, Works, and Conveniences connected therewith, and may enter upon, take, and use such of the Lands delineated on the said Plans and described in the deposited Books of Reference as may be required for that Purpose. The Railways and Pier herein-before referred to and authorized by this Act are,— Power to make Railway according to deposited Plans.

1. A Railway, Four Miles and Two Furlongs Nine Chains and Forty Links in Length, commencing in the Parish of *Thorpe-le-Soken* at or near the Road marked on the Plans deposited for the Purposes of the *Tendring Hundred Extension* Railway No. 2. with the Clerk of the Peace for the County of *Essex* in *November* 1862, and thereon numbered 17, in the Parish of *Thorpe-le-Soken*, and terminating in the Parish of *Great Clacton* at *Clacton-on-Sea* at a Point Sixty Yards from the Cliff or thereabouts, and Two hundred Yards or thereabouts to the Westward of the *New Gap :*
2. A Railway, Three Furlongs One Chain in Length, situate wholly in the Parish of *Thorpe-le-Soken*, and commencing by a Junction with the *Tendring Hundred Extension* Railway, now in course of Construction, at a Point Three Miles and Four Furlongs or thereabouts from the Commencement of the said *Tendring Hundred Extension* Railway No. 2. as shown upon the said deposited Plans, and terminating by a Junction with the intended Railway No. 1. at or near the Southern Extremity of the Field numbered on the said deposited Plans 25, in the Parish of *Thorpe-le-Soken :*
3. A Pier at *Clacton-on-Sea*, to be situate wholly in the Parish of *Great Clacton*, commencing at a Point opposite and adjacent to the Termination of the intended Railway No. 1. herein-before described, and running out into the Sea in a South-easterly Direction, and terminating Three hundred Yards or thereabouts from High-water Mark.

6. The Capital of the Company shall be Forty thousand Pounds, in Four thousand Shares of Ten Pounds each. Capital.

7. The Company shall not issue any Share created under the Authority of this Act, nor shall any Share vest in the Person accepting the same, unless and until a Sum not being less than One Fifth of the Amount of such Share shall have been paid in respect thereof. Shares not to issue until One Fifth paid up.

8. One

An extract from the Thorpe and Great Clacton Railway Act 1866 that gave permission for Clacton Pier to be built.

the salubrity of the place and its suitability for becoming a watering place. Whatever picture Bruff painted of his new town must have worked as William Jackson agreed that the Woolwich Steam Packet Company would finance the building of The Pier in return for the exclusive right of their steamers to call there.

In June 1871, the local papers were reporting that building was going well and that The Pier should be ready to receive visitors within the next couple of weeks and that a new watering place called Clacton-on-Sea would soon be open for the season. An opening date of Saturday 15 July, just one day before the five year deadline expired, was announced.

However, as 15 July approached, the Essex Herald reported that there had been a slight delay to the opening of The Pier, as, owing to adverse weather conditions and very rough seas, work had had to be suspended for a few days. Nevertheless, it was agreed that, for the purposes of beating the five year deadline set down by Parliament for the work to be completed, that 15 July would be announced as the completion date.

Following this slight delay, work quickly recommenced and it was just three days later, on 18 July 1871, that The Pier was finally opened to welcome the first steamer to call there, the SS Queen of the Orwell.

Peter Bruff, together with a large party of workmen and a few curious Great Clacton residents, were on hand at the landing stage to greet William Jackson, who had made the trip from London. As the ship drew alongside, a gun boomed from the steamer to announce the opening of the new town. Once safely landed on The Pier, the party whetted the baby's head with a toast of champagne, which the local paper says was "heartily drunk". After allowing for a very short time on shore, the Queen of the Orwell left for Ipswich with the gun booming once again to announce that a new era had begun.

Not wishing to waste time in bringing visitors to the resort, a new regular daily service from London to Ipswich via Clacton was inaugurated the very next day, July 16th, with one ship each way calling at The Pier.

Just over a week later, on 27 July 1871, the Woolwich Steam Packet Company brought 300 guests on board the SS Albert Edward to take part in the official celebrations. As The Pier was only 300 yards long, it only allowed vessels to berth during high tide and the visitors therefore had a limited stay. One couple however wandered too far inland and when they returned to the beach they found that the Albert Edward had already cast off. A small rowing boat was found to take them out to the steamship, but, as they were boarding, the lady fell into the water, apparently much to the amusement of those on board ship. Perhaps it was a symbolic baptism for the new town.

Although Peter Bruff still maintained his interest in the town by becoming a shareholder in the Woolwich Steam Packet Co., direct control for many of its undertakings now passed over to the

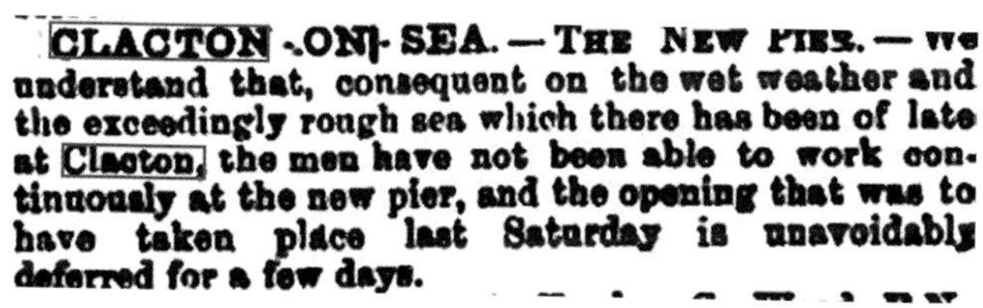
CLACTON-ON-SEA. — THE NEW PIER. — We understand that, consequent on the wet weather and the exceedingly rough sea which there has been of late at Clacton, the men have not been able to work continuously at the new pier, and the opening that was to have taken place last Saturday is unavoidably deferred for a few days.

The local newspaper article announcing the delay to the opening of The Pier.

Company under Jackson. Their next project was to build a hotel "*in order to induce people to visit the place*". It therefore floated a new company in October 1871 called the Clacton-on-Sea Hotel Co. Ltd.

The directors included Jackson and Bruff and the Royal Hotel eventually opened on 17 August 1872, just over one year after Clacton-on-Sea's official beginning.

And so, with the opening of The Pier and the Royal Hotel, Clacton-on-Sea and The Pier moved on to their next stage of development.

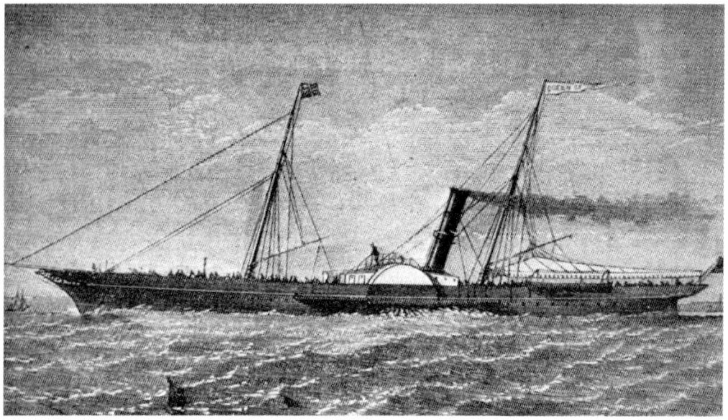

The S.S. Queen of the Orwell, the first boat to arrive at Clacton Pier on 18 July 1871, announcing the opening of both Clacton Pier and Clacton-on-Sea itself.

William Parry Jackson, Chairman of the Woolwich Steam Packet Company Ltd., the company that financed the building of Clacton Pier.

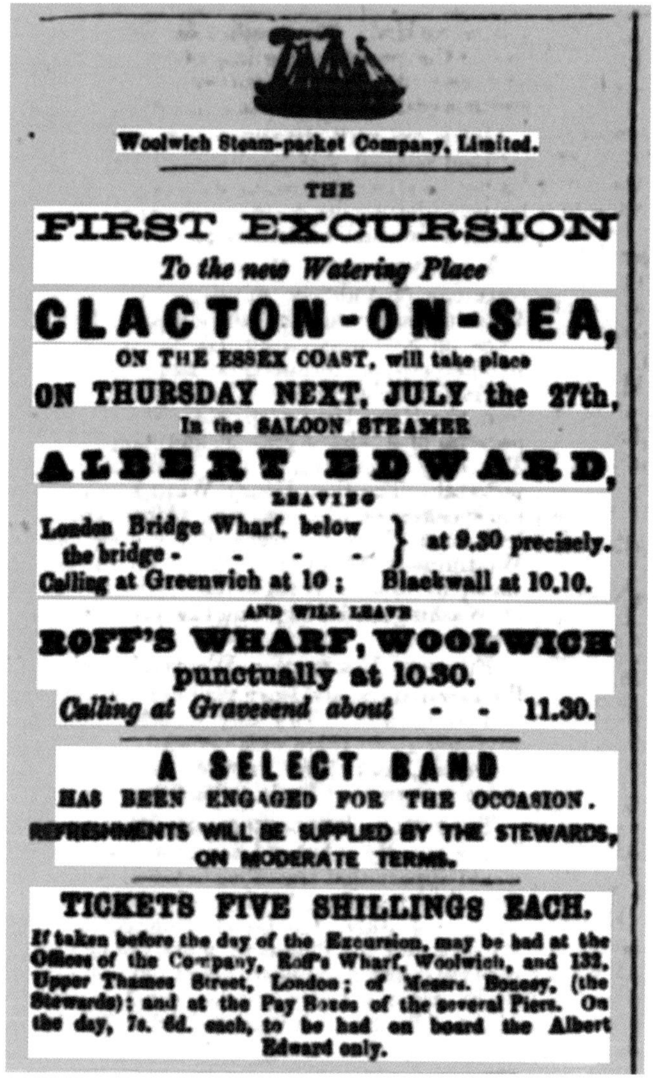

Woolwich Steam-packet Company, Limited.

THE

FIRST EXCURSION

To the new Watering Place

CLACTON-ON-SEA,

ON THE ESSEX COAST, will take place

ON THURSDAY NEXT, JULY the 27th,

In the SALOON STEAMER

ALBERT EDWARD,

LEAVING

London Bridge Wharf, below the bridge - - - - } at 9.30 precisely.

Calling at Greenwich at 10 ; Blackwall at 10.10.

AND WILL LEAVE

ROFF'S WHARF, WOOLWICH

punctually at 10.30.

Calling at Gravesend about - - 11.30.

A SELECT BAND

HAS BEEN ENGAGED FOR THE OCCASION.

REFRESHMENTS WILL BE SUPPLIED BY THE STEWARDS, ON MODERATE TERMS.

TICKETS FIVE SHILLINGS EACH.

If taken before the day of the Excursion, may be had at the Offices of the Company, Roff's Wharf, Woolwich, and 132, Upper Thames Street, London; of Messrs. Boosey, (the Stewards); and at the Pay Boxes of the several Piers. On the day, 7s. 6d. each, to be had on board the Albert Edward only.

The advert from the Woolwich Steam Packet Company announcing the official opening of Clacton Pier on 27 July 1871.

This is an engraving that appeared in the London Times to mark the opening of The Pier and the birth of the new watering place of Clacton-on-Sea and is the first known pictorial representation of both Clacton-on-Sea and The Pier as, at the time this was published, this was Clacton-on-Sea. There was nothing else, just The Pier.

And this is how Clacton would have looked to those early passengers who arrived in Peter Bruff's new town from an artist's impression of that first visit.

Chapter Two The Early Days

A view from 1884 after the Royal Hotel Hot and Cold Sea Water Baths had been opened but before the lifeboat slipways were added in 1885.

At first The Pier continued to act mainly as a landing stage for paddle steamers and as a promenade for visitors to take the air.

As Clacton-on-Sea began to grow it attracted more and more visitors and there were the first tentative moves towards providing facilities and attractions on The Pier. The first buildings for visitors to enjoy on The Pier came in the early 1880s when the weatherboard offices at the front of The Pier, which hitherto had been used by The Pier superintendent, were converted into The Pier Dining Rooms and then, in 1884, to Hot and Cold Sea Water Baths, leased by the Royal Hotel opposite.

The first alteration to the structure of The Pier came in 1885. The RNLI had established a lifeboat station at Clacton in 1877, with the lifeboat initially being housed in a lifeboat house at Anglefield and pulled down to the beach when needed by horses and launched straight into the sea. In 1884, a new bigger lifeboat was purchased which presented more logistical problems for its housing and movement, especially in the winter. And so it was agreed to build two slipways, one on each side of The Pier, to make it easier to launch with the lifeboat being stationed on The Pier from October to April.

The Pier in the late 1870s before any buildings were added.

Circa 1880 and The Pier Superintendent's offices at the entrance have now been built.

The number of visitors arriving by paddle steamer grew rapidly so that between 1880 and 1890 their number increased from 6,780 to 71,922, while the number of promenades along The Pier increased from 31,579 to a staggering 224,713.

With this ever-increasing popularity of both Clacton-on-Sea and The Pier, the Clacton-on-Sea Pier Company applied to Parliament for permission to undertake major alterations to cash in on the boom and make it even more attractive. The alterations proposed were:

1. To extend The Pier from its present 300 yards to just over 390 yards.
2. To widen The Pier by three yards each side from the shore end for a distance of 290 yards and then for a further distance of 75 yards by 12 yards each side.
3. To widen the wings of The Pier Head by the new lifeboat slipways.
4. To widen the steamer landing berth by seven yards.
5. To erect and maintain a Pavilion with all necessary and proper conveniences on the new widened Pier Head.

On 29 June 1889, the Company's solicitors, Young & Sons, were able to announce that the Bill had received Royal Assent, adding, "*these powers have not been obtained any too soon, as The Pier is very often inconveniently crowded now.*" Widening and lengthening of The Pier began almost at once and were completed in 1890.

These improvements, particularly the lengthening of The Pier, now made it easier for the paddle steamers to land at any time of the day and to stay longer before having to cast off as it was no longer necessary to wait for high tide, making Clacton even more accessible as a seaside resort and there was an even more significant increase in the number of visitors arriving in the town via The Pier.

However, with this rapid increase in the numbers of visitors, particularly from the East End of London thanks also to the eventual arrival of the railway under William Jackson, Peter Bruff's original vision of a high-class resort was changing as Clacton's image changed almost overnight, turning into the brash popular holiday resort it was to become noted as over the next century and more. Many of those who had enjoyed the peace and quiet in the early days were not happy with this change, causing one of the old school visitors to write to the local paper, the Walton and Clacton Gazette, to complain that

"*...The Pier, which was always the select promenade of the town, is now disfigured at its entrance, as I think by a stall...emitting what appeared to be a strong odour of fish. I cannot help thinking this will have some prejudicial effect on this year's receipts as the better class of visitors take a decided objection to such an affair.*"

A view of The Pier in 1893 showing much of the extension works already completed but with The Pier Pavilion still under construction.

However, the die was now cast and, with this ever-increasing number of visitors, there was a need to provide more substantial entertainments to give the visitors something to do and to make the town even more attractive. Under the provisions of the 1889 Act therefore, the Clacton Pier Company next turned its attention to building the Pavilion, which opened in 1893. Not only was this the first substantial building on The Pier to cater for visitors, but it was also the first theatre in Clacton-on-Sea as a whole.

As well as its primary purpose as a theatre, the Pavilion also provided a new restaurant on the ground floor level as well as a place to promenade on the outside of the upper deck which enabled people to obtain a good all round view of the new town.

Along with the Pavilion, other smaller attractions were built including a shooting gallery, built halfway along The Pier, as well as a Camera Obscura and various souvenir stalls.

The following year, 1894, Abraham Quick, a printer and owner of the local newspaper, the Clacton News, set up The Pier Library near the Pavilion.

THE NEW PAVILION ON PIER CLACTON-ON-SEA.

A print issued in 1893 to mark the opening of the Pavilion.

An 1884 print of the view looking along The Pier just after the Hot and Cold Sea Water Baths were opened.

This was Clacton's first lending library. Mr Quick advertised it as "*a long needed facility*", from which members of the public could "*borrow books at reasonable rates by the most popular writers of the day*", including Rudyard Kipling, Henry Wood and Wilkie Collins amongst many others. The Pier Library also sold newspapers, books and "*fancy stationery*".

So, in the space of two years, Clacton Pier was responsible for building Clacton's first theatre and opening Clacton's first lending library.

As the 19th century drew to a close, everything seemed to be going well for The Pier, which was year on year, continuing to increase in popularity and drawing more and more visitors.

However, there was a dark cloud on the horizon as, in January 1898, Clacton Pier Company was taken

The view promenaders on The Pier Pavilion balcony would have seen around the turn of the century. In the centre of The Pier are the shooting Gallery (left) and Camera Obscura (right).

A slightly stylised print of The Pier just after the Pavilion had opened which seems to have neglected the other buildings on The Pier!

over by the Coast Development Co. Ltd., which owned the former Woolwich Steam Packet fleet of paddle steamers and piers, consisting of Walton, Southwold, Felixstowe and now Clacton piers. Almost immediately they announced that, owing to difficulties arising from the silting up of the Spitway, the navigable channel off the coast of Essex, their steamers would have to approach Clacton Pier from the North, which meant they would be calling in at Walton-on-the-Naze first before coming to Clacton. Up till now, Clacton Pier had been the first port of call and many felt this was a big blow to the Clacton tourist trade as visitors would prefer to get off at the first stop and not bother coming on to Clacton any more, especially if they were day trippers as it meant the difference between two hours on shore and just a few minutes.

Clacton Urban District Council and the Clacton Graphic newspaper campaigned vigorously against this decision as they felt this reversal would prove disastrous to Clacton's growing holiday trade. Their view was that the silting up of the Spitway needed to be addressed by Trinity House, who should organise dredging, but that, in any case, just reversing the order actually made no difference to shipping as Walton was just as affected as Clacton by the Spitway silting up. Consequently, many in Clacton felt the Coast Development Company's decision had nothing to do with problems with the Spitway and more to do with trying to give Walton Pier a boost at the expense of Clacton. One councillor in particular, Councillor Daines, took it upon himself to get to the bottom of the Coast Development Company's

The souvenir stall, one of the new additions in the 1890s.

decision and made it his personal mission to "*get to the truth*".

The Council's initial response was to threaten to build a second pier and to invite another shipping company, New Palace Steamers Ltd., the opportunity to run a rival service, but Councillor Daines' dogged investigation, together with all the bad press the Coast Development Company was receiving, eventually led to the sudden "discovery" of a new navigable channel, which would allow the steamers to call at Clacton first after all. This new Channel was dubbed by the press, Daines' Spitway and, at the beginning of 1902, the Coast Development Company agreed to revert back to Clacton first.

As it happened, the disastrous effect on Clacton's holiday trade that the Council and many in Clacton had feared did not materialise as Clacton-on-Sea had, by this time, already become a very popular seaside resort with many attractions, making Clacton the object of visitors' reasons for a day out and not the trip down the Thames, so they just abandoned the Belle Steamers and took to the trains instead. Far from Clacton being affected, it was the Belle Steamer trade and the Coast Development Company which lost out. So much so in fact that by 1905, the Coast Development Company found itself in financial difficulty and was wound up and its assets taken over by a new company, the Coast Development Corporation.

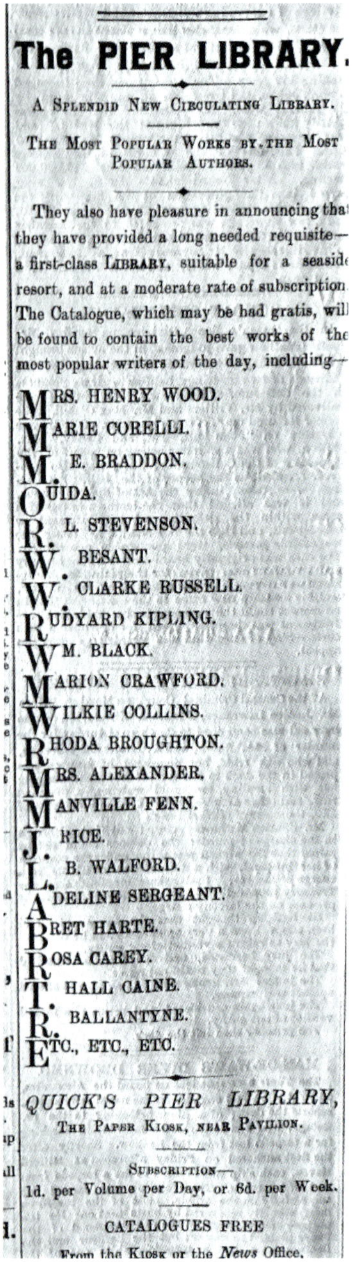

The PIER LIBRARY.

A Splendid New Circulating Library.

The Most Popular Works by the Most Popular Authors.

They also have pleasure in announcing tha they have provided a long needed requisite— a first-class Library, suitable for a seasid resort, and at a moderate rate of subscription The Catalogue, which may be had gratis, wil be found to contain the best works of the most popular writers of the day, including—

Mrs. Henry Wood.
Marie Corelli.
M. E. Braddon.
Ouida.
R. L. Stevenson.
W. Besant.
W. Clarke Russell.
Rudyard Kipling.
Wm. Black.
Marion Crawford.
Wilkie Collins.
Rhoda Broughton.
Mrs. Alexander.
Manville Fenn.
J. Rice.
L. B. Walford.
Adeline Sergeant.
Bret Harte.
Rosa Carey.
T. Hall Caine.
R. Ballantyne.
Etc., etc., etc.

QUICK'S PIER LIBRARY,
The Paper Kiosk, near Pavilion.

Subscription—
1d. per Volume per Day, or 6d. per Week.

CATALOGUES FREE
From the Kiosk or the *News* Office.

An advert for The Pier Library in the local paper, August 1894.

Following this slight hiccup to its smooth running, Clacton-on-Sea continued to grow as a popular holiday retreat, for Londoners in particular. More facilities were continually being added to The Pier during the Edwardian period, mostly at the shore end, where the baths were expanded and a new café built as well as a photographic studio, new shops and a new booking office for both the Pavilion and the steamers and it continued to attract visitors in their tens of thousands each week with many visiting The Pier just to promenade, take in a show at The Pier Pavilion or visit the other entertainments and amusements rather than use it for its original purpose as a landing stage.

However, all this was about to come to an abrupt end when the First World War broke out in 1914. Visitor numbers dropped drastically and the Coast Development Corporation fairly soon went bankrupt. But, in some ways it was this very bankruptcy that was to lead on to the golden age of Clacton Pier and of Clacton-on-Sea itself as we shall see in chapter three.

Abraham Quick's newsagent and library in 1906.

A nice late 1890s' view of The Pier Entrance.

The Pier just before the First World War showing the new additions at the front.

All the improvements to The Pier brought the crowds flocking in their tens of thousands during the late Victorian and Edwardian period.

Chapter Three The Kingsman Years, Part One, 1920-1939

The Pier shortly after the Kingsman family bought it in 1922. A new Soda Fountain is being advertised in the building on the left.

The First World War ended in 1918 and Clacton gathered itself to resume its role as a leading seaside resort. There was just one problem and that was that its main attraction, Clacton Pier, had been neglected throughout the War, it was very run-down and its owners had gone bankrupt. However, it was the arrival of one man and his family in 1920, who were to do more than anyone else to not only return The Pier to its former pre-eminent status, but to far exceed that and, by doing so, propel Clacton-on-Sea to the very top of the seaside resort league in this country. That man was Ernest Kingsman and together with his wife, Ada and his son, Herbert, known to everyone as Barney, they were to control the fortunes of both The Pier and, to a large extent, Clacton-on-Sea itself for the next 50 years.

During the Great War, he became involved with the YMCA in welfare work for former soldiers and bought up some disused army huts near Lowestoft with the idea of starting a holiday camp for them. But he needed to be able to make cheap fares available to make it pay. Consequently, he approached the railway company with a view to enlisting their support for such a worthy cause, asking them if they would provide free, or, at least very cheap transport, to take the ex-soldiers from London to Lowestoft. Unfortunately, railways were still under war-time Government control prior to reorganisation and the Government refused his request, offering return tickets at 33s 6d. The bus companies were not much better, asking for 28s 6d.

Not wanting to give up on his idea, Kingsman then turned to the steamer trade and contacted the Coast Development Corporation to see if he could charter their fleet of Belle Steamers to take the ex-soldiers to Lowestoft. It was through doing this that

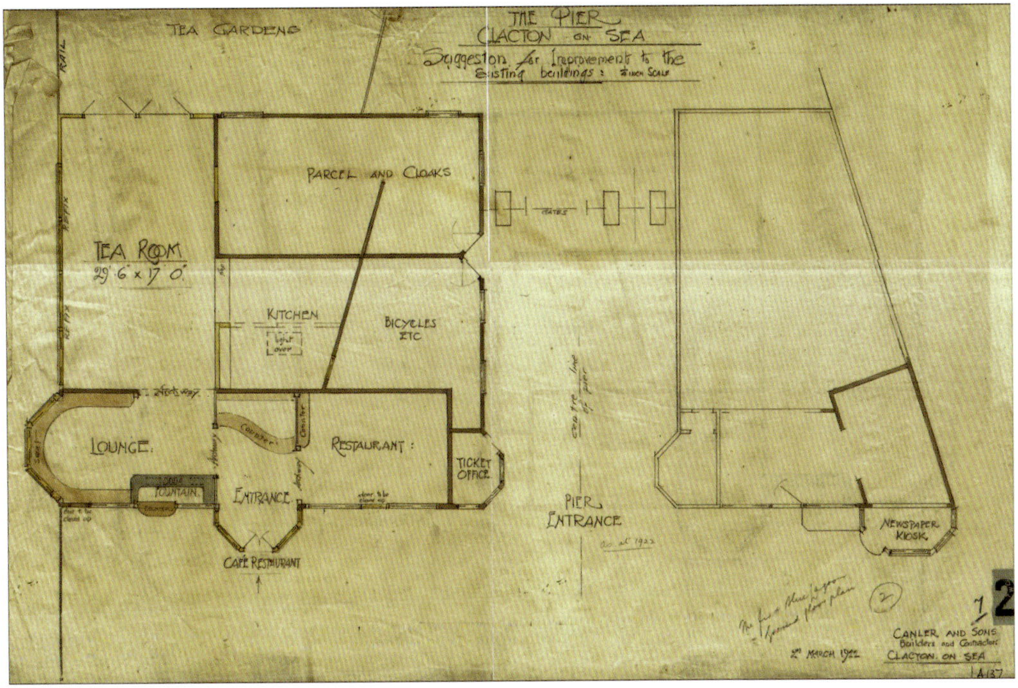

Ernest Kingsman's initial plan for improvements at the front of The Pier drawn up in 1922. The plans included a new tea room, restaurant and storage areas on the left hand side.

he learnt that the Coast Development Corporation was in liquidation and so he approached the receiver with a view to taking out a year's lease on their steamer services rather than just charter them, which was agreed. And so, in 1920, Kingsman was able to use the steamers, not only for his primary purpose of taking ex-soldiers to his camp in Lowestoft, but he was also able to re-establish the pre-war services to Clacton, Lowestoft and Southwold for the general public.

It was through this that Ernest Kingsman made his first acquaintance with the derelict Clacton Pier. At that time, all that was left on The Pier was the Pavilion at one end and a couple of small shops at the entrance, all in a poor state of repair. People still went for a walk along The Pier but there was little for them to do and it was listening to family conversations and overhearing remarks such as, "*This pier is as flat as a dead bass*" and "*Well that wasn't much, what shall we do now ?*" as they left it that it occurred to him that, with the right investment, it could be turned back into the popular pleasure pier it had been during the Victorian and Edwardian period and was just the right distance from London to attract a healthy visitor trade on the steamers. He felt that with the necessary capital and energy, it could be turned into a real money-making asset. Consequently, at the beginning of 1921, after discussing it with his wife, Ada, who was herself a very shrewd businesswoman, the Kingsmans approached the receiver with a view to buying Clacton Pier, but the liquidator was only interested in selling off the whole of the Coast Development Corporation's assets, which

Lagoon Dance Hall and Tea Rooms were built to the left of the entrance.

consisted of five steamers, four piers, two hotels, a waterworks and other odds and ends of property around the east coast, as one lot. The cost of the company was £350,000.

For the time being therefore, Kingsman renewed his lease on the Belle Steamers as well as one on Clacton Pier while negotiations continued over a permanent sale.

While these negotiations were going on, Kingsman began to spend money immediately on making the necessary repairs to the structure of The Pier to make it safe for visitors arriving both on foot at the land end and by steamer at the seaward end. He drove new piles into the bedrock and made extensive repairs from end to end.

He also managed to provide some rudimentary entertainment to give the visitors something to do by rigging up a tarpaulin roof over some poles under which visitors danced to a band. As it happened, 1921 was a particularly wet season and this makeshift dance hall was not too secure with the tarpaulin often sagging under the weight of the water that had gathered on top with water dripping in through numerous holes. Nevertheless, people still turned up to make use of the facility and the dancers held umbrellas over their heads as they danced while the band played with their collars turned up!

At the beginning of 1922, Ernest Kingsman was at last able to announce that he had finally acquired Clacton Pier and formed a new company called the Clacton Pier Company, which was wholly owned by Ernest, Ada and Barney, while all the rest of the Corporation's assets had been sold on to various buyers, including the PSM syndicate, owners of The Royal Sovereign, who bought the Belle Steamer fleet. He went on to say:

"The work of improving The Pier, of re-modelling the Pavilion and adapting them for visitors' enjoyment is being taken in hand at once, and it is hoped that by the summer all the landing stages will be again in use, the Pavilion fitted for entertainment and the decks made suitable for promenading, dancing or

The crowning of the first Carnival King and Queen on The Pier.

The early 1920s saw more building work begin at the front of The Pier to turn the whole entrance into a more attractive frontage.

Kingsman's original plan was partially implemented later in 1922 when the Blue Lagoon Lounge was opened.

seaside fetes, with every facility possible for boating, swimming and fishing.

"It is intended to arrange for a fleet of motor boats to convey visitors to various places of interest including Brightlingsea, Wivenoe, Mersea and Aldeburgh."

In March, he produced his first plans showing how he intended to improve the area around the entrance. These plans showed a new restaurant, lounge and tea rooms together with a fountain, a cloak room and bicycle store to the left of the entrance and a newspaper kiosk to the right.

Shortly afterwards, Kingsman was approached by a young man looking for employment as an entertainer. This is how Kingsman later described this meeting in an interview he gave to Tit Bits magazine in 1934:

"At the beginning of my second season, a young man wandered into my office and asked if he could give daily shows for the children.

He said he had done a little concert party work and could make kiddies laugh. I sent him along to my foreman with instructions for a small open-air dais to be set up, with a carpet in front for the kiddies to sit upon. It was ready that same night.

The next afternoon, I heard a hullabaloo and came out of my office to see the cause. At the end of The Pier a thousand people were standing, and scores of children sitting on the bit of carpet, and they were shrieking with laughter, while the young man, aided by a couple of children from the audience, played a burlesque drama...It was a riot – and that was the beginning of Clown Bertram..."

If he wasn't sure before, Ernest Kingsman was now certain that the future of The Pier lay in it becoming a large entertainment and amusement complex. Although paddle steamers were still arriving at The Pier, rail and even road travel had overtaken the sea in importance as a way of getting to Clacton and he knew there was no future in The Pier purely as a landing stage. His first major investment therefore was to build a proper theatre for Clown Bertram, called the Children's Theatre.

The new frontage saw the entrance to The Pier being moved to the right side.

Two of his other early additions that year were Skeeball, a game imported from America which became the latest craze in the early 1920s and the Blue Lagoon Dance Hall to the left of The Pier entrance as part of the already proposed restaurant and tea rooms complex.

Later in 1922, Ernest Kingsman came up with another original idea for increasing the number of visitors to The Pier when he proposed holding a three day Carnival on The Pier in August with a number of different events taking place. This was seen as such a good idea by Clacton Council and by the local business community as a way of increasing the visitor footfall to Clacton as a whole that they also became involved with the Carnival and a committee was set up to oversee the arrangements, in which Ernest Kingsman, of course, played a prominent part.

The building of new attractions continued throughout the 1920s. In 1927, Kingsman added a large amusement hall called the Crystal Casino in the centre of The Pier with all the latest slot machines and pinball tables plus football and cricket games, crane machines and What the Butler Saw machines. The Skeeball was incorporated into it as well as skittles games and something called flash-o-ball.

The following year another 1,000 seat theatre, the Ocean Theatre, was built and began putting on an annual Summer Variety Season.

In 1929, the PSM Syndicate, who had bought the Belle Steamer fleet, went broke and, with the demise of the company, the Clacton Belle and the London Belle were both scrapped. But Kingsman

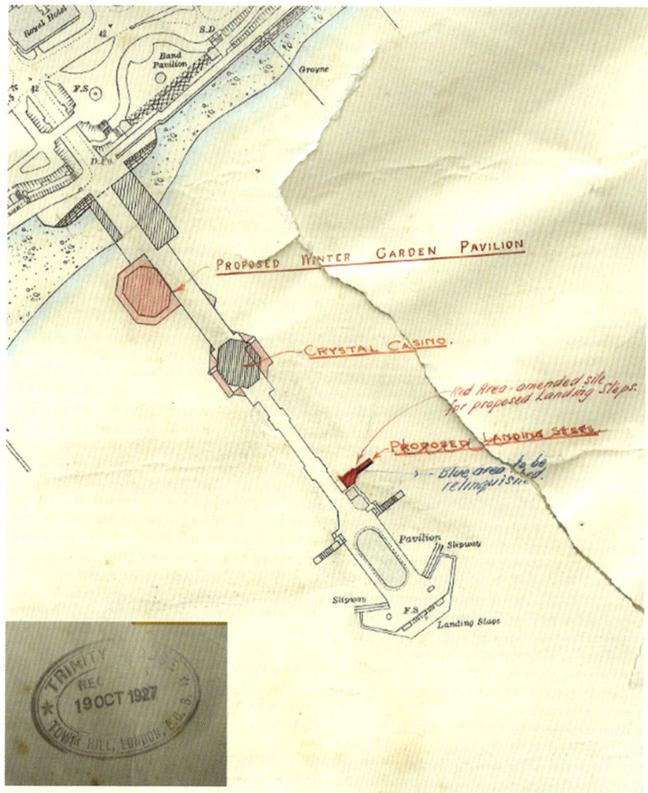

The Trinity House approved plan dated 19 October 1927 showing the proposed new Ocean Theatre building under its original title of Winter Garden Pavilion.

The Pier in 1927 after the Crystal Casino (the large building in the centre) had been built but before the Ocean Theatre.

stepped in and took the opportunity of purchasing the Southend Belle, which he renamed the Laguna Belle, and started his own service to and from London.

Also in 1929, the new lifeboat house was opened towards the end of The Pier to house the latest lifeboat, the Edward Z Dresden. Its official opening, together with the official launch of the Edward Z Dresden, came a year later in 1930 with Prince George (the Duke of Kent) performing the opening ceremony.

By the start of the 1930s, Clacton Pier was attracting visitors in their tens of thousands each week and had been turned from the derelict state it was in just ten years earlier to being well on the way to becoming one of the leading tourist attractions, not just in Clacton, but in the whole of the United Kingdom.

However, the Kingsmans wanted to go even further and on 24 June 1930, they introduced a bill into the Houses of Parliament proposing to widen the front of The Pier by some 90 feet on either side of Pier Gap, which necessitated a compulsory purchase order of land belonging to Clacton Urban District Council. The intention was to demolish the original Blue Lagoon Dance Hall and the other buildings and to build a newer much bigger building, which would include a restaurant and a new Dance Hall. The cost of the work was estimated at £60,000. The Council objected on the grounds that it would seriously interfere with the amenities of the foreshore and vehemently opposed the bill.

During the hearing in front of the House of Lords Select Committee, Mr Rowand Harker, acting as barrister for the Kingsmans, said that since purchasing The Pier they had spent something like £60,000 on improving it and turning what was a derelict pier at the time of purchase into *"a very profitable concern, one that was now central to Clacton's holiday trade with its dance hall, theatres, children's entertainment and amusements attracting tens of thousands of visitors each week during the Summer."*

In dealing with the Council's objections to the compulsory purchase order, Mr Harker quoted from the Council's own Holiday Guide, which said of The Pier:

An extremely rare photograph of the inside of the Crystal Casino showing the manager, Wally Howe on the right, with Sid Humphrys on the left.

The Pier staff in 1925. Ada and Ernest Kingsman are 7th and 8th from the left in the 2nd row from the front. 11th from the left is the "Legendary" Legerton, Robert, who was Pier Master for almost 40 years from 1891 to 1930. Pride of place in the centre of the front row is Filbert, Clown Bertram's dummy. Clown Bertram himself is 5th from the left front row.

"There is an air of welcome and a promise of entertainment about it that few can resist. It houses the largest oversea dance hall in England – the 'Blue Lagoon'; the Ocean Theatre, a large and up-to-date house for variety; and the Childrens' Theatre, where special clown entertainments are provided for the kiddies. The raised balcony surrounding The Pier Pavilion provides sheltered nooks for those who wish to enjoy the landward and seaward view at their ease."

Given the Council's own view of the importance of The Pier, Mr Harker continued, it would seem to everyone's advantage to allow the Clacton Pier Company to continue its expansion to make Clacton Pier even more attractive to visitors.

Eventually, the bill was passed in both Houses of Parliament and the compulsory purchase made.

Ernest Kingsman lost little time in taking over the foreshore around the front of The Pier and making it safe before embarking on his new improvements. His first proposal was to modernise and enlarge the existing Blue Lagoon Dance Hall in its current position and to build a new restaurant on the opposite side of the front entrance. Behind the new Blue Lagoon, he proposed building an open-air swimming pool and this was the first project which came to fruition being opened at Easter 1932 by the local M.P. and Minister for Transport, Sir John Pybus. The pool was a full size Olympic standard 50 metre swimming pool and was the first to be built on a pier anywhere in the country. Right from the start it was Kingsman's intention that the pool could be used for big national and international events, drawing in crowds not just from all over this country, but from all over the world.

1932 also saw the arrival of a fourth theatre, this time an open air theatre, Rambla, home to The Ramblas Concert Party, who were a bit of a throwback to the old Victorian style concert parties. Their stage was situated to the left of the Pavilion

The Duke of Kent, Prince George, opening the Lifeboat House on The Pier in 1930. He is shown here shaking hands with Cllr. Mrs Coleman, who was the first female Chair of Clacton Council. Notice the chalked numbers on the floor, showing everyone where they had to stand!

His next major move was to use the compulsorily purchased land at the front of The Pier and build an entirely new and much more welcoming entrance which included abandoning his original 1930 plan and completely rebuilding the Blue Lagoon Dance Hall on the right hand side of the entrance. The old Blue Lagoon held its last dance at Easter, 1934 with the new Blue Lagoon being opened on Whit Monday, again by Sir John Pybus. The new dance hall was able to cater for 750 couples on the dance floor paying 2/- per session, 10/- for a monthly pass or 30/- for the whole season.

Following the closure of the old Blue Lagoon, the building was demolished and a large circus tent erected. The circus, along with its associated zoo, proved to be a big success and continued for five seasons. It also gave Clacton an added attraction as holidaymakers flocked to see the elephants taking their exercise around the town and their daily morning dip in the sea.

A late 1920s view of The Pier entrance, showing the newly built Ocean Theatre to the right.

Along with all the changes at the front of The Pier, the Kingsmans made improvements at the seaward end with a new berthing arm enabling up to four steamers to berth simultaneously. This allowed for the companies to put on extra sailings to places other than London and the East Coast resorts, including Kent with outings to the Chatham Dockyard for example and there were even a weekly, no passports required, sailings to the continent to places like Calais, Dunkirk and Ostend, giving passengers three hours ashore including optional coach excursions to places such as Bruges and Ypres.

The Swimming Pool was opened in 1932, helping to draw large crowds to The Pier.

The Kingsmans continued to add new attractions to The Pier year on year and in 1937 a new roller coaster was erected at a cost of £2000. Named the Steel Stella, it became the iconic symbol of Clacton Pier. The following year, a new covered indoor arena was built to house the circus ring as well as a number of other amusements and rides including the dodgems.

All of these major extensions and improvements didn't come without cost, pitting Ernest Kingsman in a seemingly never-ending battle with the Government as piers were controlled by the Ministry of Transport, and, every time a major extension or improvement was made, Parliamentary approval had to be given and other departments had to have their say. For example, the Marine Department of the Board of Trade wanted to know if navigation would be affected, the Admiralty had to mark any extensions on their charts and Trinity House had to agree how The Pier was lit.

On top of that Mr. Kingsman had to buy up some of the sea-bed as the Crown owns the seabed below medium tide mark and the 3-mile limit. It was not necessary to buy all the seabed under The Pier as Kingsman bought only those parts on which the piles of The Pier were to rest. Nevertheless, it was still a costly matter. So, for example, Kingsman had to pay £1,500 for a site for the supports of his swimming pool. In all, he had to apply for nine Acts of Parliament, each of which left him "*with an extra battle-scar*", as he once explained to a magazine journalist.

By the time War broke out, something like £250,000 had been spent on improvements. A sum that today would equate to approximately £18 million. By the end of the 1930s, as well as the big structural improvements and exciting rides such as the dodgems, racing cars, the Monte Carlo Rallye Ride and the Ghost Train, many smaller attractions had been added, including an aquarium, electric boats, a mirror maze and a radio robot as well as many

With the arrival of the Rambla Open Air Concert Party, there were three theatres next to each other at the end of The Pier. From l-r, they are the Rambla Concert Party, Pier Theatre (later the Jolly Roger) and the Children's Theatre.

Lobby Lud was a popular character in the 1930s, who visited seaside resorts giving away £5 to anyone who recognised him and approached him saying, "You are Lobby Lud and I claim my £5 reward."

smaller rides for younger children, such as "Toy Town Taxis", roundabouts and small carousels. Some of these were let out as concessions and before he built his holiday camp in Clacton, Billy Butlin owned some of these. In particular, it was he who had introduced the dodgems and the racing cars on to The Pier.

In addition to the fixed attractions, Clacton Pier was also home to a number of one-off entertainments and exhibitions throughout the 1930s. One of the strangest of the former occurred in 1931 when New Zealander, William Edmund Ormerod, who was actually born in London, but had spent many years in New Zealand, where he was, as the saying goes, "known to police", set out to beat the World fasting record, which stood at 62 days. Under the stage name, Raymond Tac, he chose Clacton Pier as the place to attempt the record. He sat sealed behind a glass wall, through which spectators could view him. Living on just eight bottles of lemonade and 26 cigarettes per day as his only nourishment he managed 68 days, thus beating the World record.

As for exhibitions, there was a rose show, a "Fruit Packers" show and, in 1938, a travelling exhibition portraying a large scale model of the RMS Queen Mary.

An exhibition of a different sort came to The Pier in 1933, when a new game craze called Looparoo was introduced. In June that year, experts came along and set up by the side of the swimming pool to instruct people how to play the game, the object of which was to make a rope dance through a series of different spins. As members of the public became more proficient, the swimmers forgot about swimming and left the pool in their swimming costumes to try out the new game. The instructors returned in the evening for a repeat performance and found 2,000 members of the public waiting for them. For the rest of that season, Looparoo took Clacton Pier by storm.

A close up aerial view of the Crystal Casino and the Swimming Pool.

A mid 1930s advertising leaflet showing many of the new buildings on The Pier.

There was also a Pets' Corner on The Pier, which exhibited some common types of pet as well as the more unusual, though there was an unfortunate occurrence in 1939 when a West Indian parrot called George put on a display in front of the cage of a baboon who seemed to take exception to the display and grabbed George's tail feathers pulling them off completely.

In addition to all these shows and exhibitions, The Pier Carnival also continued as a major attraction for three days in the Summer until 1935. In 1936, however, the Carnival was taken over by Clacton Council, who centred its activities on their own newly opened Band Pavilion. But being so close to The Pier, no doubt the great majority of Carnival-goers also went on to The Pier.

By the late 1930s, there is no doubt that, with all these attractions, entertainments and amusements, Clacton Pier had become one of the best known – if not the best known - piers in the country and through the season was attracting visitors in their millions with anything up to 40,000 people in a single day passing through the turnstiles. In line with this pre-eminent status it began using the tag line "Clacton Pier – The Pier of the Realm".

In America, Atlantic City Pier had been similarly transformed and the Kingsman Family took a keen interest in its development to see if they could gain any ideas. One idea in particular that struck Barney was that Atlantic City Pier had adopted the telegraph address of No.1 Atlantic Ocean, so on 20 May 1938, he announced that from then on Clacton's telegraph address was to be No.1 North Sea, a name which became adopted to describe The Pier itself, supplanting The Pier of the Realm tag line, and how it has become affectionately known ever since.

Clacton Pier was undoubtedly a major factor in the rise of Clacton-on-Sea itself, and, by the time War broke out in 1939, though it may be hard to think of it as such these days, it was right up there with the likes of Blackpool and Brighton as one of the premier seaside resorts in the country, attracting hundreds of thousands of visitors each week during the season.

The new Blue Lagoon, opened in 1934 completing the improvements to the right side frontage.

With the old Blue Lagoon now redundant, the building was demolished and a new amusement hall built in its place. This photo shows work on the new construction taking place.

A 1934 plan showing all the new attractions.

In 1936 a large circus tent was pitched at the front of The Pier, which became home, at first to the "Old English Circus" and then later to the Royal Bengal Circus as well as a zoo.

The Circus also gave Clacton a new attraction as holidaymakers could witness the elephants daily dip in the sea.

1937 saw the construction of the new Roller Coaster, the Steel Stella. This photograph shows it in its very early stages of construction.

Building the Steel Stella continues. It is said that the steel scaffolding poles were from those erected for the spectator viewing areas at King George VI's Coronation in London.

Finished. A photo showing all the workers engaged on its construction. Ernest Kingsman is In the centre.

The first car arrives for the Steel Stella in 1937.

Ernest Kingsman (left) takes the first ride on his new attraction.

In 1938, The Pier was once again widened and a new building constructed to house both the circus in a new indoor arena as well as the amusements from the original amusement hall, including the dodgems shown in the next illustration.

The dodgems before moving into the amusement hall.

Ernest Kingsman liked to try out all his new rides to make sure they were safe and exactly as he wanted them. This shows him on the Bumper Boats.

And this shows him on the Toy Town Taxis, advertised as "Run by electricity, safe and absolutely silent."

An aerial view from the late 1930s showing all Ernest Kingsman's improvements including the new berthing arm.

Before he became famous for his holiday camps, Billy Butlin operated many fairgrounds around the country. He was also given the concession for a number of rides on Clacton Pier, ranging from this merry-go-round for young children to the more adult "Supercars", shown here.

One attraction that had survived since before the First World War, although improved and moved to a new location, was the Shooting Gallery, shown here on the left as Bisley Shooting.

Raymond Tac, who broke the world fasting record on Clacton Pier.

"Looporoo"'s enthusiasts at Clacton yesterday.

RICH BREWER KIDNAPPED

£20,000 RANSOM

PARIS, Sunday.

Mr. William Hamm, a wealthy brewer, of St. Paul, Minnesota, was kidnapped last evening and held for £20,000 ransom, and to-day the police withdrew from the case to leave the family free to carry out negotiations for his return, says the "New York Herald," Paris edition.

Mr. Hamm, who is 39 years old, was seized while walking to his home from his office. The family immediately called the police and refused to deal with the kidnappers, but later threats that Hamm would be killed caused his relatives to ask the police to withdraw.—Central News.

U.S. AND FRENCH DEBT

WASHINGTON, Sunday.

A Note addressed to France by the United States Government regarding the French war debt default says:

"The Government of the United States must in all frankness call attention to the problems raised by the failure of the French Government to meet the payment due on Dec. 15, 1932, which have not yet been solved or even discussed between the two nations."—Reuter.

GIBRALTAR TUNNEL PLAN

From Our Own Correspondent

MADRID, Sunday.

The proposed tunnel under the Straits of Gibraltar, linking Europe with Africa, now seems to be on the way towards realisation. The Minister for Home Affairs yesterday visited Algeciras, Ceuta and Tarifa, where preliminary soundings and tests are being carried out.

"Looporoo" Captures Clacton

From Our Own Correspondent

CLACTON-ON-SEA, Sunday.

"Looporoo"—the new vastly popular rope-spinning art—took Clacton-on-Sea by storm this afternoon. On the pier young and old were trying the fascinating game.

The game is mainly spectacular, the object being to make a rope dance through a number of different spins, and in the swimming pool enclosure the public were eagerly awaiting the demonstration by the experts.

Don Ray, with his clever manipulation of the looped rope, drew many bursts of applause.

Then the public tried their skill, and soon dozens of twirling ropes were seen.

"I'VE GOT IT, GIRLS!"

One young woman tried again and again, but could not get control of the whirling rope.

Suddenly a cry was heard, "I've got it, girls!" and it was seen that at last she had mastered the trick, and was competing with the experts.

Ex-Seaman Harvey, after long persuasion, tried his hand and soon became proficient. Bathers left the pool, and, clad only in their costumes, stood round the edge of the water trying a variation of the simple spin.

A film operator had no trouble in finding plenty of subjects for his pictures.

As far as Clacton-on-Sea is concerned, "Looporoo" has come to stay.

By popular demand, an extra performance of "Looporoo" was given to an audience of about 2,000 people on the Clacton Pier this evening by the instructors.

PENALTY OF THRIFT

Because she had saved sufficient to purchase an annuity of £70, Miss Mary A. Burton, formerly ward sister at the Eastern Hospital, is to lose a special gratuity recommended for payment by the London County Council.

Miss Burton retired after 32 years' service with the old Metropolitan Asylums Board, and it was recommended by the L.C.C. General Purposes Committee that she should receive a special gratuity of £82 10s.

This, in view of her savings, was half the usual gratuity.

The Minister of Health, however, stated that he was unable to sanction the proposal, and the Committee assume that this action was taken because of her savings.

Both this Committee and the Central Public Health Committee thought it inequitable that Miss Burton should lose her gratuity through making provision for her retirement.

They urged the Minister to reconsider his decision, but he has intimated that he cannot alter it.

The matter will be reported to the Council to-morrow.

BOMBING FROM THE AIR

Reservation by the British Government of the right of bombing from the air in certain circumstances, in spite of the fact that other Powers are ready to agree to abandon this weapon entirely, was severely criticised at Birmingham last night at a combined Anglican and Free Church meeting.

Among those associating themselves with the protest were the Bishop of Birmingham (Dr. Barnes), the Rector of Birmingham (Canon T. Guy Rogers), Mr. and Mrs. Barrow Cadbury, and Mr. George Cadbury.

The new Clacton Pier craze of Looparoo was reported in many of the national daily newspapers.

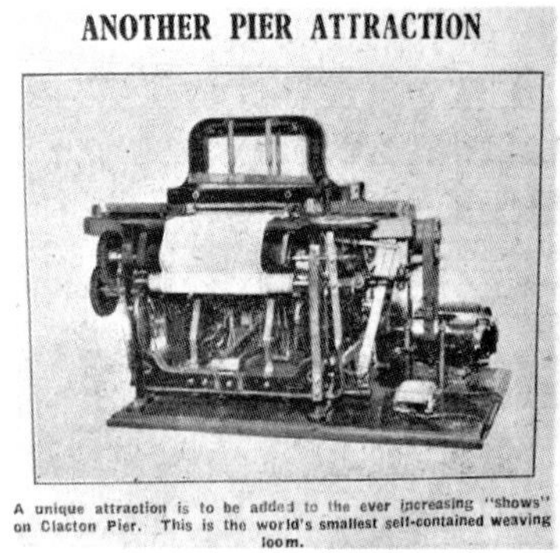

ANOTHER PIER ATTRACTION

A unique attraction is to be added to the ever increasing "shows" on Clacton Pier. This is the world's smallest self-contained weaving loom.

Nothing was too small to exhibit as this, the "world's smallest self-contained weaving loom" shows!

Ernest Kingsman arranged many exhibitions. Here he is seen to the left of the Apple Stall, part of the Fruit Packers' show.

There were also some larger exhibitions, such as the "Queen Mary Exhibition". The RMS Queen Mary made its maiden voyage in 1934, following which a nationwide exhibition tour was undertaken, with Clacton Pier being included on its itinerary.

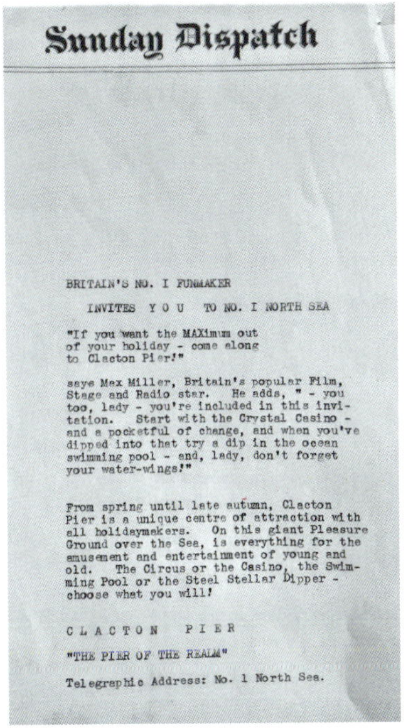

Sunday Dispatch

BRITAIN'S NO. I FUNMAKER

INVITES Y O U TO NO. I NORTH SEA

"If you want the MAXimum out of your holiday - come along to Clacton Pier!"

says Max Miller, Britain's popular Film, Stage and Radio star. He adds, " - you too, lady - you're included in this invitation. Start with the Crystal Casino - and a pocketful of change, and when you've dipped into that try a dip in the ocean swimming pool - and, lady, don't forget your water-wings!"

From spring until late autumn, Clacton Pier is a unique centre of attraction with all holidaymakers. On this giant Pleasure Ground over the Sea, is everything for the amusement and entertainment of young and old. The Circus or the Casino, the Swimming Pool or the Steel Stellar Dipper - choose what you will!

C L A C T O N P I E R

"THE PIER OF THE REALM"

Telegraphic Address: No. 1 North Sea.

No expense was spared in advertising The Pier. Even the "Pure Gold of the Musical Hall", Max Miller, was roped in to endorse and advertise Clacton Pier in national newspapers and on billboards.

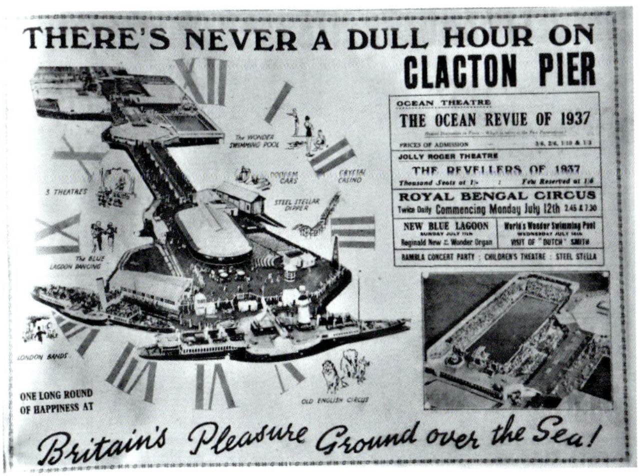

A newspaper advert showing all the attractions on The Pier.

The first cablegram sent to "No.1 North Sea" was from Clacton Pier's counterpart in America, "No.1 Atlantic Ocean", Atlantic City Pier.

By the end of the 1930s, Clacton Pier was one of the leading attractions in the country, drawing in upwards of 40,000 visitors in a single day and making Clacton-on-Sea itself one of the leading seaside resorts in the UK.

Chapter Four Clacton Pier in Wartime

With the outbreak of War on 3 September 1939, The Pier was forced to close. Although the local council was hoping it could salvage some sort of Summer Season in 1940, a number of events in the early part of the year, put paid to that idea. The first was when, on 30 January, two sea mines washed up on to the beach. Although neither exploded it was an early warning of the dangers that might befall anyone trying to enjoy a holiday on the beach, A warning that became much more stark and vivid eight days later when another floating mine did explode, this time against The Pier itself, blowing a hole sixty feet across.

The first Ernest Kingsman knew about it was when he was sitting at home having breakfast and heard an explosion. Shortly afterwards the phone rang and a voice said, *"It's your pier sir, a mine has blown it up."* Kingsman raced to the scene and found a gaping hole which had almost cut The Pier in two. The whole of the pumping plant was gone with steel girders smashed and buckled and glass from shattered glass up and down The Pier littering the ground.

Two of the lifeboat crew, including the 84 year old Tom Fairweather, were on The Pier when the explosion happened. They had just entered the lifeboat house, which fortunately escaped the worst of the blast. Tom's first words apparently were, *"I think I could do with a drink!"*

The damage caused to The Pier by the floating mine that hit it on 6 February 1940.

Alfred Colby, one of The Pier attendants was also on The Pier. He said afterwards, *"I could hear some bumping below The Pier and then there was a frightful roar and up went everything in a huge black cloud. I hung on to a post otherwise I would probably have been blown into the sea. It was a terrible sight to see great chunks of concrete being hurled about over my head."*

The gaping hole in the decking left The Pier very unsafe and made it impossible for the lifeboat crew to get to the lifeboat should they be called out. This particular problem was solved by placing a rope ladder and foot board bridges across the gap. Albert Scott, who was eight years old at the time, recalled later, *"My father took me across it a couple of times to visit the lifeboat house. I found it quite scary as the wooden slats moved in front as you walked across and it was all very open to the elements."*

The next major event came on 30 April when a German plane on a mine-laying mission was shot down and crashed on a row of houses in Victoria Road causing the first civilian deaths of the War anywhere on mainland Britain. The War and what it would mean was brought home vividly to the people of Clacton and its exposed position on the East Coast saw the Government declare Clacton-on-Sea a front line town, ordering the evacuation of all citizens who had no essential reason to remain in the town.

On 4 June, towards the end of the Dunkirk evacuation, a small boat with 30 Belgian and French soldiers landed on The Pier. They were immediately handed over to the military for cross-examination as there was some concern they could be German spies, as, at the time, the whole country was on high alert about possible fifth columnists and told to be on the look-out.

84 year old Lifeboatman, Tom Fairweather, said he "could do with a drink!"

Ernest Kingman assesses the damage caused to The Pier with a Clacton Council official.

Soon after this, the Royal Engineers arrived in Clacton to carry out defensive works, which included demolishing The Jetty, a small pier which stood at the opposite end of the beach to the main pier in the area where Billy Butlin had built his holiday camp in 1938. They also removed some of the shelters along the seafront and erected defensive barriers including anti-tank concrete blocks, barbed wire and other obstructions.

As one of their defensive measures they also intended to blow a large hole in The Pier to prevent it being used as a landing stage in case of invasion. But they had reckoned without Ernest Kingsman's personal assistant, a 24 year old young lady by the name of Clare Hamey. When the Royal Engineers

In the foreground is Clare Hamey, who single-handedly prevented the army blowing a hole in The Pier until Mr Kingsman had been consulted.

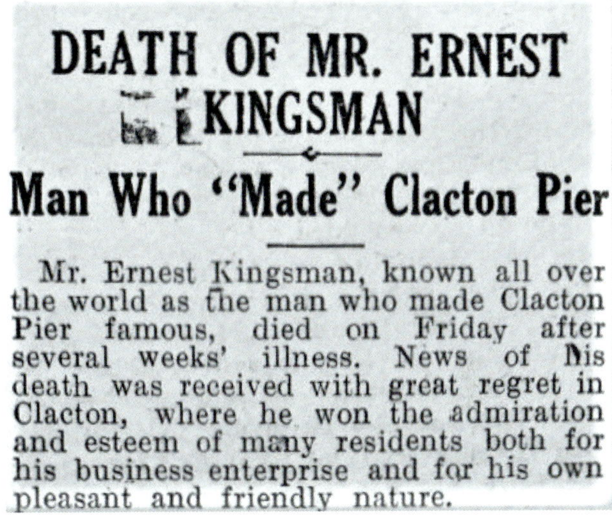

DEATH OF MR. ERNEST KINGSMAN

Man Who "Made" Clacton Pier

Mr. Ernest Kingsman, known all over the world as the man who made Clacton Pier famous, died on Friday after several weeks' illness. News of his death was received with great regret in Clacton, where he won the admiration and esteem of many residents both for his business enterprise and for his own pleasant and friendly nature.

The obituary notice to Ernest Kingsman which appeared in the local paper on 14 November 1942.

turned up, Clare was the only person present on The Pier and their senior officer announced that they were going to blow a hole in The Pier. She said, *"Have you asked Mr Kingsman's permission?"* The officer replied that he didn't need permission as it was being carried out under War Time emergency regulations. Clare maintained that she was sorry but she couldn't allow them on The Pier until they had spoken to Mr Kingsman. The officer was not amused, but his men seemed to find it all highly amusing. It was probably the strangest stand-off of the War!

In the end, Clare got her way and the army left without blowing their hole. They then contacted Mr Kingsman and told him that they intended not only to blow a hole in the centre of The Pier, but also to demolish the Children's Theatre and the Crystal Casino. The work was to be carried out over a several weeks and, on 25 May, the Royal Engineers returned to start their work with what should have been a controlled explosion but, in fact, managed to shatter windows and panes of glass in many of the neighbouring seafront properties, including the Band Pavilion, nearby tea shops and as far away as the Beaumont Hall Hotel, while a column of black smoke, 100 feet high, could be seen from miles away.

Naturally, Kingsman was not too happy about having his pier blown to pieces and several of the buildings demolished, but it was when he was told that the Steel Stella was next on the list for demolition that he dug his heels in. After consulting his solicitor, Kingsman wrote to the army, saying:

"For some considerable time the military have been demolishing parts of our pier. We have no requisition for the damage already done, which runs into several thousands of pounds. We have now been told by the military that they want to take the Steel Stella down, which cost us ten

The space left behind by the Crystal Casino after it had been dismantled by the army can clearly be seen in this late 1940s photograph.

thousand pounds to erect, and which would cost us considerably more to re-erect, as they want the material. Our solicitors say, until we get the property requisitioned and an agreement as to the value, we are not to let it be moved."

Eventually the Army gave way on this point and the Steel Stella was saved, but, ironically, in August 1941 a German plane was shot down and crashed into the sea causing some damage to the Steel Stella. Fortunately, it was only minor and the Steel Stella lived to fight another day.

The greatest tragedy to befall The Pier during wartime however was not actually connected with the War and came on 6 November 1942, when Ernest Kingsman, the man who had owned The Pier for just over 20 years and whose ambition, foresight, energy and sheer determination had transformed Clacton Pier from a derelict landing stage to one of the leading amusement and entertainment centres in the whole country, died. On his death, his wife, Ada, took over the running of The Pier along with their son, Barney.

Later on, in December 1942, The Pier found itself embroiled in an inter-service controversy not of its own making. Because of its unsafe nature, the Admiralty had banned all fishing from The Pier. It was reported however that the local army officers had issued permits for military personnel to be able to fish. As soon as the Admiralty heard about this, the First Lord contacted Clacton's M.P., Stanley Holmes, to tell him that he had personally cancelled the permits and that if Mr Holmes, or the Council, wished fishing to resume they would have to take this up with the local Flag Officer (the senior local Naval Officer). Following a report of this appearing in the local papers, the Army issued a flat denial that they had ever issued such permits and that it was all a misunderstanding and the whole matter was dropped.

For the last two and a half years of the War, Clacton Pier led an uneventful existence while Ada and Barney began preparations for its re-opening after the War.

Chapter Five The Kingsman Years, Part Two, Post War, 1945-1971

The War in Europe ended on 8 May 1945 and just one month later, Mrs Kingsman announced to the local press that Clacton Pier would be reopening on 7 July. There was, of course, much structural work to be put in place to make The Pier safe before it could fully reopen and, in fact, the only thing that reopened on 7 July was the Blue Lagoon Dance Hall with a dance to the music of Teddy Dobbs and his Band. The following day, the Blue Lagoon café opened.

The extension to the Queen Mary Building across the old Crystal Casino, with the sun deck above the new amusement arcade, also named the Crystal Casino.

Two weeks later, the amusement hall to the left of the entrance also had a limited opening, though the circus was no longer housed there.

And then on 15 August, a show entitled "A Midsummer Night's Scream – a Victory Revudeville" was held in the Ocean Theatre to celebrate VJ Day. The show was jointly staged by Ada Kingsman and Sergeant Jerome Bowick of the 16th Holding Regiment, Royal Artillery. The show was repeated the following night. Later in the year, a one-nighter was held, when local performer, Jack Chugg, staged a show called "Stardust" and then Clown Bertram re-appeared for just one children's show matinee appearance. These were the only shows performed at the Ocean Theatre that year and, for the rest of the year, the only activity on The Pier was centred on the Blue Lagoon and the Amusement Hall.

The Cresta Run Helter Skelter, another new addition built over the open space left by the demolition of the old Crystal Casino.

Roger, which staged a Variety season called The Lagoon Follies. The last major pre-War attraction to re-open was the Rambla Open Air Concert Party, which did not stage its first show until 1950.

Three major pre-War attractions did not return to The Pier at all, the Children's Theatre and the Crystal Casino, which had been demolished, and the Circus, which had to wait until the 1980s before seeing a revival. The Crystal Casino was partly replaced by an extension to the Queen Mary Building which ran along the side of the swimming pool. This extension contained a new amusement arcade, also called the Crystal Casino, downstairs with a sun-deck above. A new attraction, the Cresta Run Helter Skelter, was also built on the site of the old Crystal Casino, while a new ride for young

Many of the amusements and rides returned to action the following year as did the Ocean Theatre, which staged the first post-War edition of the Ocean Revue. However, there were still a few attractions which remained closed including the Swimming Pool, the Jolly Roger and the Rambla Concert Party.

In early 1948, Mrs Kingsman was able to announce that, apart from one or two minor areas which were still under repair, The Pier would be fully open as from Whit Saturday that year, including the swimming pool and the Jolly

The plan for the layout of the Peter Pan Railway, dated 20 April 1950.

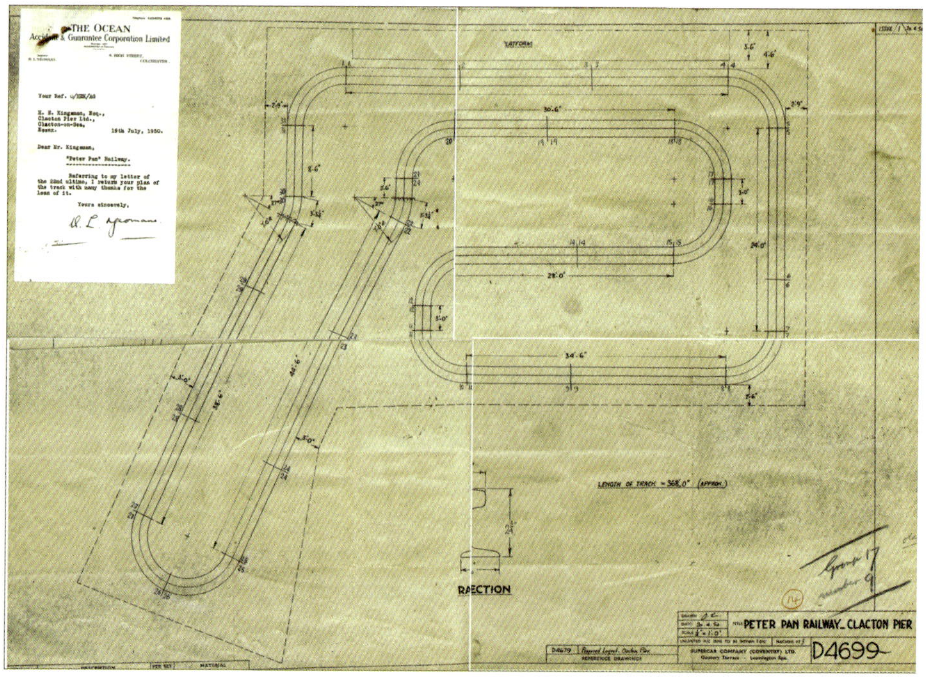

The new Peter Pan Railway.

children was added in 1950, the Peter Pan Railway, in front of the Steel Stella plus a new indoor amusement in the new Crystal Casino, the Mirror Maze.

Steamers made their come-back to The Pier in 1947 with the Golden Eagle, owned by the General and Steam Navigation Company (GSN), operating daily trips to London (Tower Pier), Greenwich and Southend. In 1951, she was replaced by the Queen of the Channel, which continued in service until 1965. As well as the service to London the No Passport trips to Calais were also reinstated.

There were also hourly trips of 12 miles along the coast from The Pier Head on the M.L. Gay Commodore for 3s 6d. with a special three hour evening cruise up the River Blackwater on Wednesdays and Sunday evenings for 7s 6d. For the more adventurous, there were short trips on Ernie Cobb's speedboat from the side of The Pier.

In the late 1940s and early 1950s, both Clacton Pier and Clacton itself continued to enjoy the boom in holidaymakers and day trippers it had enjoyed in the 1930s, with estimates putting visitor numbers at an even higher figure than the pre-War peak.

In spite of (or perhaps because of) these increasing numbers, apart from the Cresta Run and the Peter Pan Railway, there were no more large scale changes or structural improvements and for the next 10 years or so, The Pier continued to enjoy a more basic stability than it had done in the 1930s when Ernest Kingsman seemed to be making major alterations year on year.

However, the good times were not to last forever. Moving into the 1960s, with post-War austerity now receding and travel abroad becoming easier, families began deserting Clacton as a holiday destination, preferring instead to travel to places like Spain, where the warmth and the sunshine could more or less be guaranteed. At the end of the 1962 season, for example, the East Essex Gazette

The Mirror Maze.

EAGLE AND QUEEN LINE STEAMERS

SEA TRIPS AGAIN

THE FAMOUS LONDON STEAMER

"GOLDEN EAGLE"

will operate Afternoon

Sea Cruises Daily

(FRIDAYS EXCEPTED)

(Weather and other circumstances permitting)

from CLACTON PIER

FARES: 3/- and 4/- (Children Half Price)

DAILY SERVICES (Fridays excepted) to LONDON (Tower Pier), GREENWICH and SOUTHEND

ALL CATERING FACILITIES — FULLY LICENSED

BOOK YOUR TICKETS IN ADVANCE FROM

8, ELECTRIC PARADE & PIER OFFICE, CLACTON

Telephone: Clacton 1252

The announcement that steamship sailings would recommence after the War, both to and from London as well as local outings up and down the coast.

reported that it had been the worst season in Clacton for many years with holidays abroad and the wet weather being cited as two of the main reasons for this. The knock-on effect of this was felt very strongly on The Pier as less visitors meant less income.

Barney Kingsman now had some very difficult decisions to make. As, in addition to the general fall in visitor numbers, those holidaymakers that were still coming to Clacton were tending to stay at the many newly opened caravan parks taking the place of the hotels and guest houses which were now closing at a rapid rate. A survey carried out that year showed that only 3,000 hotel and guest house beds were available as opposed to 30,000 caravan places. This created a big problem not just for Clacton Pier but also for the other entertainment venues in the town as the caravan parks were providing their own entertainment making it difficult to attract holidaymakers off their camps.

Things were getting so bad that, by the end of the 1964 season, Barney Kingsman was seriously considering selling The Pier but eventually decided against it, instead settling on a series of drastic cost saving cuts, particularly to the entertainment on offer. The first to go was the Rambla Concert Party. The Ramblas were the last open-air concert party to be operating anywhere in the country, so their demise was not wholly unexpected because, as well as the general lowering of visitor numbers, this form of entertainment was now more increasingly being seen as old hat in the modern world of the Swinging Sixties. But this was just the start of Kingsman's cuts as the closure of the Rambla

The Golden Eagle taking on passengers at The Pier Head in 1950. To the left, the M.L. Gay Commodore is being advertised

Concert Party also meant the closure of the Jolly Roger, which had been used by The Ramblas on wet days and for evening performances. This left just one theatre on The Pier, the Ocean Theatre, three down from its pre-War peak of four.

The next to go was the Blue Lagoon. Kingsman announced that 1964 was its last year and that he would be replacing it with a ten-pin bowling centre. Although the bowling centre never happened, 1964 was to prove the final year for the Blue Lagoon as a dance hall. It remained closed until 1967 while the building was renovated, re-opening that year as the "Fully licensed Lagoon Bar – adjacent to the Ocean Theatre".

1966 saw the last year of regular steamship services to and from The Pier and the last no passport required day trips to France, operated in this final year by the M.V. Royal Sovereign.

1950 and visitors are returning to The Pier in large numbers. There is an advert for the Gay Commodore on the left.

The M.L. Gay Commodore. This was one of five Commodore class Fairmile B motor launches which were built in 1940 for the Royal Navy, serving in several wartime roles. After the War, the Gay Commodore came to Clacton to serve as a small pleasure boat, taking passengers on hour long trips of 12 miles along the coast for 3s 6d with a special three hour evening cruise on Wednesdays and Sundays for 7s 6d.

As if these cuts weren't bad enough, Kingsman announced his real bombshell in 1964 with his most drastic closure of all, that of the Swimming Pool. This announcement caused uproar in the town. Many of the town's businesses were aware that the swimming pool was a major attraction and one which brought many visitors to Clacton, especially when there were regional and national swimming galas, not to mention the international water polo matches. The Clacton Swimming Club was devastated by the announcement and many local schools complained as they used the pool for their own galas and swimming lessons.

In the end Clacton Council itself was forced to step in and guaranteed to underwrite any losses made on the pool during the year enabling Barney Kingsman to agree to reopen the pool in 1965.

But this was only a temporary reprieve as, in 1968, Kingsman once again decided the swimming pool had to close. He said, "It has lost money over the last three years despite all the Council's assistance, so we have decided we should shut it." Once again the town's businesspeople felt they could not allow this to happen and, this time, a consortium of the town's businesses stepped in to underwrite the costs.

For Barney Kingsman the writing was well and truly on the wall and in 1971, he took the very difficult and emotional decision that he would have to sell The Pier. And so, 50 years after he, along with his mother and father, had first taken out a lease on Clacton Pier and provided a makeshift tarpaulin roof over some poles for visitors to dance to a band, the Kingsman era came to an end.

There is no doubt that the Kingsman Family had totally transformed Clacton Pier, turning it in to the largest and most utilised pier in the country and one of the UK's leading entertainment centres and, by so doing, were responsible too for Clacton-on-Sea's rise as a holiday resort to the very top league of seaside resorts on a par with places like Blackpool and Brighton. Sadly, changing times had brought all this to an end and Barney felt he now had no alternative but to get out and leave others to take over.

An early 1950s aerial view showing the Queen of the Channel at the Pier Head.

Poster advertising No Passport Day Trips to Calais.

Passengers boarding the Queen of the Channel for a day trip to France in 1958.

The Steel Stella, Ghost Train and Peter Pan Railway, three of the very popular attractions in the 1950s.

Ernie Cobb's speedboat disembarking on the west side steps.

The Pier Head in the 1950s.

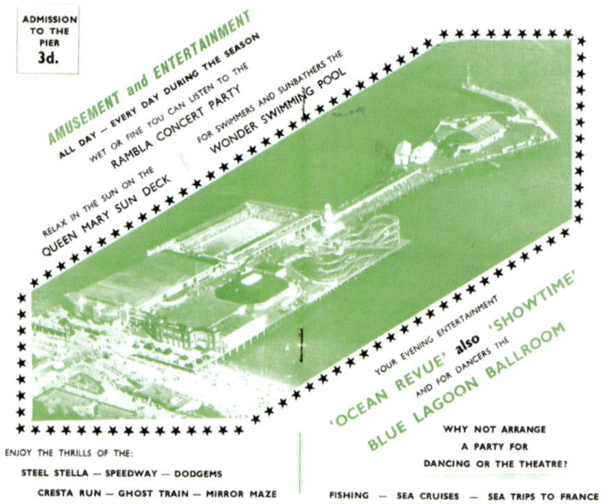

A leaflet advertising what was on offer on The Pier in the 1950s.

As well as the many amusements, there was also plenty of space and facilities available for those just wanting to relax. This photo shows the well-used shelters down the centre and the seats on either side of The Pier.

An aerial view showing many of the amusements and entertainments to be found on Clacton Pier.

By the mid 1950s, with plenty of facilities catering for every taste, The Pier was once again drawing in crowds in their tens of thousands every day during the Summer.

There was just one slight hiccup that interrupted The Pier's smooth running in the mid 1950s, when strong winds blew the Cresta Run over in 1956.

Sadly, by the early 1960s, with holidays abroad becoming more popular, the number of visitors began to drop off. This photo from c.1962, is witness to the fact there weren't as many people around.

EAST ESSEX
GAZETTE

No. 2576 FRIDAY, JANUARY 8, 1965 Price 4d.

BALLROOM LIKELY TO BECOME BOWLS CENTRE

No planning consent needed from council

Should a safety boat advertise?

BLUE LAGOON NEGOTIATIONS IN ADVANCED STAGE

CLACTON PIER Blue Lagoon ballroom is likely to be turned into a ten-pin bowling centre, complete with licensed bar and catering facilities.

This news, given yesterday by Mr. H. E. Kingsman, of the pier, puts an end to weeks of speculation and rumour about the future of the ballroom and adjacent annex.

As the 1960s wore on and with less and less paying customers, there was a whole series of newspaper headlines announcing attempted money-saving closures. This first was the closure of the Blue Lagoon Dance Hall at the beginning of 1965.

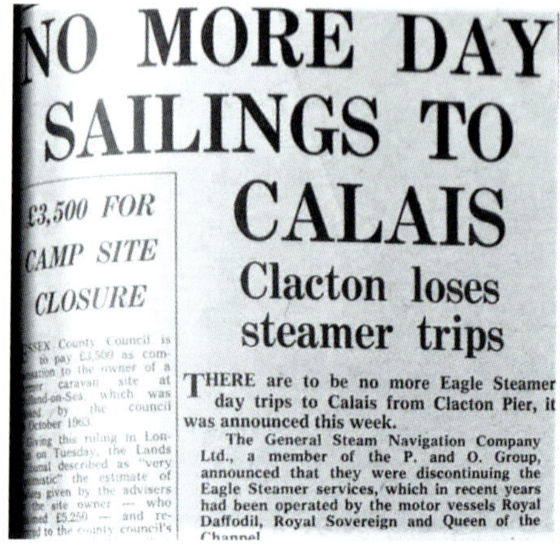

NO MORE DAY SAILINGS TO CALAIS

Clacton loses steamer trips

£3,500 FOR CAMP SITE CLOSURE

THERE are to be no more Eagle Steamer day trips to Calais from Clacton Pier, it was announced this week.

The General Steam Navigation Company Ltd., a member of the P. and O. Group, announced that they were discontinuing the Eagle Steamer services, which in recent years had been operated by the motor vessels Royal Daffodil, Royal Sovereign and Queen of the Channel.

And here, that the No-Passport trips to Calais were to cease at the end of the 1966 season.

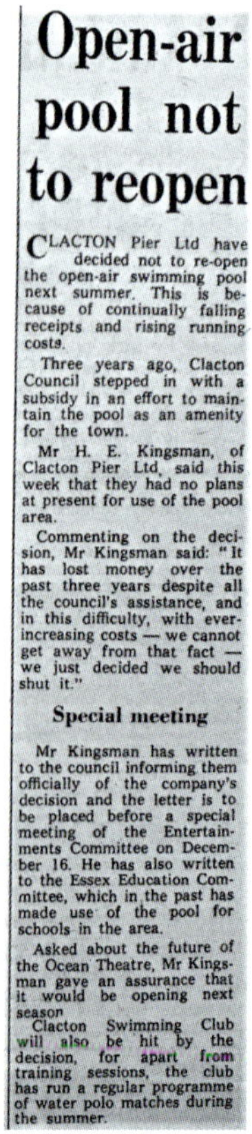

Open-air pool not to reopen

CLACTON Pier Ltd have decided not to re-open the open-air swimming pool next summer. This is because of continually falling receipts and rising running costs.

Three years ago, Clacton Council stepped in with a subsidy in an effort to maintain the pool as an amenity for the town.

Mr H. E. Kingsman, of Clacton Pier Ltd, said this week that they had no plans at present for use of the pool area.

Commenting on the decision, Mr Kingsman said: "It has lost money over the past three years despite all the council's assistance, and in this difficulty, with ever-increasing costs — we cannot get away from that fact — we just decided we should shut it."

Special meeting

Mr Kingsman has written to the council informing them officially of the company's decision and the letter is to be placed before a special meeting of the Entertainments Committee on December 16. He has also written to the Essex Education Committee, which in the past has made use of the pool for schools in the area.

Asked about the future of the Ocean Theatre, Mr Kingsman gave an assurance that it would be opening next season.

Clacton Swimming Club will also be hit by the decision, for apart from training sessions, the club has run a regular programme of water polo matches during the summer.

And finally, the biggest blow of all, that the Swimming Pool was to close. As it happened it did receive a temporary reprieve, but it was very short-lived.

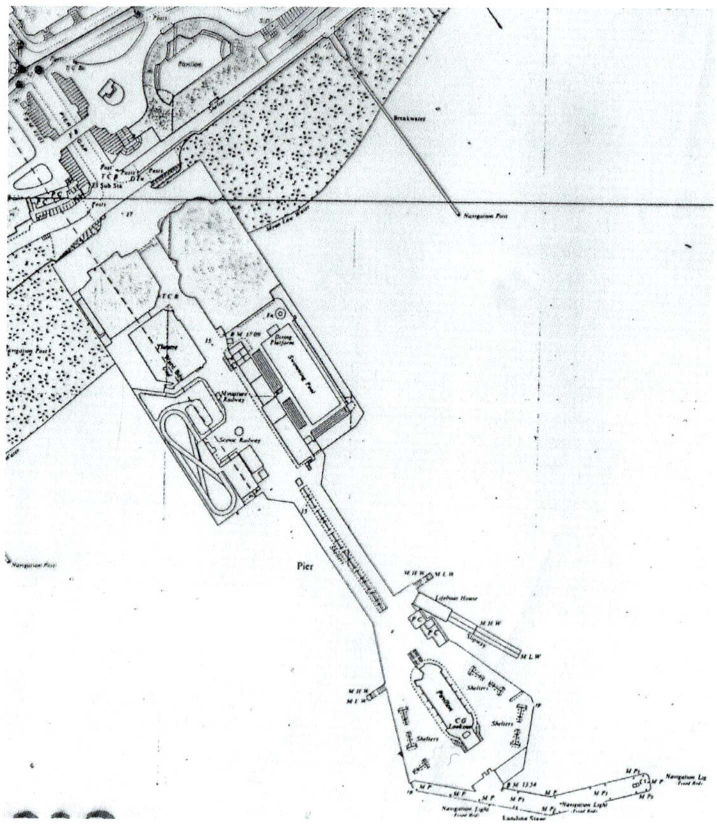

A plan of The Pier as it looked in 1971 when Barney Kingsman sold Clacton Pier, ending 50 years of ownership by the Kingsman Family.

Chapter Six

The Goss Days, 1971-1981

On 30 June 1971, the local press were summoned to a press conference at The Pier to be told that Barney Kingsman's Clacton Pier Company had sold Clacton Pier to the Goss family, the owners of Walton Pier. Although it transpired that negotiations had been going on for some time, the news came as a complete surprise to the newspaper reporters and to Clacton itself. Michael Goss, began the press conference by saying simply, "We have bought Clacton Pier."

Michael Goss became the new Managing Director, while his father, Charlie Goss, became Chairman. Soon afterwards, their company split, with Charlie continuing to run Walton Pier, leaving Michael and his wife, Sandra, to look after Clacton Pier.

With the continuing fall in visitor numbers, Barney Kingsman had been struggling to make ends meet and had made a number of alterations and cuts to try and keep The Pier afloat. One thing he had tried on at least two occasions was to close the swimming pool, but this move had been met with great opposition in the town and firstly the Council and then the Chamber of Trade and the town's businesses had stepped in to offer subsidies.

But, even with the subsidies, the swimming pool had been and was still proving to be a great drain on The Pier and so the first thing Michael Goss did was to close it. In its place he opened a dolphinarium.

Barney Kingsman sells Clacton Pier to the Goss Family. L-r standing new company chairman, Charlie Goss; outgoing Pier Manager, Len Tomlinson; driving Barney Kingsman; new managing director, Michael Goss.

Less than a year after their purchase, the Goss Family had already made some big changes, This shows the front of The Pier in 1972, with adverts for the Dick Emery Shows at the Ocean Theatre, the new Dolphinarium and the new Bingo Hall at the back of the old Blue Lagoon where the New Lagoon Lounge had been.

The new Soli Big Wheel, which replaced Kingsman's original Ferris Wheel. [Photo: Paul Angel]

The idea for the dolphinarium came after a visit to The Pier by an old school friend of Goss's called Reg Bloom, who lived in Walton. Bloom had introduced the very first dolphin displays to the United Kingdom in the 1960s at Flamingo Park in Yorkshire. During his visit, Goss asked him if he had any idea what he could do with an Olympic swimming pool that was losing money. Bloom replied, *"As a matter of fact I do."*

Coming from a showman family, Goss was a frequent visitor to America, always on the lookout for new amusement park ideas he could introduce into this country, so he knew that dolphinariums were very popular over there and could be a big crowd-puller here too, so he asked his friend to take on the swimming pool and its conversion, which Bloom readily agreed to.

Wanting to get it started straightaway, he initially used the swimming pool area as a "Dolphin Training Ground", with just one dolphin, Maria, performing five 45 minute shows per day. This new attraction, Goss's first major change, opened on 1 August 1971, just one month after he bought The Pier. During his first winter, with more time to work on it properly, the area was modified to form a proper dolphinarium and a new marine exhibition known as North Sea World.

Another drastic change followed on swiftly as Goss announced that the traditional Ocean Theatre Summer Season would be enhanced, and that, from the 1972 season, he proposed bringing in the very biggest names in show business to star both in the Summer Season itself and in special Sunday Concerts. 1972 therefore saw Dick Emery star for the season with Sunday shows that included the likes of Bob Monkhouse and Leslie Crowther. He also took the decision to open the Theatre up for morning and afternoon Children's Shows in an attempt to maximise its potential.

The Waltzer, the scene of much lost change down the back of the seats! [Photo: Paul Angel]

His next move was to cover the whole of the area between The Pier Entrance and the Ocean Theatre with translucent roofing and converting the former Blue Lagoon bar into an amusement and bingo arcade which was heated to allow it to be opened earlier and later in the year.

The Gallopers [Photo: Paul Angel]

After these changes, he turned his attention to the rides, introducing three new ones, a Soli Big Wheel to replace the former Ferris Wheel, a large carousel called the Gallopers and the Waltzer as well as updating the dodgems with 20 new cars.

All this was followed by what he hoped would be one of the biggest new attractions, a chair lift, known as the Skyliner, which carried people from the Ocean Theatre to the end of The Pier, going out over the sea for part of the way. One person who found it to be a great new attraction was Mary Hooks, who can remember having "*happy memories of going on this ride multiple times. Lost a few shoes over the side too.*"

With all these major changes and innovations in just his first year, Managing Director, Michael Goss, had come in like a whirlwind, making more changes to The Pier and introducing more attractions than it had seen at any time since The Pier's pre-War heyday under Ernest Kingsman.

The Steel Stella, still a major attraction in Goss's days.

New rides introduced in place of the Steel Stella included The Paratrooper. [Photo: Paul Angel]

Having brought about all these major changes in their first year, the Goss Family were looking to settle down and bring a bit of stability to The Pier in 1973. Sadly, it wasn't to work out like that, as in August of that year, another major change was forced on The Pier when the Steel Stella, to many the iconic symbol of The Pier, caught fire and had to be dismantled.

The Skyliner running down towards the Jolly Roger.

Michael Goss decided not to rebuild the Steel Stella, for two interlinked reasons. The first being health & safety considerations; the second, commercial considerations, both of which combined made the cost of rebuilding a 1930s structure not financially viable. As he said at the time, *"It is a difficult decision to dismantle such an iconic ride but from a business sense, it seems wiser and more sensible to bring in a number of smaller new rides to take the place of this one ride."*

A number of new smaller rides were therefore erected to take the place of the roller coaster. Those included the Caterpillar, Calypso and the Paratrooper Ride.

Michael Goss, the son of the owner, who was a young boy in the 1970s, remembers these new rides well. *"For a while we lived upstairs on The Pier, where the offices are now. We later moved to a house in Lancaster Gardens. Early in the morning, I used to ride my bike to The Pier from my new home. The bike had a basket on the front and I would ride up The Pier, round to all the rides, collecting the takings*

The Caterpillar [Photo: Jack Leeson. Reproduced by kind permission of National Fairground and Circus Archive, Sheffield University]

An overall view of the new rides in the area formerly occupied by the Steel Stella.

and take the money back to the office. I also used to walk along The Pier with two greased sticks, which I'd poke down between the boards to pick up any loose change that had fallen down them. After this, I would then cycle off to school."

Calypso [Photo: Jack Leeson. Reproduced by kind permission of National Fairground and Circus Archive, Sheffield University]

Goss later introduced ticket booths where you could buy tickets for the rides instead of paying for each individual ride. An innovation that under various guises, tickets, wristbands, etc., has continued to this day.

Meanwhile, at the Ocean Theatre, things were not going so well either and the hoped-for big crowds looking to see the big names of Variety didn't work out as numbers continued to fall. It was inevitable therefore that, at the end of the 1977 season, Goss took the decision to pull the plug on the Theatre and it was closed, never to re-open.

The East Essex Gazette summed up the feelings of many in its editorial when it said, *"Of course we shall miss the Ocean. But how many people have patronised its shows weekly or even twice weekly as they did in the old days?*

The Goss era in full swing. The Pier entrance in 1975.

Ghost Safari, the new ride that took the place of the Ocean Theatre. [Photo: Paul Angel]

We should be thankful that [Pier] owner Michael Goss has not given up the fight altogether. Instead, he is using his flair and foresight to adapt the building to a use that he is confident will not only give him a return for his money but will be what people want. No businessman can say fairer.

"Final curtain for the Ocean is like the passing of an old friend. Even owner Mr Goss admits to a tinge of regret. But as long as he is prepared to meet the challenge of change regardless, it must be seen that the future prosperity of both Clacton and Pier is as secure as when engineer Peter Bruff drove in his first pile in 1871."

The adaptation that Michael Goss made was to create a new ghost train ride, Ghost Safari, and a shooting range.

The Ghost Safari occupied the main part of the former Ocean Theatre, which as Michael Goss had hoped did, indeed, prove to be an extremely popular ride. Gil Clasby remembers "*going on the ghost train when I was little and a piece of the machinery came lose and hit me on the forehead. I got told off for making a fuss by my mum in the car behind me. When we got out into the light my face was covered in blood!"*

Steve Forward also has fond memories, *"I remember going on the Ghost Safari when I was about eight or nine on my own. Then once, on a Saturday night, it broke down right at the long corridor section. Scary! When the operator came on and turned on all the emergency lighting I could see the track and the props and layout. It began my fascination with ghost trains."*

It was also popular with pier workers as Ian Hammond recalls, "I worked on The Pier in the summer of 1981 and was mainly on the ghost train. There were short cut doors inside that we could run through and scare the passengers during their ride!"

An emergency light was fitted up in Ghost Safari and when anything went wrong, for example someone getting out of their car while going round, this light would light up and the ride was stopped immediately. On seeing the light, all The Pier managers and anyone else available, including the

Goss's schnauzer, Hugo, would drop anything they were doing and rush to the ride to sort out the problem.

The shooting range, a large 'Hill Billy' electronic/pneumatic shooting range, was set up at the former corner entrance to the theatre, while the Bingo was extended to utilise the rest of the side of the theatre that opened on to the newly covered main central concourse of The Pier.

Michael Goss introduced the idea of ride tickets. This is a selection of ride tickets over the following years. [Design and photo: Robert Gunthorpe]

While all this work was going on to make use of the space made possible by the closure of the Ocean Theatre, a bad storm struck The Pier in January 1978 causing much damage. At one stage the whole structure rocked under the force of the gigantic 30 ft waves and it was thought The Pier might collapse as it received a terrible battering. As it was, the whole of The Pier head was submerged, while at the land end, giant cracks and holes appeared on the car park platform.

The high tide and winds pounded the carpenters' shop and workshops, ruining electrical equipment and washing away a 1,000 gallon fuel tank. The lifeboat house was also severely damaged. Amazingly, and with the typical bravery of the lifeboat crew, mechanic, Bernie Cobb, and his assistant, Micky Lynn, spent three hours in the lifeboat house risking their lives in case the lifeboat needed to be launched.

Fortunately, the two dolphins, Bubble and Squeak, were away in their winter quarters at Whipsnade Zoo, but the sealions and the penguins had to be rescued as the Dolphinarium too was badly damaged with the flooring in the non-public area being ripped out as its reinforced concrete floors and beams were swept away. Where the food freezers had stood, there was just a gaping hole.

The following day another high tide hit The Pier with even more decking being lifted and pieces of the concrete floor that had been loosened on the first day being washed away completely. In addition, the police came along and sealed off The Pier when a fractured gas main was discovered.

Damaged caused to the planking during the 1978 storm.

Ready to open on 9 March 1979 after the second disastrous storm in as many years.

Following the two days of storms, Michael Goss said, "*We have lost every tool, every bit of machinery from one side of The Pier and all the shelters at the sea end and we have had to find new homes for the animals from the Dolphinarium. But we shall rebuild the damaged areas and shall reopen as planned on 5 March, even though some parts may have to be closed off for a while.*"

Although the storm had caused a lot of damage to The Pier and cost in the region of £150,000 for repairs, amazingly, Goss was right and it was ready to open on 5 March.

In spite of the damage suffered, Clacton Pier fared better than some other East Coast piers. Most of Hunstanton Pier, for example, was destroyed, leaving just a small section at the shore end, while Margate Pier was so badly damaged that it had to be demolished completely.

Disastrously, almost exactly one year later, in January 1979, another freak storm hit Clacton Pier. This time, although much of the exposed planking on the east side of The Pier was torn up, the real concern this time was for the Dolphinarium, which bore the brunt of the high tides. There was real anxiety for the sea life as waves continued to batter The Pier supports leaving the killer whale, Suzie Wong, the sea lions and the penguins in desperate need of rescue.

A concerted superb all-round team effort was launched by Pier staff, which fortunately proved successful in saving all the animals and they were eventually evacuated in a fleet of lorries which then had to battle through the snow to take them to Windsor Safari Park.

The rescue was supported by many from the town, who turned out to lend their support in saving the sea creatures as well as generally clearing up and helping to remove damaged items to make The Pier safe, while others brought refreshments to help those working and clothes outfitters, Ernest Newson, sent up bundles of dry clothes for the workers to change into.

Once again, the repair bill ran into six figures but once again The Pier was ready to open on its designated opening date of 9 March, though the Dolphinarium was completely out of action for a couple of years.

As part of the repair work, Goss was able to introduce a new "space age" ride to The Pier, the Century 2000, at the time said to be the only one of its kind in Britain. Garry Champion still remembers it to this day as *"terrifying if you hadn't seen it and got on it without knowing."*

The Red Arrows display over The Pier on 24 June 1978.

The new Century 2000 ride, described as "terrifying" by some. [Photo: Paul Angel]

Later that year, Clacton Pier had yet another scare, though of an entirely different nature, as on 25 June, the Red Arrows put on a display over The Pier and it was reported that visitors were "*scared stiff*" when one of the planes flew very low. Many people said the pilot of this particular plane had been very reckless and had flown at high speed between the Big Wheel and the Helter Skelter, a fact that seemed to be

The photograph in the East Essex Gazette that seemed to confirm that one of the Red Arrows had flown between the Big Wheel and the Helter Skelter.

confirmed by a photograph in the following week's Clacton Gazette.

But a spokesman for the Red Arrows, Warrant Officer D.H.Thorne, said it was an optical illusion caused by the angle of the photograph.
He continued, *"People manage to photograph the Red Arrows seemingly doing weird and wonderful things, but really their flying is very safe. I can't see from that photograph how it can possibly have flown between the Big Wheel and the Helter Skelter. We don't take any chances. We can't afford to. For one thing the pilot would be looking for another job if he really tried that!"*

On behalf of The Pier, Sandra Goss said, *"Some people were scared stiff, but most enjoyed the spectacle immensely, especially those on the Big Wheel at the time."*

Notwithstanding these various setbacks and "scares", The Pier remained a thriving concern throughout the 1970s, thanks in no small measure to the enthusiasm, foresight and energy of Michael and Sandra Goss with their feel for giving the public what they wanted and their commitment to bringing in new innovations, whether that be new rides, new entertainments or even new buildings.

But by the early 1980s, Clacton, as a seaside resort, was suffering from an ever-decreasing number of visitors as more and more people were holidaying abroad with the knock-on effect this had on The Pier. Michael Goss also felt very strongly that the local Council was not doing enough to encourage tourism to the area and were, in fact, quite negative about it. Both these factors, combined with his own continuing love affair with America, led to him finally deciding to leave Clacton behind and move his family to America.

And so, in 1981, the Goss Family sold up and a new era in The Pier's history was about to begin.

Chapter Seven The McGinty Era, 1981-1994

On 31 July 1981, it was announced that a new consortium, headed by Francis McGinty had bought Clacton Pier from Michael and Sandra Goss.

The Consortium consisted of four people, all of whom had had many years' experience in the leisure industry. Francis himself became the new Managing Director. He already owned an amusement firm in Austria and currently held the Bingo concession on Clacton Pier and it was under the name of his Austrian Company, Anglo Austrian Automatics, that McGinty set up the consortium, which consisted of himself; his brother, Denis; John Threadwell, who owned the amusements at Point Clear Caravan Park and David Howe, who had been a manager on Clacton Pier since 1955.

The Consortium that took over The Pier in 1981. L-r: John Threadwell, David Howe, Francis McGinty, Denis McGinty.

Right from the outset, the new consortium announced major plans to transform The Pier. In a statement to the press, McGinty said they intended to spend £10,000,000 over the next ten years. He said their biggest priority was to bring back the dolphinarium which had been closed since the bad storm of 1979 had caused extensive damage to it. Next, they intended to re-open the Blue Lagoon as a bar and disco and finally they were looking to bring several new rides on to The Pier.

Tendring District Council Chief Executive, Richard Painter, who had been stung by some of the comments made by departing owner, Michael Goss, announced that he would be meeting the new owners as soon as possible and said, *"I am very pleased to hear of the proposals for The Pier and I know my council will give all the help and encouragement it can to the new owners."*

McGinty also put forward the idea of abolishing ride tickets and instead putting up the price for entry but giving free access to all the rides, allowing people to use each ride as many times as they liked. However, this idea didn't come to fruition as many people complained that all they wanted to do was talk a walk along The Pier and didn't want to use the rides. Instead the price of admission was put up from 4p to 10p, with anyone wanting to go on the rides still having to buy individual tickets or purchase a wristband for unlimited rides.

Right from the start, Francis McGinty had big plans for The Pier and drew up this plan for how he envisaged the frontage. Sadly, it was to remain unbuilt.

Good as their word in other respects however, the consortium's first major act was to re-open the Dolphinarium, bringing in three killer whales. The full story of the killer whales and the impact they had on The Pier over the next three and half years is detailed later on in the book in the "North Sea World" chapter. Suffice to say here, it was not a very happy time and it brought a lot of negative publicity to The Pier.

Continuing to press ahead with their major development plans, the following year, 1982, saw

A postcard issued to mark the opening of the Whirlwind on 18 May 1982.

The frontage in November 1982 being made ready for a number of changes – Slots of Fun on the left and Cockney Pride on the right. In the foreground is the Century 2000 ride being packed up ready for removal. [Photo: Anthony Allston]

a number of changes to The Pier. The first was the arrival of a new spectacular roller coaster ride, The Whirlwind.

The Whirlwind was a double corkscrew MK-1200 model built by the Dutch company, Vekoma. Unbeknown to the rest of the consortium, Francis McGinty travelled to Germany and brokered a deal to buy the Whirlwind on a repayment plan for £750,000, which was only £50,000 less than they had paid for The Pier!

In spite of its cost, McGinty was certain he had done the right thing. *"I am over the moon about it,"* he said, *"and I am hoping it will bring a bit of life to The Pier. What we are trying to do is have the place open 52 weeks of the year."*

On 18 May 1982, the ride was given a grand ceremonial opening with Tendring Council Chairman, Len Parrish, cutting the ribbon. Council Chief Executive, Richard Paintrer, was also present, as was the Council's head of Economic and Tourism

The Cockney Pride public house, opened at Christmas 1982.

department, Rex Stevenson, who was so impressed that he opined, *"It's the greatest thing that's happened to Clacton for years."*

One young man at the opening ceremony, Karl Fuller, wasn't quite so impressed. *"I can remember,"* he said later, *"that it was announced that the ride would be opened by the Ipswich Town football squad which of course was managed by Bobby Robson. Bring an avid Ipswich fan, my Dad took my brother and me along to meet the squad and get their autographs. I remember standing at the front of The Pier with a big crowd all eagerly awaiting the arrival of Robson and his players. In the event, only defender Steve McCall turned up. This was disappointing of course but I was still able to get his autograph on a Kevin Beattie testimonial programme which I still have today."* Mind you, it wasn't all bad, as he added, *"A great memory despite the disappointment."*

At the end of its first week, it seemed that McGinty's optimism was justified when it was reported that in that week alone, more than 10,000 people had experienced the thrill of hurtling round the one minute long ride at 45 m.p.h., partly upside down. One young Colbayns' student, Keith Walker, enjoyed it so much that he travelled on it over 140 times during its first weekend.

Night time at the front of The Pier in 1983 with adverts for the Ice Rink and Oscars. [Photo: Anthony Allston]

The circus returns to the Jolly Roger in 1982.

The newly opened Fun Lido.

At the end of that first week, Francis McGinty said, *"It costs a lot of money and it uses more power than the rest of The Pier put together, but it has proved its worth."*

But that was just the start for 1982, as there were to be more innovations. The next being the reopening of the Jolly Roger for the first time since 1964, when Sally Chipperfields' Circus was staged inside. As part of the revamp, the outside of the Jolly Roger was covered in an attractive red and white cladding. The cost of hiring the circus was £96,000 with admission price to The Pier put up to 30p to help cover the cost of hiring it in. Sadly, it was just a one-off and the Jolly Roger returned to being used mainly as a store in 1983.

However, there were more permanent changes taking place at the front of The Pier as the former Blue Lagoon Dance Hall and Ocean Theatre areas were undergoing major changes. Firstly, the Ghost Safari was removed and replaced by the amusement arcade which was moved from its current location to allow space for two new features. The first of these was the Cockney Pride public house, which opened at Christmas 1982. Behind that, major alterations were taking place to turn the former amusement area into a night club, which was to become Oscars, though that did not open until the Summer of 1983.

Also in 1982, on the other side of The Pier, in the under cover section next to the dodgems, a new "Pleasure Dome" (as it was christened) was created. This included a new ice skating rink. Francis McGinty had a winter resort business in Austria and was therefore a frequent visitor to the country. As a result of this, he had plans to build an "Austrian Centre" on The Pier which included the skating rink.

The rink proved to be very popular and in its second year was extended to about twice the size but this increase in size led to it becoming very difficult to keep the temperature sufficiently cold to maintain the ice and it sometimes got a bit thin and slushy. In fact, the ice rink's fate was sealed after a couple of

The Whirlwind undergoing a test run before opening to the public. In the background is the Jolly Roger with its red and white cladding.

A general view looking at The Pier in 1985, showing Slots of Fun, the Fun Lido with water chutes, the Big Wheel and the Whirlwind.

years when someone fell through a trap door into the sea below. It was closed soon after that and the area turned into a roller skating rink instead.

The roller skating rink also proved to be very popular, especially as it stayed open until 10 p.m. at the weekend with a Disco session. It had a professional hardwood floor and was decorated in a glitzy Hollywood style with photos of leading film stars around the walls in keeping with the name it was given, "Flicks". Music played throughout and there was an exciting light and video show. There was also a coffee lounge attached. On popular nights at Oscars it was also used as an overflow area with often a second stage, when it would stay open until the early hours – or even all night!

Another innovation in the Pleasure Dome was "The Fourth Dimension". In the words of an advertisement of the time, this was *"A unique experience in light, sound and motion to thrill and delight. Four separate space adventures that will appeal to the young at heart. Definitely not for the faint-hearted."*

The four separate rides, all of which took place in the dark, were Star Cruiser, Space Shuttle, Star Fighter and Driving School.

The Roller Rink, Flicks, decorated in glitzy Hollywood style.

By 1985 there was a total of 23 rides on The Pier ranging from the Whirlwind and The Fourth Dimension to children's roundabouts. The Consortium had also converted the building on the left at the front entrance to a new amusement arcade called "Slots of Fun".

Although there were a lot of new innovations in the first two years, a couple of Michael Goss's rides from the 1970s disappeared quite quickly. These included the Gallopers, the Century 2000 ride, which was dismantled and removed in 1982 and the chair lift, the Skyliner. This had a very unfortunate end as Pier worker, Robert Kendall, recalls, *"The Skyliner broke down on a busy day while it was full of children. Luckily, I had a scaffold tower on wheels already set up so I went along The Pier and got the children off one at a time with other members of Pier staff. Each time to a round of applause from the public. The ride was closed down permanently a short while after."*

Over the next couple of years, development continued, but at a slower rate. The next major addition was the Fun Lido. Following the departure of Nemo, the last remining killer whale, on 22 June 1985 (see "North Sea World" chapter), it was decided to remove all the sea life apart from the sea lions and to convert the Dolphinarium into the Fun Lido, which consisted of three water chutes of differing sizes plunging the intrepid thrill-seeker down the spiraling chutes into the tranquil and sparkling waters of the small swimming pool beneath.

But this was to prove to be the last of the major new attractions opened by Anglo Austrian Automatics as, in December 1985, it was announced that Clacton Pier was up for sale.

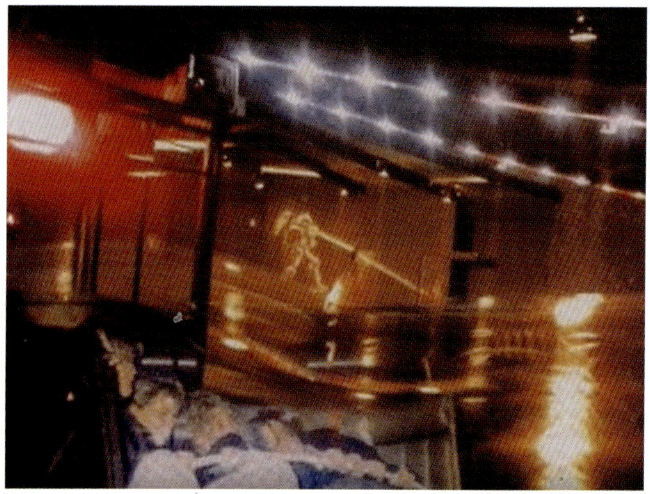

Star Fighter, part of the Fourth Dimension.

The Whirlwind being dismantled at the end of the 1986 season. [Photo: Anthony Allston]

Looking at The Pier after the removal of the Whirlwind.

By the mid-80s, Clacton-on-Sea itself as a seaside resort was undergoing a serious decline in its fortunes. This had started in the 1960s due to the advent of cheap summer holidays abroad and the general increase in living standards and, as far back as Barney Kingsman's days, had already led to cutbacks on The Pier. The decline had been accelerating ever since with the result that many of the town's hotels and guest houses, not to mention other entertainment venues, had been closing at an alarming rate. But the nadir of Clacton's fortunes came at the end of the 1983 season when Butlin's announced it was closing its holiday camp. This had attracted 6,000 people a week plus many day visitors, something in excess of 100,000 visitors during the season.

In 1983, Clacton Pier received 1,000,000 visitors. In 1984, the year after Butlin's closure, that number was halved. Unsurprisingly, the knock-on effect of this was that The Pier was getting into financial difficulties. To add to the problems, 1985 was a very bad one weatherwise, keeping visitor numbers even lower.

In late October 1985, Anglo Austrian Automatics called in the receiver who froze all its debts and assets. Francis McGinty said that the company that owned The Pier was in financial difficulties and that the recovery hoped for in the summer season had not materialised. He added, *"We've had good local support but the number of visitors has been down. The prospect of a long hard winter is not a very pleasant one and we will be very vulnerable during this period."* A spokesperson for the Receiver said, *"We will be looking to ensure that The Pier and the facilities it has to offer will stay for the future."*

The helicopter flights which only lasted a couple of years.

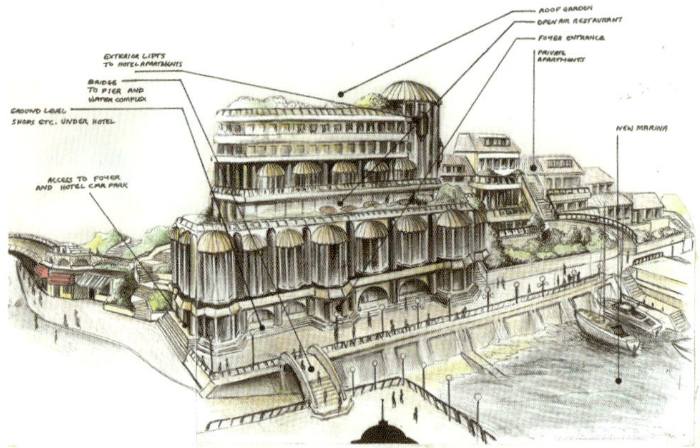

In the early 1990s, Tendring District Council decided to lease the Band Pavilion and tenders were asked for. This is Francis McGinty's proposal for the Pavilion, which he wanted to link to The Pier by means of a bridge to make it all one big enterprise. Needless to say, the plan never came to fruition.

In December, the Financial Times and the World Fair trade paper carried adverts for the sale of Clacton Pier. Within the first week, 40 inquiries had been made. The receivers said they were looking for offers in the region of £1,000,000 but there was no fixed sale price.

Eventually, Francis McGinty restructured his consortium and with financial backing from a local businessman, formed a new company, TotalQuest Ltd. and, made an offer himself, buying The Pier back for £400,000 and was ready to open up again for the 1986 season.

At the end of the 1986 season, The Pier said goodbye to the Whirlwind as the roller coaster was dismantled and removed to Särkännieman amusement park in Finland.

Following the demise of the Whirlwind, some other smaller rides were added, including a ride for young children, Go Gator.

Another attraction that was added in the late 1980s was helicopter rides from The Pier. However, this only lasted a couple of seasons due to a change in legislation regarding landing places and the types of helicopters that were permitted to land on places such as oil rigs, boat helipads and piers.

Clacton Pier did pull off one coup in 1989 reminiscent of the Kingsman era when the National Angling Championship Final was held over the weekend of 25th and 26th November, attracting 450 anglers.

In spite of TotalQuest's ongoing investment in new attractions and new ideas, visitor numbers still continued to fall in the late 80s and early 90s during the worst recession Clacton had ever suffered, The Pier remained in trouble and the Fun Lido was closed with the area it had occupied becoming mostly derelict apart from a small section for the aquarium and the sea lion show area which continued.

By the early 1990s, the only parts of The Pier that were making money were Oscars and the amusement arcades but both of those had been let out as concessions.

And so, in 1993, Francis McGinty once again called in the receivers, this time Grant Thornton, well-known insolvency services specialists. Tony Bostock was installed as the new general manager of The Pier. Recognising that Oscars was the main source of income, this was brought back under the control of The Pier itself and was placed under Grant Thornton.

In a letter to all Pier staff, Melvin Childs, on behalf of Grant Thornton, said, *"The potential income of the nightclub is considerable....I am confident that with the current management in place the venue will soon be more popular than ever. I would ask you all, therefore, to support the efforts of Busta Brooker and his staff in ensuring the safe and prosperous future of the night club operation."*

As for The Pier itself, Melvin Childs expressed disappointment about the recent trading results and planned to put in place a programme of cosmetic and structural improvements which would attract visitors back. Their first big improvement was to refurbish the Big Wheel, which was described as the *"focal point of The Pier"*. Another early change was to make a new entrance to the roller rink and it was hoped that with better marketing this would provide an increase on income previously achieved.

In the middle of all the turmoil and plans for improvements, BBC's Eastenders turned up to film an episode on The Pier!

But there was soon to be a change for the better in Clacton Pier's fortunes...

A photograph of the Jolly Roger taken in August 1992, not long before McGinty called in the receivers for the second time, showing what a poor state of repair much of The Pier had got into. [Photo: Anthony Allston]

EastEnders get taste of the seaside

EASTENDERS Pat and Ricky Butcher have got something to smile about — they have escaped from London to sunny Clacton seafront.

Pat and Ricky, alias actors Pam St Clement and Sid Owen, have been filming in the town all week for the BBC's top-rated soap opera.

And the trials and tribulations of life in Albert Square seemed to be forgotten as they tucked into ice creams during a break in their schedule.

How the visit of Pat and Ricky from Eastenders was reported in the Clacton Gazette. [Photo: Roy Mullen]

Chapter Eight

The Harrison Years, 1994-2009

On 6 October 1994, the local press carried the news that, after a year in administration, Clacton Pier had been sold to E & M Harrison, *"the owners of several amusement arcades in Clacton."*

In fact, not only did the Harrisons own several arcades in Clacton but they also held the concession for all the amusement outlets on The Pier and it was because of this, that they were given first refusal to purchase The Pier.

With The Pier now in the hands of Ted Harrison and his son, also Ted, they issued a statement saying, *"We as a company are fully aware of the responsibility of taking over The Pier. The whole town is relying on what we do here and if we can bring the people back it will benefit everyone."* The young Ted added, *"Our family were originally travelling showmen and we are rooted in the fairground tradition. We want to open The Pier up to family fun and create a fairground atmosphere here."*

They immediately announced a three year plan to turn The Pier's fortunes round but promised that people would see a difference as early as the first year. Good as their word, within the first month work had begun, brightening it up and providing the structure with a much needed facelift.

By the start of the 1995 season, the Harrisons had already made a significant number of changes; the first being the removal of the Fourth Dimension, replaced by a large new Waltzer, the Twist, Truck

The Harrisons on the day it was announced they had bought Clacton Pier, 6 October 1994.

Convoy and Teacups. As Ted Harrison Jr. said, *"We are trying to please everybody. We want parents to be able to see their children on the rides and having a good time – not walking down some dark tunnel and coming out the other end."*

As well as this major change, the roller skating rink, which had been closed during the time The Pier had been in the hands of the receivers, was also removed and The Dodgems was restored on traditional fairground lines with new cars. At the front left of The Pier, the Slots of Fun amusement arcade was replaced by a fish & chip shop while a second amusement arcade was closed and converted into fairground stalls along with a German-style sweet shop.

Before buying The Pier, the Harrisons already held a number of concessions, including this one, "Harrisons Kiddies Corner".

Along with these customer-facing improvements, essential maintenance work had not been forgotten with new decking being installed and outdated wiring and plumbing renovated, while below The Pier 30 pylons were replaced.

But, in spite of all these visible changes, perhaps the biggest change of all was the abolition of The Pier's 50p entrance charge. The Harrisons felt that the high entry fee was proving a bar to many families going on The Pier and, for the first time in The Pier's history, entry to The Pier was granted free of charge,

Ted Harrison Jr. said later, *"it was the best decision we could have made. Right from the start we noticed a big increase in trade. Ironically, because many more people were coming on to The Pier, there was an immediate drop of a quarter of all income in our Pier Avenue Amusement Arcade. Nevertheless, it showed our idea was the right one for The Pier."* Local residents agreed as one of them, Maurice Williams, said, *"I think it's great. We often come down here and*

An advert for Clacton Pier just before the Harrisons took over showing the attractions they inherited.

the free entry is wonderful. I find it's very invigorating to walk along with the fresh sea air."

Purchase of Clacton Pier had naturally included the Cockney Pride Pub and Oscars Nightclub both of which the Harrisons committed to keeping open 52 weeks a year, something they saw as vital to The Pier's overall success. However, they had big

One of the first things they did was to introduce free admission to Clacton Pier for the first time in its history.

plans for the Cockney Pride which they envisaged as a family pub and proposed to transform the front forecourt into a children's play area with more tables and chairs for adults to sit at with their fish and chips or pizza enjoying the sea view.

With phase one of their improvement plan completed, the Harrisons moved on to phase two for the start of the next season. The 1996 season therefore saw the plans for the Cockney Pride

An announcement posted at the front of the Jolly Roger at the beginning of 1995.

achieved which also included entertainment by a jazz band outside on the concourse and a new roller coaster designed for younger children, The Speedy Pedro, later renamed the Wild Mouse, installed. A new underground fairground was also opened.

Other new innovations during these first two years included placing a number of young children's rides in the centre section, free deck chairs, a Punch & Judy show outside the Jolly Roger operated by Clacton favourite, Peter Battey, and the introduction of special fireworks nights.

1996 saw The Year of The Pier, a national celebration of seaside piers organised by The British Piers' Society and the British Association of Leisure Parks, Piers and Attraction with 30 June nominated as "The Year of The Pier Day". Clacton Pier played an active part in the celebrations. A traditional Victorian atmosphere was created which included all-day attractions such as a troupe of dancers performing the can-can at regular intervals, clowns, a juggler and a visit from "Postman Pat".

The end of The Pier as it looked at the start of the Harrisons' ownership with the Paratrooper ride at the back on the left and the Peter Pan Railway at the front right.

Skydancer Aviation, an aerobatic display team, visited Clacton Pier during the day as part of their attempt to set a British record for the most aerobatic flying displays by one organisation in one day with four aeroplanes being used to stage events at 16 piers throughout the UK. Along with this more up-to-date mode of transport, the world's last sea-going paddle steamer, PS Waverley, made a welcome return visit to The Pier.

The day also featured a long distance balloon competition organised at 20 piers throughout the country at which balloons were released with the winner being the person whose balloon label was returned from the furthest distance. Towards the end of July, it was announced that the winning balloon had been released from Clacton Pier and had reached the Polish city of Leszno.

The day was chosen for Clacton Pier's latest attraction to be announced, a new reptile house, whose main attractions were a 20' python and a "*crocodile infested swamp*".

The whole highly successful day finished with a grand fireworks display starting at 9 p.m.

By the end of just their second year in charge, the Harrisons had achieved many changes and had brought the buzz back to Clacton Pier, bringing with it a large increase in the number of visitors. But there was more to come as, in 1997, a new attraction, Terminator, was added.

The Big Wheel undergoing renovation in March 1995.

The entrance as it looked at the start of the 1995 season.

Clacton Gazette's reporter, Mark Beales, tried out the new 16 tonne ride and described his experience, *"There are 16 colourful seats to choose from in line. Just as you are settling in, it starts up. At first it swings left and right, going right to the top of its arc before settling down to go the other way. But almost immediately the ride picks up and without warning goes flying all the way around. With each turn your stomach flips up and returns to its traditional position before flipping over again. It is an incredible sensation that is repeated again and again."* His verdict: *"Clacton Pier's newest arrival is a sure-fire success, even if it does give you a G-force of five, and is set to pull in visitors all summer."*

The following year, 1998, a new bone-shaking simulator, Morphis, was introduced on to The Pier. It was promoted as a "Flight Simulator", but it offered a variety of rides, including TT Racing and an Astro Canyon run. In fact, the actual Flight Simulator package was generally only used during Clacton's Air Show.

Putting up Morphis was a bit of a nightmare in itself, as a floating base (not fixed to The Pier) had to be provided because The Pier's concrete deck was not quite suitable for its movement and vibration. Pier maintenance manager, Peter Watts, remembers, *"Seven tons of steel and concrete were fabricated and there was also a lot of welding on site that fell to me, to provide a suitable base. When the ride eventually went, it took longer to break up this base, than move the actual ride."*

Not quite so bone-shaking, trampolines were another new addition that year.

As well as introducing more thrill-making rides and children's attractions, some attention was also paid to style and to making The Pier look more attractive to the casual visitor. A new look entrance, with little fountains dotted along the walkway giving a lighter feel, was introduced along with a nod to the traditions of The Pier by reintroducing Victorian style seating along the open deck plus Victorian style lampposts and signage (designed by Ray Jessop, a well-known local sign writer).

The Harrisons introduced a new logo as part of their planned improvements to give The Pier a more family image.

The newly styled entrance to The Pier showing the new logo in prominent positions.

Clacton Pier hit the national news in 1998 and 1999. Firstly in 1998, when 6ft security fences were erected to prevent children risking their lives by leaping into the sea from The Pier. During the past three years something like 60 children, aged between eight and 12, had been known to jump. The Pier's general manger, Mark Baird, said, "*We had to put up the fences in the name of safety. The problem has been getting steadily worse.*" He added, "*This should make a safer summer, it had become quite a hazard.*" A far cry from Professor Webb and the days when the Clacton Swimming Club used to actually organise Pier jumping contests!

And then in 1999, when a helicopter landed at the end of The Pier and the pilot was prosecuted for "*causing the helicopter to endanger people and property.*" The pilot, Mr Derek Hammond from Broadstairs in Kent, had landed his helicopter to pick up his wife. In his defence he claimed that The Pier itself ran helicopter rides from The Pier so he couldn't see the problem. The problem was, of course, that helicopter rides had been banned from The Pier 10 years previously!

Continuing the policy of adding of a new white-knuckle ride each year, the Skymaster, which featured two gondolas swinging from side to side 60 feet in the air was added for the 1999 season. Within a week of its installation, it became the most popular ride on The Pier, particularly with teenagers. Andrew Smith told Gazette reporter, Mark Beales, "*It's the best ride around here,*" while 15 year old, Richard Hall, added, "*It was mental!*"

The introduction of the Skymaster led to a bit of a shake up on The Pier as the Big Wheel was removed and the Terminator moved to its former position, with the Skymaster erected in its place.

In the four years since taking over Clacton Pier, the Harrisons had transformed its fortunes but there was one significant change still to come when it was decided to close Oscars. For much of the 1980s and the early 1990s, Oscars had been the main money-

The Tea Cups, one of the first of the new young children's rides introduced.

The new fairground style dodgems.

The front of The Pier showing some of the changes made by the Harrisons. On the left is the new Fish & Chip shop and on the right, the outdoor seating area for the Cockney Pride pub.
[Photo: Anthony Allston]

spinner on The Pier, but by the late 1990s, times were changing and musical tastes had altered and Oscars was attracting fewer and fewer clubbers. Its final night came on 11 September 1999. After which it was closed and the appropriately darkened room turned into a new ghost train ride, known as the Haunted Mansion, for the 2000 season, while the front portion of Oscars was converted into a café called The Lagoon Tea Room, taking inspiration for its name from The Pier's past.

Later in the 2000 season, a special Radio London studio and mast was set up at the end of The Pier, creating a real "blast from the past" as 1960s music, along with the former Pirate Radio station's jingles and promos, were broadcast 24 hours a day throughout August. The DJs included some of the original Radio London DJs, such as Keith Skues and Dave Cash. All money raised went to the Royal National Lifeboat Institution.

2001 saw the arrival of The Twister, while, in 2002, The Frog joined the ever-growing list of attractions and, in 2004, Techno Jump. Pier manager, Mark Baird, described Techno Jump as *"Semi-white knuckle,"* adding *"it is certainly exhilarating. We think it will be the star attraction this season."*

By the time of their retirement from Clacton Pier after 15 years they had accomplished a major refurbishment programme that saw most of the old Pier rides removed or upgraded and many new rides introduced. They had put into place a much-needed maintenance programme and had improved the look of the whole Pier with a number of major cosmetic changes. In particular they had completely reinvented the Seaquarium with a new front entrance and had cleaned out the tanks so that, in the words of Ted Harrison Jr., *"You could actually see the fish!"* They had also removed the sea lion stage, which was falling into disrepair.

A closer view of the right hand side showing the new outdoor seating area in front of the Cockney Pride.

They had improved the under cover area at the front of The Pier with new lattice work and had painted the ceiling with Hammerite.

Probably their one regret with regard to the refurbishment programme was not to have been able to re-open the Jolly Roger. They had had plans to turn it into a "mini Covent Garden" by forming a large tropical garden in the centre, overlooked by a balcony, with the possibility of a children's theatre and an exhibition centre with craft stalls. However, it was not

Peter Battey with his Punch and Judy show became a permanent feature of The Pier entertainments.

to be, but they did at least manage to preserve the building by removing the rotting plywood cladding and replacing it with sheet steel cladding.

There is no doubt the Harrisons had run a highly successful operation, bringing back visitors in their hundreds of thousands during what was not a great period for many British seaside resorts.

At the beginning of 2008 however, they made their decision to exit the leisure industry and sold The Pier to the current owners, Billy and Elliot Ball, with the deal completing in March 2009.

Speedy Pedro, later renamed the Wild Mouse.

A view of the crowded front of The Pier in 1996, "The Year of The Pier". [Photo: Anthony Allston]

The can-can dancers getting ready to perform on 30 June 1996, "Year of The Pier" day.

The balloons released by the West Cliff Theatre's Summer Show dancers on "Year of The Pier" day.

Clacton Pier "dares" visitors to ride The Terminator.

Morphis, the flight simulator.

Some of the seating and lampposts placed on The Pier as a reminder of The Pier's Victorian origins for those seeking a bit of tranquility away from the all-action white-knuckle rides.

Astro Canyon, one of the most popular simulations in Morphis.

The Lagoon Tea Rooms, another reminder of The Pier's history.

The Haunted Mansion which took the place of Oscars nightclub.

Techno Jump, one of the last rides introduced by the Harrisons.

Skymaster, introduced in 1999.

From finding Clacton Pier in this sort of state when they took over, the Harrisons did a magnificent job in restoring and renovating the 125 year old pier and once again making it a leading tourist attraction.

Chapter Nine

The Latest Phase, Billy and Elliot Ball

In 2004, Ted Harrison Snr retired and his son, Ted Jnr, took over the business, but by 2008 he was looking to pursue other interests and felt it was time to sell up.

It was no surprise – and it was probably meant to be – that he turned to the Balls and offered them the exclusive chance to buy The Pier. The deal was agreed at the end of January 2008 but it took a further 14 months to get across the line and complete, mainly due to the onset of the 2008 financial crisis which made business deals more difficult to deliver.

Even then it was far from straightforward. On Friday 13 March both parties met, along with their respective lawyers, to get the deal finalised. The last piece of the jigsaw was the transfer of funds, but it did not happen! There had been a fire at the bank department that was making the payment and so the sale was delayed further.

"Everything was signed up in anticipation of the funds going through and we were legally bound to buy The Pier," said Billy. *"It was an agonising wait over the weekend and again on Monday morning, but we finally got ownership at 4pm on 16 March.*

"It all felt like a huge anti-climax. We were waiting and wanting to celebrate but it just dragged on throughout the Monday until we got the all-important phone call. By that time, it was a feeling of disbelief and 'is it really ours?'"

Billy Ball Sr in the centre, with Elliot (left) and Billy Jr (right) not long after purchasing The Pier.

Billy was 28 and Elliot, 25 when they got the keys.

The first employee to greet the boys when they rushed down to The Pier was Peter Watts. He has worked at the attraction for 40 years – for three different owners - and it still employed by the brothers now.

"Within an hour of taking over The Pier, everyone went home because it was the end of the working day (at that time)," Billy remembers. *"Myself, Elliot and our cousin, Arthur, stayed on until the early hours and by the time the staff turned up the next morning we had emptied the whole amusement arcade except for two pieces of equipment.*

One of the first projects was to convert the Cockney Pride into The Boardwalk. This is the bar of the new Boardwalk.

"The rest went on the scrapheap, and we had made our very first changes in the department of the business we understood best, having been involved with amusement arcades all our lives. Within 24 hours lorry loads of new equipment were arriving.

"On the day we took over we had just enough money to buy The Pier but no working capital. We had enough in the bank to pay one month's wages.

The Lanes Bowling Centre, autumn 2011 a few days before this new facility opened to the public.

There were just three weeks till Easter and we were literally banking on a great bank holiday to get us through and luckily that's what happened."

One of the other things that needed urgent attention was The Cockney Pride pub, which had been closed for 7 months and was in a poor state of repair. The outlook was also poor as all the window openings on the front of the building had been blocked up preventing any view to the outside terrace (then a car park) or the sea and beaches.

Work commenced on renovating the pub on the same day they took over and was re-opened as the Boardwalk Bar and Grill in July 2009, the Balls having felt that a rebrand and new name would be important to the success of the venture.

In the early years they capitalised on both the day time and the late night market with the bar providing family entertainment and food in the day and a music/club offering over weekend evenings. As the years went by and the rest of The Pier became more family oriented, it was decided to drop the late night offering to align with the rest of The Pier's business model.

Stella's Revenge, opened in 2011 – a nod to The Pier's history, occupying the same space as the former iconic roller coaster, the Steel Stella. It was dismantled in January 2020.

The flyer for Oscar's last ever night, 29 August 2010.

The Balls continued their improvements by buying in a Helter Skelter and a Wave Swinger Chairoplane ride as statements of intent.

"Family, friends and contractors played a positive part in our success, and we owe them a great deal as we could not have done it on our own in those early days," said Elliot. *"There was always huge potential, but it came at a cost and that's where their backing was so crucial."*

One time Billy remembers well was about three or four days before their first Easter. He was questioning exactly what they had done – they had spent 14 months trying to buy the attraction and had to make it work.

"We had laid everything on the line including all the family assets," he recalls. *"It was massive pressure, I spoke to Elliot and said something like 'we're never going to make this work!' Rather than offer the reassuring words I was hoping for he said: 'I know, you are right'!!!"*

"We had a bit of a meltdown and wondered what we were going to do. At that moment dad walked in and had overheard what we had been saying and said that if we could not turn The Pier around with all the support and knowhow we had gained there was something wrong. He gave us a strong pep talk and by the time he had finished with us we probably felt like we could have flown to the moon!"

Billy said their father had earlier told them both they could do whatever they wanted to achieve their dream of buying The Pier. He had said they could use everything the family had to make the deal happen – there was however one condition; it was all as long as he didn't have to go back to work – unless he wanted to.

"He had rolled the dice and had confidence in us," said Elliot. *"He felt it was a risk worth taking and an opportunity that was never likely to come again. Dad had worked so hard over the years to give us the best opportunities he could and yet here he was risking his own future to help us better ourselves. To many*

The damage to the Helter Skelter on 28 October 2013.

The new Bumper Boats and the Go Kart track which between them led to the final closure and demolition of the last vestiges of the old swimming pool.

people this would have been strange but this really only underlines the kind of person our Dad was."

That first Easter turned out to be good due to some fantastic weather and just what they needed; it gave the business momentum. The brothers worked long hours and were very hands on; they had the skill sets needed to drive the company forward and applied those skills.

"I liken owning a pier to restoring a classic car," said Billy. *"If you take your time, reinvest and pay attention to detail then the benefits will appreciate, but if you neglect it to deal with unimportant elements you will end up with a worthless headache. We realised early on what had to be done and much of the development in attractions that you see today was planned from the day we took over, the less seen projects have been huge too, we have replaced the infrastructure, heating, rewired and sorted out the gas and electrics – some of which went back to the 1930s".*

"It is not possible to mothball this type of asset. If you close certain areas, they will deteriorate and then you are in reverse. Every square inch of the 6.5 acres must pay for itself. If you can't monetise them, you can't maintain them."

Because there was not a huge amount of money behind the brothers they had to organically evolve. They could only make the improvements as and when they could get their hands on enough money to pay for them. The good thing about that was that as people came back, they were always seeing new changes. They believe this has been part of The Pier's success, an evolving attraction creates interest and people come back to see what's new.

Billy and Elliot always had a master plan which was basically the business plan they put before the banks to secure the borrowing they required. Everything that has been achieved was part of that original plan with some of it still to happen. What visitors see now is all part of the vision they had before they bought The Pier.

It included a bowling centre, bar, adventure golf, children's soft play, a big wheel and a bigger roller coaster. The seeds were there, it was just a case of when to plant them.

Billy admits that this was not always achieved in the order the brothers envisaged but in one that made good sense for the business. The main aim

The rebuilt Helter Skelter reopened in 2016.

overall was always to create a 52-weeks a year attraction. Work on this began with the building the Lanes Bowling Centre in the place where the Haunted Mansion was situated. This also happened to be the space previously occupied by Oscars. Work to remove the Haunted Mansion took place in early 2010, with the machinery and dividing walls removed.

With the peak summer season around the corner they realised there was an opportunity to monetise the space that had essentially now been stripped back to the former night club. Looking at a chance of increasing their income, especially as The Pier's takings weren't huge at that time, a decision was made to re-open Oscars for three nights in August. Each and every night was a huge success with sell out attendances as clubbers travelled from as far afield as Scotland to soak up the atmosphere and take their one last chance to enjoy the club that back in the 1980s and 90s had become an institution in this music genre.

One major improvement that flowed from the conversion of the Haunted Mansion was connecting various areas of the site to make it flow naturally. Originally, the amusement arcade and the Bowling Centre were separate buildings, but they were joined up at the end of 2011.

When the Balls took over, The Pier ran on an Easter to October season, but they knew that had to change. If it virtually closed in the winter it was almost impossible to keep up with the running costs of administration, legal, employment laws, insurance, health and safety and there was a large seasonal loss incurred.

Boards showing the plans for the new Discovery Bay project were erected along The Pier.

The last of the rides awaiting removal to make way for the Discovery Bay area.

Even the snow didn't stop the redevelopment and opening of Discovery Bay on time!

"The business was not viable when we took it over," explained Billy. *"We needed to take more cash if we were to be progressive."*

"We also had to look carefully at the rides on offer – get rid of some older ones and bring some new ones in. We hired in guest rides and refreshed the offer, all to help the cashflow."

"Our pier offers a good clean and active day out, families interact together, make great memories away from screens, smart phones and social media. We truly believe a day at The Pier positively helps with visitors' welfare and well-being.

"At the same time there has never been more competition for the secondary spend so you have to get the whole experience just right."

There were many ups and downs over the first 10 years and there was constantly the financial struggle they had always anticipated with a few unexpected setbacks. In 2013, for example, the iconic Helter Skelter blew down in a storm. It had been bought from a good friend of the Balls and because of the sentimental value they knew they had to rebuild it.

The brothers trawled the four corners of the Earth to search out the right attractions and equipment at the right price. This included the Go Kart track from Germany, point of sale software from India, adventure golf from America, numerous rides from Italy and the amusement arcade equipment from all over the world.

Working holidays were used visiting other parks for ideas along with attending trade shows. In 2013/14 for example the Balls entered a foreign market when they took the Go Karts and Scalextric children's ride to the Global Village in Dubai in association with the Mellor's Group for six months.

The pace hotted up in 2016 when the Helter Skelter returned after its rebuild and refurbishment;

Discovery Bay opens on 21 July 2019.

Billy had drawn up detailed sketches and the architects converted them into technical plans for the vision ahead which had been created by the family. They had to be sure the concept would work before it was handed over to the engineering professionals.

At that very time the Balls took the massive step of changing their primary bank. The one they were with was willing to only part fund the project while the one they changed to came up trumps and was very keen and supportive.

Bumper Boats were introduced and the Miami Beach Party ride was commissioned especially for Clacton Pier. The deep end of the former swimming pool was refurbished and repurposed as part of the boats project, having been derelict and unused since 1993.

The following year planning got underway for the biggest investment to date. This involved a multi-million project to develop the main building on the east side of the site to provide Skull Point Adventure Golf, Discovery Bay Soft Play, Dockside Dodgems, The Galley Restaurant and The Captain's Table Food Outlet.

The scheme also involved a complete revamp and new roof for the concourse.

"First we had to remove rides such as the old Dodgems, Waltzer and Twister so that we would be ready to get to work quickly in 2018," said Billy. *"It was like a huge game of chess, moving equipment into various locations until we were able to get them where we wanted them, but it was all part of the long-term plan."*

Welcome to Discovery Bay!

Part of the new complex included the Skull Point all weather adventure golf course.

Then came the biggest gamble. Although the brothers did not have the final bank letter in their hands, they decided to start the development as they needed it completed and ready to take money for the start of the main summer season. Demolition started and six weeks passed before the letter finally arrived.

Work began on 8 January 2019 as the contractors and in-house maintenance teams broke ground on the new development by removing the old roof of the concourse.

Almost immediately bad weather hit the project but the teams battled through the Beast from the East and managed to make up lost time. *"I can still remember a snow plough clearing the deck so we could carry on fixing the steel,"* Billy recalled later, *"We would do anything we could to press on as everything – and I mean everything - was riding on it."*

The toughest part of the scheme was the removal of timber deck for concrete floors on the central concourse which was a huge civil engineering project in itself on what is the spine of The Pier. That had to be finished by Easter 2019 otherwise the volume of customers at that time of year would not have suitable access to the rest of The Pier, and it caused the greatest stress. Billy says he only slept through sheer exhaustion.

The new dodgems, also part of the newly revamped Discovery Bay area.

Elliot (left) and Billy (right) Ball receive the National Piers Society's Outstanding Achievement Award from Tim Wardley, the Society's Chairman. This was only the second time the award had been made in 40 years.

The demolition of the old Queen Mary building in October 2019.

In spite of everything, the project finished on time and on budget on 21 July – the day it opened to the public. The opening went entirely to plan and was well-received with footfall and visitor numbers as predicted.

Just six weeks later, Billy received a call from his cousin in Aberdeen, offering him the Log Flume and the Looping Star Roller Coaster. They had been key attractions at Codona's Park for 20 years.

The immediate reaction was to decline as it was just not the right time. The cousin returned with an offer he simply could not refuse, and he agreed to the deal.

In the first week of September, Billy & Elliot headed up to Scotland to see what they had got into. It turned out to be the start of the next project while snagging was still taking place on the previous one!

The brothers were not happy with the standard of offering on the ride deck and these two attractions were just the answer to that problem. It allowed them to progress quicker than they had expected.

In February 2019, a team of five from Clacton – including Billy and Elliot – travelled up to the Aberdeen coast to dismantle the Log Flume. The weather was particularly kind for the time of year and they completed the job, in shirt sleeves, in eight days. They returned triumphant with various parts of the ride deposited across Tendring to be totally refurbished. It provided work and money for more than a dozen local firms in the district.

In June 2019, Clacton Pier hosted the National Piers Society which had chosen the town for its annual meeting. At the meeting Billy and Elliot were presented with the society's Outstanding Achievement Award to mark their efforts over the first ten years of their reign. it was only the second time the award had been made in 40 years.

In November it was time to return to Aberdeen with a larger team of ten to dismantle the Looping Star. This time it was a different story. To begin with it was sitting on top of a building 40ft off the ground!

The damage caused to the west side of The Pier following Storm Ciara in February 2020.

The Log Flume, opened in August 2020.

Two 100-ton cranes and one 66-ton crane were brought in. Work continued for ten days, sometimes from 6am to 1am. This time the weather was very unseasonal and many layers of clothing were essential.

"At one point I returned to the site in a lorry and I looked at a tired, weary and cold bunch of men and I realised I had a mutiny on my hands," recalled Billy. *"A union meeting was taking place and I had to pacify the troops."*

Winter 2019/20 proved to be the most eventful with a large team of concrete deck specialists preparing the site for a new layout. The pressure was also on The Pier's own in-house team at this point. The 1930s Queen Mary building was demolished and every single ride, bar two, was relocated.

Everything was going well but on Valentine's Day 2020 that all changed. The team was working on the west side of the structure four days after Storm Ciara, which, unbeknown at the time, had temporarily weakened the piles holding up The Pier. New concrete was applied to the deck and the piles sank with the modest weight on top and there was a partial collapse of the west corner of the deck.

This all added to the workload and structural engineers had to be brought in.

"The world's leading engineering authority at HR Wallingford near Oxford was consulted and agreed we had done nothing wrong, and it had been down to the effect of the storm," said Billy. *"It all added to the workload and we ended up with significant delays all round."*

To make matters worse, just weeks later, the world was struck by the COVID pandemic and the contracted workforce had to be laid off.

If there was a positive side, the small in-house team with greatly reduced numbers than planned, worked every day through the pandemic to complete the project. The Log Flume eventually opened in August 2020 and the Looping Star in October 2021.

The Looping Star, which replaced Stella's revenge, opened in October 2021.

The Elegant Wheel experience shortly after it opened to the public in the Summer of 2021.

Also on a very positive note, in 2020 Clacton Pier picked up the prestigious Pier of the Year Award from the National Piers Society. It was a further honour and recognition for the efforts made under the Balls' ownership and a real accolade for the family.

The Pier had beaten off stiff competition from 60 others around the country. There were further honours for Clacton Pier from the Tendring Blue Ribbon Business Awards. It won the Hospitality and Leisure category in 2017; the Business in the Community category in 2018 and Team of the Year in 2019.

As part of the bounce back from COVID, the brothers also brought in another major attraction, the Elegant Wheel Experience, which was initially leased for the summer of 2021, but, after a successful first season, was purchased outright.

Billy and Elliot Ball are as keen as ever to embellish and improve the existing attractions on the site of the largest pleasure pier in Europe. There are still areas that need rejuvenation and regeneration.

Future projects will see them turn their attention to the west side of The Pier where they are looking to vastly improve the fabric of the buildings and refresh the offerings within.

There is also the deck-down structure which needs constant attention as it is basically over 150 years old and provides the platform for everything above.

The neck of The Pier will also come under scrutiny going forwards with uses being looked at for both the former Lifeboat House and the Jolly Roger.

A Government grant was provided to kick-start investigations into plans for the Jolly Roger. For two and a half summers it was home to Matthew Wingate's Circus Fantasia (2017 to 2019) and in the past couple of years has been used as a workshop.

In terms of the rides the end of 2022 will see the return of the ever-popular Waltzer after a major £100,000 facelift.

Clacton Pier has stood for just over 150 years and is now in as good a shape as at any time in its illustrious history and in excellent shape to face the next 150 years.

Clacton Pier once again proudly displays its unique address to the world, first announced by the Kingsman Family in the 1930s, as Billy and Elliot Ball revive its glory days.

Chapter Ten

"Underneath the ocean rolled and foamed and roared" The Pier Pavilion and Jolly Roger

The origins of The Pier Pavilion go back to the 1880s, when bands used to play in the open-air at the end of The Pier. The earliest we have any record of dates back to 1881, when the band of the 2nd Essex Rifle Volunteer Regiment, who were encamped nearby on the East Cliffs, gave two public performances on The Pier.

The blueprint drawn up in 1892 by Kinipple and Jaffrey for The Pier Pavilion.

Following on from this, in 1882, The Pier engaged a band, under the direction of Mr Harry Phillips, to play concerts throughout the season. These concerts also included other stage acts, comprising comedians, acrobats, dancers, jugglers, illusionists and even a Punch & Judy show.

Over the next few years the band appeared under different directors including Mr Sydney Dewics, Mr C Herbert and Mr Sydney Davies.

By the end of the 1880s, the band concerts were becoming so popular that a small enclosure was built for the band and the audiences.

When the Clacton-on-Sea Pier Company decided to lengthen The Pier (see chapter two), one of the improvements that was deemed to be absolutely necessary was the provision of a proper building to house the very popular band concerts and so the idea of The Pier Pavilion was born.

Plans were drawn up in 1892 by engineers, Kinipple and Jaffrey of Victoria Street, London, for a new steel structure, 156' long, 66' wide and 38' 6" high.

Building work underway.

The whole to be built on the widest part of the new Pier extension and erected on creosoted fir bearers laid under the deck planking.

The building work was carried out by Murdock and Cameron, a Glasgow firm. The Pavilion was glazed along both sides and contained an outside viewing gallery, which was sheltered from the rain by an overhanging balcony. Access to this was obtained

The new Pier Pavilion opens to the public.

The viewing balcony became an immediate success with the public.

from two sides within the main hall and from an internal stairway in the passage between the main hall and the refreshment room which was at the end nearest the sea.

The main concert hall was 75' x 45' 6 and could accommodate up to 1,500 people seated in the stalls and the balcony. The balcony floor also contained the ladies' rooms and toilets. There were five entrances, two on each side, with the principal entrance at the opposite end to the refreshment room. Between the entrance and the main hall was a vestibule containing eight small shops. There was a glazed screen between the vestibule and the main auditorium which could be opened if more space was needed during a performance. The whole building cost £12,000 (well over £1.5m in today's money).

The first concert given inside the new Pavilion took place on the afternoon of 17 July 1893, making it the first theatre to open anywhere in Clacton-on-Sea. Although it was now open to the public, it was still not yet fully built and there was no seating available in the balcony. The doors were left open around the Pavilion so people could stand outside and hear

The interior of the Pier Pavilion.

The new refreshment room, the cause of much controversy when it applied for a liquor license.

the band. Because the building was not complete yet, no charge was made to either those inside or outside.

This state of affairs continued for the next two weeks and the local paper reported that for the concert on 24 July, both inside and outside, the Pavilion was crowded and that the audience very much appreciated the musical selections chosen by the director, Sydney Davies, who was to be congratulated for the *"excellent vocalists and orchestra"*. In particular, the musical sketch by Walter Banks *"caused much amusement and was encored."*

The following week, beginning 31 July, the Pavilion was fully open and a small charge was now made to attend the concerts but, in spite of this, the concerts were just as crowded as before with soprano, Miss Rose Moss, being a particular favourite.

From then until the end of the season, the Pavilion continued to play to capacity audiences of 1,500 and became firmly established as the leading holiday attraction in Clacton.

In August 1893, Mrs Wallis, the licensee of the Royal Hotel, applied for a liquor license for the refreshment room and bar, supported by Clacton Pier. A public meeting was organised in Clacton by the Temperance Society and local churches to object.

Some of the interior iron work showing the initials of the Clacton Pier Company.

An advertisement for one of Harry Baynton's Easter Concerts

When the hearing took place, Mrs Wallis argued that now that the Pavilion was open there was a real need for a licensed refreshment room at The Pier Head not just for the Pavilion itself but also for the many visitors arriving by paddle steamer. *"After their long voyage from London, many would be In need of refreshment,"* she said.

Mrs Wallis added that she had an agreement with The Pier to provide refreshments rooms with one bar and two rooms for teetotallers at a rent of £220 per annum.

Speaking for the objectors, local solicitor, Mr Thompson Smith, said that his clients wished only that the quietude and peace of Clacton should not be disturbed by the granting of a license *"which might lead to noise and disturbance"*. He added *"those arriving by paddle steamer had the opportunity to buy drink on board and that people sometimes arrived the worse for liquor."*

As far as adding to the attractiveness of The Pier Pavilion, he thought the opposite was the case and that it could lead to the concert hall degenerating into a second class Music Hall.

Finally, he referred to the public meeting which, he said, had been open to everyone and yet only one person had supported the granting of a license. He then handed in a petition signed by 456 visitors and 243 residents objecting to the granting of a license.

In the end, the magistrates found in favour of the objectors and so the Pavilion refreshment room was forced to open without a liquor license and it was several years before the decision was eventually overturned.

The Pavilion opened for its second season on 11 June 1894. Once again, The Pier Band was under the direction of Sydney Davies and the two leading vocalists on the opening night were Miss Emily Foxcroft and Mr Walter George.

Over the next few weeks, the guest artists appearing with the band changed weekly and

Harry Baynton and The Pier Pavilion Orchestra on the stage.

A notice on the front of The Pier for The Court Jesters, one of the companies who leased The Pier Pavilion during the early Edwardian period.

included straight singers such as Miss Florence Croft (contralto), Mr D'Arcy Clayton (tenor), Miss Maisie Riversdale (soprano) and Mr Barry Lindon (bass) as well as more specialised acts. These included Mr Oswald Sharpley with his two *"highly amusing songs"*, *"The Proposal"* and *"That Awful Club"*; Mr Arthur Melrose, *"the celebrated coster comedian & siffleur"* and Miss Maud Kempton in her *"celebrated skirt dance, tarantella etc."*

By the middle of that first full season, The Pier Pavilion was already receiving excellent reviews. The East Essex Advertiser and Clacton News noted that the concerts were, *"a most attractive feature for the town and a point of no little importance that in the columns of the London papers notices should appear of the new songs being sung in The Pier Pavilion, Clacton-on-Sea,"* while an early visitor to the Pavilion was the later-to-be famous novelist, Edgar Wallace, who was then earning a living (15s a week) as a builder's labourer in Clacton. He wrote in his diary,

"Went on The Pier, into the Pavilion. Very good vocal and instrumental concert. It was hard to realise that underneath us the ocean rolled and foamed and roared."

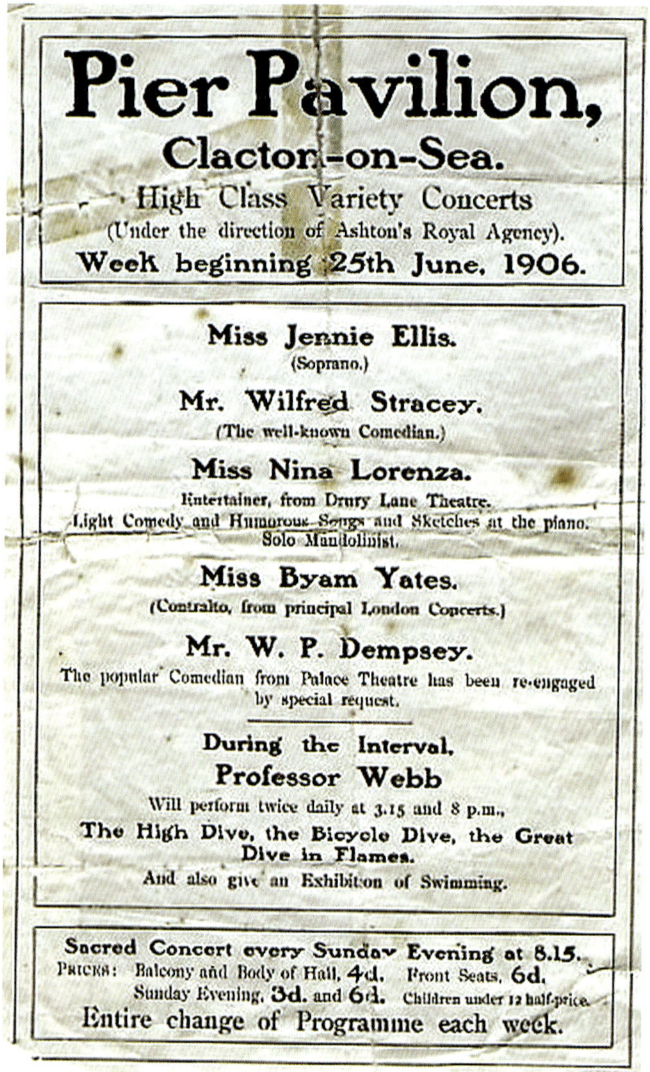

Pier Pavilion,

Clacton-on-Sea.

High Class Variety Concerts

(Under the direction of Ashton's Royal Agency).

Week beginning 25th June, 1906.

Miss Jennie Ellis.

(Soprano.)

Mr. Wilfred Stracey.

(The well-known Comedian.)

Miss Nina Lorenza.

Entertainer, from Drury Lane Theatre.
Light Comedy and Humorous Songs and Sketches at the piano.
Solo Mandolinist.

Miss Byam Yates.

(Contralto, from principal London Concerts.)

Mr. W. P. Dempsey.

The popular Comedian from Palace Theatre has been re-engaged by special request.

During the Interval,

Professor Webb

Will perform twice daily at 3.15 and 8 p.m.,

The High Dive, the Bicycle Dive, the Great Dive in Flames.

And also give an Exhibition of Swimming.

Sacred Concert every Sunday Evening at 8.15.

PRICES: Balcony and Body of Hall, 4d. Front Seats, 6d.
Sunday Evening, 3d. and 6d. Children under 12 half-price.

Entire change of Programme each week.

A programme for 1906 during the period the Pavilion was leased by Ashton's Royal Agency, showing Professor Webb and his diving feats as an interval attraction.

The sign at the front of The Pier in 1907 shows Harold Montague is now the lessee of the Pavilion.

On 2 August, as the Summer season was reaching its height, a weekly "Fashionable Night" was introduced every Thursday with an augmented orchestra of 24 performers and special artistes including Arthur Melrose and Maud Kempton.

In September, as the season was coming to a close, a series of benefit concerts was held. The first of which, held on 3 September, was for the musical director, Sydney Davies, himself. The advert for the concert promised, "*A splendid array of talent, and we strongly advise everyone not to miss the treat provided.*"

Five days later, a special fund raiser for the Clacton Lifeboat was held. Sydney Davies announced in the local paper that he "*will be glad to receive the names of ladies and gentlemen of talent willing to assist this noble institution. The Lifeboat Crew will appear in costume during the evening, and a description of the past years' work will be given by Mr F W Lewellen, hon sec.*"

The final benefit concert was given in aid of Mr Legerton, The Pier Master, and The Pier staff. As well as a full orchestra and vocalists, artists included Mr R B Hopkins, royal campanologist; Mr Cecil Barnard, musical sketch and Mr W F Rawles, elocutionist.

The final concert of the season was given on 30 September, the weekly Sunday "Sacred Concert".

Following the end of the Summer Concert Season, on October 1st, 2nd and 3rd, Mr Noakes' Stereorama & Optical Tableaux from the Crystal Palace and London Halls was engaged with a change of programme each evening:

"*October 1st, Chicago and the Exposition, or a Visit to the World's Fair*

October 2nd, Manx Land, its Beauties and its Legends

October 3rd, Rural England and its picturesque water ways"

The advertisement noted that the "*subjects are beautifully illustrated with realistic natural photographs and each evening Mr C W Locke will introduce a selection of magnificent mechanical changes and dioramic effects. A selection will also be given from Mr D W Noakes' latest invention entitled Optical Tableaux reproducing in the highest artistic fashion some of the most famous pictures of the day.*"

Doors opened at 7 p.m. and the performance commenced at 7:30 p.m. Admission prices were, front seats 6d, balcony and area 4d, back seats 3d.

For the next decade or so, entertainment in The Pier Pavilion followed a similar pattern with daily concerts during the Summer, Sacred Concerts on Sundays and special fundraising concerts towards the end of the season, which included an annual Lifeboat Benefit Concert. The only difference being that towards the end of the 19th century, Mr Harry Baynton took over as Musical Director.

Harry Baynton was a well-known figure around Clacton who owned a music shop in Station Road and was a local music teacher. As well as becoming musical director of the Pavilion Orchestra, he was also the musical director at the new West Cliff Gardens Theatre.

In the early years of the 20th century, the Pavilion became available on annual lease. In 1906, for example, the Pavilion was leased by Ashton's Royal Agency, one of the country's top entertainment agencies who put on shows at St James's Hall, the leading concert hall in London, where they produced Music Hall and Concert Party type shows. And, although they continued the tradition of the daily orchestral and vocal concerts, including the weekly Sacred Concert, they introduced more novelty and variety into the proceedings. A programme from 1906, for example shows that Professor Webb's diving feats now became part of the concert shows.

Ashton's was followed in 1907 by Harold Montague, a well-known Music Hall star of the time, who ran a highly successful Music Hall group known as The Vagabonds. Although The Vagabonds were the mainstay of the season, other groups appeared during the year, including the The Tatlers and The Willow Pattern Serenaders.

Following these annual changes, 1909 saw the establishment of a company who were to take over the Pavilion for the next 15 years when Will C. Pepper's White Coons moved in. The White Coons were already a well-known Concert Party, founded in 1899 by Will C. Pepper in Mumbles, South Wales. From there they toured the country, setting up concert parties in places like Felixstowe and Bray in Ireland.

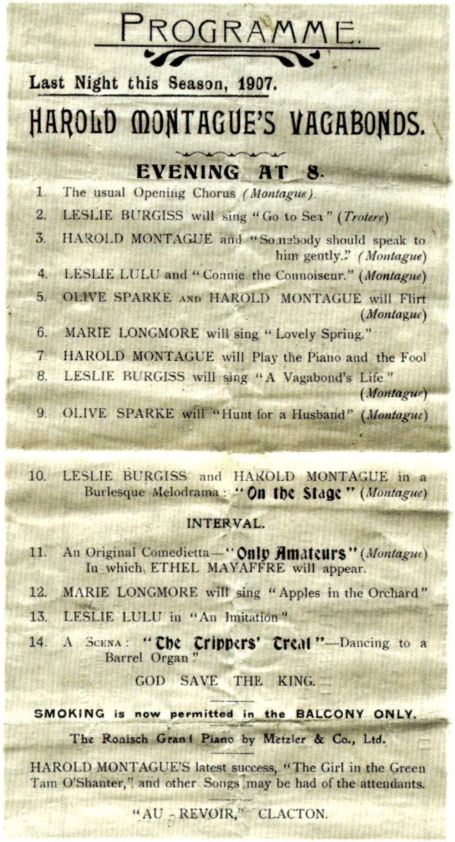

PROGRAMME.

Last Night this Season, 1907.

HAROLD MONTAGUE'S VAGABONDS.

EVENING AT 8.

1. The usual Opening Chorus *(Montague)*.
2. LESLIE BURGISS will sing "Go to Sea" *(Trotere)*
3. HAROLD MONTAGUE and "Somebody should speak to him gently." *(Montague)*
4. LESLIE LULU and "Connie the Connoiseur." *(Montague)*
5. OLIVE SPARKE AND HAROLD MONTAGUE will Flirt *(Montague)*
6. MARIE LONGMORE will sing "Lovely Spring."
7. HAROLD MONTAGUE will Play the Piano and the Fool
8. LESLIE BURGISS will sing "A Vagabond's Life" *(Montague)*
9. OLIVE SPARKE will "Hunt for a Husband" *(Montague)*
10. LESLIE BURGISS and HAROLD MONTAGUE in a Burlesque Melodrama: **"On the Stage"** *(Montague)*

INTERVAL.

11. An Original Comedietta—**"Only Amateurs"** *(Montague)* In which ETHEL MAYAFFRE will appear.
12. MARIE LONGMORE will sing "Apples in the Orchard"
13. LESLIE LULU in "An Imitation"
14. A SCENA: **"The Trippers' Treat"**—Dancing to a Barrel Organ"

GOD SAVE THE KING.

SMOKING is now permitted in the BALCONY ONLY.

The Ronisch Grand Piano by Metzler & Co., Ltd.

HAROLD MONTAGUE'S latest success, "The Girl in the Green Tam O'Shanter," and other Songs may be had of the attendants.

"AU - REVOIR," CLACTON.

The 1907 last night programme for Harold Montague's Vagabonds.

They were typical of a concert party of their period with songs, humour, sketches and specialty acts and fitted in well with the mood of the times, becoming hugely popular with Clacton audiences. So much so that the White Coons became The Pier's major attraction until the outbreak of the Great War in 1914, with the main sign at the front of The Pier being given over to advertising them.

When The Pier re-opened after the War, the first entertainment to be offered was the return of the White Coons to the Pavilion at Easter 1921. The local paper reported that holidaymakers were *"given a real treat"* and that the White Coons immediately

1909 and the White Coons begin their 15 year run at the Pavilion.

regained their former popularity, particularly comedian, Wal Barker, who, *"put his audience in a state of hopeless hilarity."* Will Pepper's son, Harry played the piano.

The White Coons continued to appear throughout the Summer Season with full houses at every performance. The concerts were *"varied by confetti fights and other attractive items, proving irresistible to visitors bent on having a good time."*

From the following year, 1922, special Sunday Concerts with top stars from London, including Leslie Sarony, who was billed as *"appearing by kind permission of the London Palladium"*, were added to the daily White Coons diet.

The White Coons remained until the end of the 1924 season, at which point a number of changes were made as Kingsman drew up new improvement plans for the Pavilion. Firstly, to accommodate the ever-growing audiences, plans were drawn up to add boxes and an upper circle to accommodate more audience seating and secondly the installation of a new grand wrought iron staircase at the front so that visitors could go straight up to the balcony level from the outside. As a result of these changes, the name of the theatre was changed to The Pier Theatre.

The first resident company to appear in the newly named theatre was a Cabaret Revue Company called the K.N.'s, who took over the daily performances. The local paper found this new company to be *"most mirth provoking."*

Variety and Revue continued until 1932, when The Pier Theatre changed direction altogether and put on a repertory season, mostly farces, performed by Arthur Gibbons' Popular Players. One play was "The Ghost Train", written by Arnold Ridley, later famous, of course, for his role as Private Godfrey in Dad's Army.

At the end of this season, Ernest Kingsman decided on an even more drastic rebuilding and reorganisation of The Pier Theatre. To enable these new major additions and improvements, the winter was spent on the immense work of installing piling under the structure with screw and concrete piles to hold the weight of the new building.

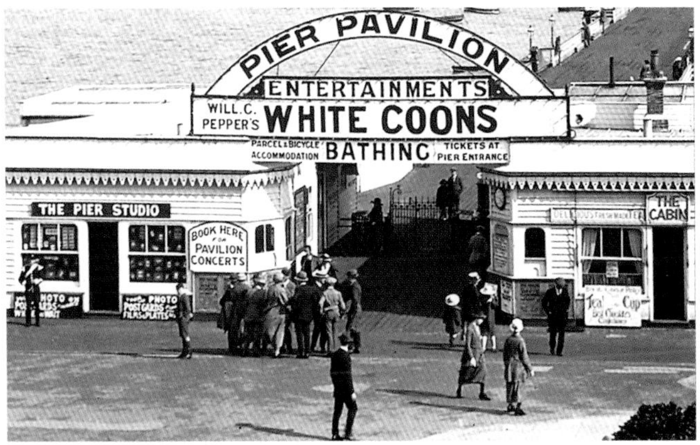

The White Coons became The Pier's major attraction.

The White Coons on stage during a performance.

Once this was completed, the old stage and dressing rooms were removed and the balcony was re-decked and extended to the full width of the structure. By Spring 1933, glazed slides were being fitted all around the old promenade on the balcony level, giving a new splendid floor with seating for 1,200 and a similar capacity below. New embossed sheet steel wall coverings known as Steleonite and Crimpstele were also installed.

This new improved and modernised Pier Theatre was relaunched at the Clacton Trade Fair and Exhibition in May 1933 as the Jolly Roger.

The newly named Jolly Roger was opened to the public for the first time on Whit Saturday, 3rd June with a new Summer Season as Ada Kingsman presented Hal Bryan's Revue, Happy Days, with full cast supported by Walter Snelling and his Jolly Roger Band.

The following day, a grand christening ceremony staged by top Music Hall star, Wee Georgie Wood, supported by a full London Company including Bennett and Williams on their phono-fiddles. The music was provided by the Blue Lagoon's Teddy Dobbs and his orchestra.

In addition to changes to the theatre itself, a new amusement hall was opened beneath the theatre on 3 June 1933. It was to have been opened by Labour Party leader, George Lansbury, but he was unable to attend. Instead, the M.P. for Stratford and Mayor of East Ham, Tom Groves, did the honours. *"The splendour of the new hall,"* he said, *"paid tribute to those behind the work,"* and he was *"sure it would make a big contribution to the pleasure of thousands of visitors to Clacton."*

In 1936, the Jolly Roger became the setting for the Rambla Concert Party's evening performance under the title, Jolly Revellers, while in 1938, the theatre was renamed the Jollity Theatre as Clown Bertram also staged his children's shows there twice a day, morning and afternoon. These three daily shows remained until the closure of the theatre on the outbreak of War.

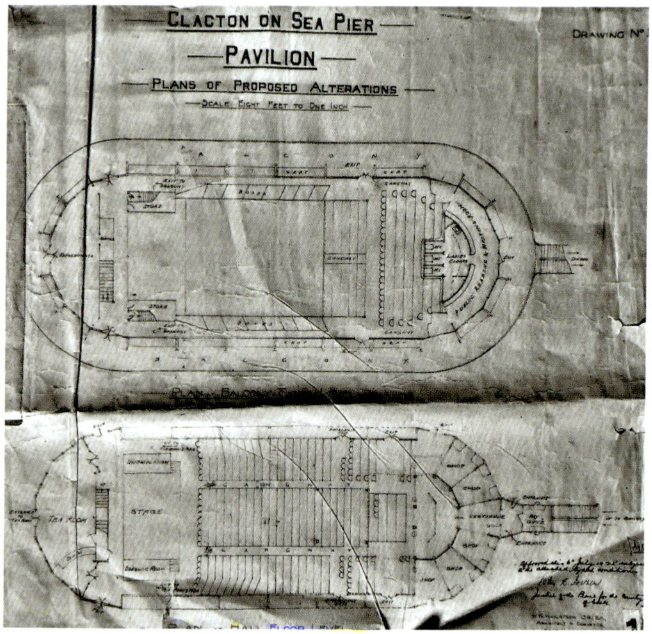

Plans for the 1924 alterations. The new external staircase is marked on the right.

A K.N.s programme from 1927 showing the new name, Pier Theatre.

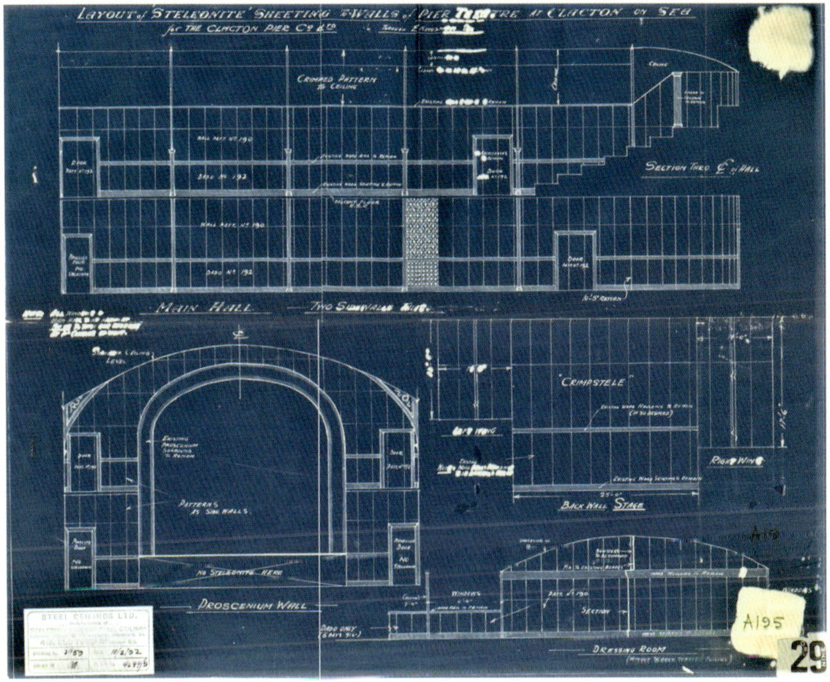

The blueprint for the new steel walls drawn up in 1932 by Steel Ceilings Ltd and executed in 1933.

The theatre re-opened once again as the Jolly Roger in 1948 again with three shows per day. In the morning and afternoon, "Uncle Tommy", billed as *"television's favourite childrens' clown"*, put on shows at 2:00 p.m. and 6:00 p.m. and in the evening, the theatre was leased to London theatre manager, Richard Stone, who staged a variety show at 8:15 p.m., called Lagoon Follies, with a programme change each Thursday.

Richard Stone chose as his producer a young comedy actor just beginning to make a name for himself in the theatre, Ian Carmichael. The show itself consisted of just seven performers, three men (two comedians and a singer), three women (one comedienne, a singer and another who was described as an "all-purpose girl") and a pianist. One of the comedians was a young 21 year old comic actor just out of the Navy, having his first Summer variety season, by the name of Terry Scott.

Uncle Tommy and Lagoon Follies reappeared in 1949, but, in 1950, with the return of the Rambla Concert Party, the Ramblas resumed their evening shows in the Jolly Roger as they had done before the War.

From then until the demise of the Ramblas at the end of the 1964 season, the Jolly Roger continued to be their evening home as well as their morning and afternoon home in case of poor weather. When the Ramblas closed, so did the Jolly Roger.

Following its closure, the Jolly Roger quickly fell into a state of disrepair and was used mostly as a

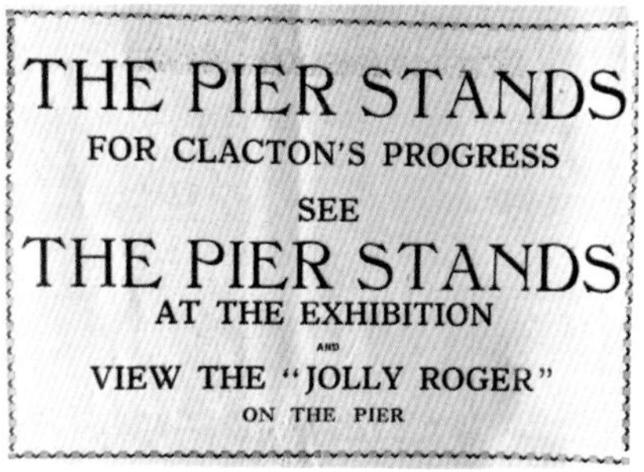
THE PIER STANDS
FOR CLACTON'S PROGRESS
SEE
THE PIER STANDS
AT THE EXHIBITION
AND
VIEW THE "JOLLY ROGER"
ON THE PIER

The first public mention of the name Jolly Roger in a newspaper advert for the stand at the 1933 Clacton Trade Fair and Exhibition held at the Town Hall in May.

Clacton-on-Sea
The Pier
Whit - Attractions
The Wonder Swimming Pool
Grand Opening Gala
WHIT - SATURDAY AFTERNOON
at 3 o'clock
INTERNATIONAL AND INTER-CLUB
Diving Contests and Team Races
Special Visit of VAN-DE-VEN, Diving Champion of Belgium
Mammoth Firework Display at Night
WHIT-SATURDAY at 8 o'clock
First Performance in
THE JOLLY ROGER
"HAPPY DAYS"
with HAL BRYAN and Full London Company
Reserved Seats 2/-, 1/6 and 1/- (including Tax and Pier Toll)
Blue Lagoon
Grand Opening
Whit - Saturday
at 8 o'clock
Bertram & His Happy Family
in the
Children's Theatre
DAILY at 3 and 7.
The Rambla
Alfresco Performance
Daily at 11 and 3
by
The Ramblas
15 ARTISTES
Open-Air Physical Culture Classes
Free Instruction. Directed by WALLY DAKIN, the Well-known Gymnast
WHIT-SUNDAY at 8 o'clock.
Grand Christening Ceremony of
THE JOLLY ROGER
by
Wee Georgie Wood
Supported by Full London Company.
OCEAN THEATRE at 8
RANDOLPH SUTTON
and Full London Company
Crystal Casino. Miniature Speed Boat Lake.
Jolly Roger Amusements. Electric Water Dodgems.

A Clacton Pier notice from the local paper advertising the Jolly Roger's opening performance on Whit Saturday followed by its official "Grand Christening" by Wee Georgie Wood the following day.

storage area. In the early 1980s, after Francis McGinty took over The Pier, the steel frame and cast iron tread plates from the front grand staircase were removed, some being re-used to repair the east boat landing stage. The raised stage floor was also removed and the floorboards and timbers used in the building of Oscars.

The sea end of the building became a temporary wood shop and later an amusement arcade for a very short period. It was then taken over by Pauline McGinty, who returned it to its original use as a tea room and restaurant known as the Jolly Roger Cafe. Pauline has run the restaurant ever since.

With the intention of re-opening the Jolly Roger as a circus, the next major removal was the whole first floor up to the stage including the front grand staircase giving a large flat floor space that could be used as a circus ring entered from deck level. The inside was completely gutted and everything inside removed. Peter Watts, who helped with the renovation said he can remember the *"St. Osyth Trading Co. sand lorries running up and down The Pier collecting the material that was thrown in over the balcony. This included a few hundred directors' deck chairs, a baby grand piano and rolls of back drop scenery."*

As part of the preparations for the circus, the outside of the Jolly Roger was covered in red and white vinyl type tarpaulins, that hung from the gutters, with the roof painted in matching colours to give a better impression of a circus big top marquee.

Once the demolition, clearance and redecoration work was completed, the Jolly Roger was able to re-open to the public for the first time in almost 20 years as Sally Chipperfield's Circus performed for the 1982 season. Sadly, it was just for one year, at the end of which the theatre closed again.

A programme for the Jolly Roger from 1937.

Although the theatre itself closed, the Jolly Roger as a building did remain open to the public for a short while when the Jungle Safari ride was removed from the front amusement hall and placed inside but, following its removal the following year, the Jolly Roger returned to its use as storage facility, with old arcade equipment amongst other things stored there.

By the time the Harrisons took over The Pier in 1994, the Jolly Roger had once again deteriorated badly and, although not re-opening the theatre, they spent money on restoring and renovating the building to preserve it for any possible future re-opening, removing the plywood cladding and the window frames, which were by then rotting away, replacing them with the profiled sheet steel cladding that still survives to this day.

The Jolly Roger again lay dormant until 2017 when Billy and Elliot Ball decided to open it once again for public use by staging Circus Fantasia inside. A brand new brightly coloured fascia was erected at the front while, inside, the 1982 circus area was renovated with sections of the 1982 seating at each side of the ring pressed into service with seven tiers of brand new tip-up seating also installed, facing the ring.

The circus lasted for three years and then from the end of 2019 to 2022, the Jolly Roger was once again used as a storage area.

It has now re-opened in 2022 to stage an exhibition and series of short talks to celebrate the launch of this book, the 150th Anniversary of The Pier and the centenary of Clown Bertram and Filbert's first

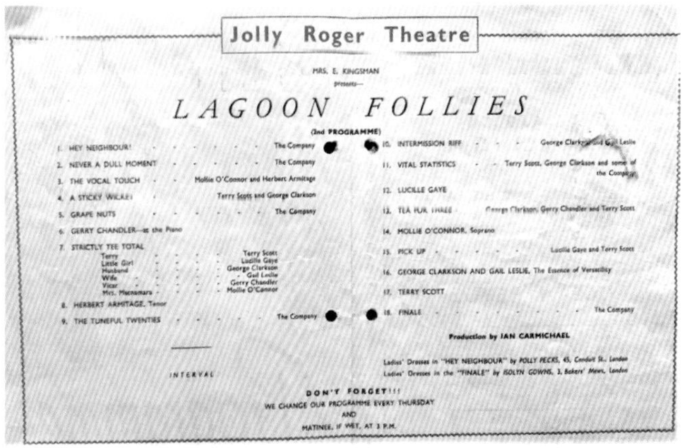

Jolly Roger Theatre

MRS. E. KINGSMAN presents—

LAGOON FOLLIES

(2nd PROGRAMME)

1. HEY NEIGHBOUR! - The Company
2. NEVER A DULL MOMENT - The Company
3. THE VOCAL TOUCH - Mollie O'Connor and Herbert Armitage
4. A STICKY WICKET - Terry Scott and George Clarkson
5. GRAPE NUTS - The Company
6. GERRY CHANDLER—at the Piano
7. STRICTLY TEE TOTAL
   - Terry - Terry Scott
   - Little Girl - Lucille Gaye
   - Husband - George Clarkson
   - Wife - Gail Leslie
   - Vicar - Gerry Chandler
   - Mrs. Macnamara - Mollie O'Connor
8. HERBERT ARMITAGE, Tenor
9. THE TUNEFUL TWENTIES - The Company

INTERVAL

10. INTERMISSION RIFF - George Clarkson and Gail Leslie
11. VITAL STATISTICS - Terry Scott, George Clarkson and some of the Company
12. LUCILLE GAYE
13. TEA FOR THREE - George Clarkson, Gerry Chandler and Terry Scott
14. MOLLIE O'CONNOR, Soprano
15. PICK UP - Lucille Gaye and Terry Scott
16. GEORGE CLARKSON AND GAIL LESLIE, The Essence of Versatility
17. TERRY SCOTT
18. FINALE - The Company

Production by IAN CARMICHAEL

Ladies' Dresses in "HEY NEIGHBOUR" by POLLY PECKS, 45, Conduit St., London
Ladies' Dresses in the "FINALE" by ISOLYN GOWNS, 3, Bakers' Mews, London

DON'T FORGET!!!
WE CHANGE OUR PROGRAMME EVERY THURSDAY
AND
MATINEE, IF WET, AT 3 P.M.

The programme for the 1948 Lagoon Follies, produced by Ian Carmichael, with Terry Scott as one of the cast.

appearance on The Pier and the centenary of the Clacton Carnival which began in 1922 on The Pier.

It is hoped that in the very near future the Jolly Roger will once again return to public use. Watch this space - if you'll pardon the pun!

The Ramblas evening performances in the Jolly Roger were called Showtime.

A 1961 Showtime programme.

A 1958 Showtime programme.

The interior of the Jolly Roger.

Following the closure of the circus, the Jolly Roger returned to being mainly a storage area as it had been between 1965 and 1981.

The Jolly Roger was given a red and white striped external make-over ready to house Sally Chipperfield's Circus in 1982.

Between 2017 and 2019, Elliot and Billy Ball reopened the Jolly Roger to house Circus Fantasia.

Pauline McGinty's Jolly Roger Café, open for the last 40 years in roughly the same position as the original refreshment rooms back in 1893 when the Pavilion first opened.

Chapter Eleven

Professor Webb and Friends

A popular event that used to take place on – or rather off – Clacton Pier in the early days was stunt diving. One of the earliest of the stunt divers was Professor Jules Gautier, who, for two weeks in August 1889, performed a season of high dives and swimming stunts daily from Clacton Pier. He was just 5ft 4 inches tall and weighed 10 stone. He once swam 3 miles in the River Thames with his hands and feet tied. He promoted himself as 'National Champion of France' and that he was born in Caen. In fact he was born in Islington and his 'French' accent was terrible! One of his stunts including diving into the sea off The Pier and then swimming back, singing, smoking and peeling and eating an orange under water.

He was followed in 1898 by Professor Reddish who used to perform his 'Great Monte Cristo Sack Feat.' This involved him being thrown into the sea with a 56lb weight attached. One afternoon the crowds gasped and shouted out when Professor Reddish didn't surface. The piermaster, Robert Legerton, and another boatman rescued him, dragging him out of the rough sea. The diver seemed grateful but was very upset at losing his 56lb weight which remained at the bottom of the sea.

Following him came the most famous and best remembered of the diving "professors", George Webb. Webb performed throughout the Edwardian period up till the First World War. Professor Webb was a local Clacton man, living first in Oxford Road, later moving to Ellis Road. He performed many different stunts but his best remembered ones both had unexpected and unfortunate consequences of differing degrees of seriousness.

The first was his "Cigarette Dive", in which he would dive in to the sea with a lighted cigarette in his mouth and come up out of the water with the cigarette still alight. The way he used to do this was to flip the cigarette inside his mouth just as he reached the water and then flip it out again as he came back up. One day, however, he flipped so hard that he flipped his false teeth out and they were lost forever beneath the waves.

The second, and his most famous dive of all, which he would use as the finale to all his sessions, was to ride his bike off the end of The Pier, diving in to the water off the bike. On one occasion, in 1911, just as he commenced his dive a rowing boat come round the end of The Pier and the professor landed smack in the middle of the boat. The poor woman passenger in the boat never knew what hit her and was rushed off to Clacton Cottage Hospital suffering from concussion. Webb received nothing more than slight bruising and was ready to dive again the next day.

Although he retired from professional diving when the First World War broke out he continued to keep fit and just one week off from his 74th birthday, he was given the honour of performing the first dive from the top board of The Pier Swimming pool at its opening ceremony on 2 July 1932.

Webb put his continued fitness down to the fact that he continued to walk six miles every day and never smoked or drank. He also worked hard, owning two provisions shops in Clacton and was often to be seen cycling round Clacton delivering goods to customers. The cycle he used was very rusty and he was once asked if this was the same bike that he used for his dives off The Pier. He just laughed! Apart from still being able to dive at the age of 74, his fitness stood him in good stead generally as he died at the age of 95 on 11 July 1954, having, it is said, never had a day's illness in his life until then.

Professor Reddish advertising his "Great Monte Cristo Sack Feat" in 1898.

Although he was a regular performer and the most popular, Professor Webb wasn't the only diver to dive off Clacton Pier during the Edwardian period. At least two others appeared. The first was Bert Powsey, another "Professor". He had begun at Herne Bay, moving to Brighton and then to Clacton in 1906/7. He also performed a bicycle dive as well as his 'Sensational Dive in Flames' in which he was placed in a sack with cotton wool affixed and then doused with petrol set alight just before jumping.

A portrait of Clacton's own diver, Professor George Webb.

The other diver was Walter Tong, who had also been diving at Brighton before coming to Clacton in 1910. He had learnt to swim at the age of nine and throughout his teens he attained various awards from the Royal Life Saving Society. As an entertainer, Tong was a great exponent of the daring 'Mollberg Dive' invented by eccentric Swedish acrobat Anders Fredrik Mollberg. This involved what was described as an "eye-watering" backward somersault from a height of 40 to 50 feet. To spice things up a little he sometimes performed this dive in a full suit, shirt, tie and shoes and would then completely undress underwater. The audience's reaction to his appearance when he climbed out of the water with no clothes on back on to The Pier doesn't seem to have been recorded anywhere.

The 1920s saw more stunt divers including one legged diver, Montague Wesley, and Mona de Gray, who both performed stunts dives in 1924. Mona dfe Gray was billed as 'the Champion Underwater Contortionist of the World' dived off the end of The Pier. She performed a Fire Dive, the "*biggest ever ventured by anyone*". The poster advertising her appearance said, "*Mona will be bound in 4 yards of cotton wool saturated with 2 quarts of paraffin oil-set alight and dive from The Pier IN REAL FLAMES.*" At the bottom of the poster was written - "*Failure means BURNT TO DEATH.*"

Another female diver in the 1920s was Madge Goodhall, who, at one time had been Harry Houdini's stage assistant. She was forever announcing that she was going to swim the English Channel – but she never did! Her most famous dive was one based on the "sack dive" as performed by her former boss, in which she was tied in a sack and thrown into the sea, escaping from it while under water.

One other slightly different act was that performed by the Daring Brothers, who undertook a double act with various synchronised dives, including the Mollberg Dive from a diving board over 60 feet above the sea as well as the "backward-forward" dive, two and half somersaults and jack knife etc. The climax to their act was a double bicycle dive.

During the 1920s, diving off The Pier had become so popular that Clacton Swimming Club held an annual competition in which divers were judged on a programme of three dives. There was a regular entry of between five and ten entrants each year.

Professor Webb's high dive from the side of Clacton Pier.

Professor Webb caught in mid dive.

Professor Webb's bicycle dive off the end of The Pier.

Professor Webb making the first dive at Clacton Pier's newly opened swimming pool in 1932.

Walter Tong.

THE BIGGEST SENSATION IN CLACTON

END OF THE PIER

TO-NIGHT

at 10 p.m. Saturday, June 14 at 10 p.m.

Dare-Devil Mona deGray

WILL PERFORM THE BIGGEST

FIRE DIVE

EVER VENTURED BY ANYONE

Mona de Gray will be bound in 4 yards of cotton wool saturated with 2 quarts of Paraffin Oil – set alight and dive from the Pier IN REAL FLAMES.

Failure Means 'BURNT TO DEATH.'

An advert for "Dare-Devil" Mona de Gray and her "Fire Dive", "The biggest ever ventured by anyone".

Madge Goodhall performing one of her dives off The Pier in the 1920s.

Chapter Twelve

"Dancing over the Sea" The Blue Lagoon

When Ernest Kingsman acquired The Pier in 1922, he set about transforming the buildings at the front to give The Pier a much more welcoming feeling and to provide facilities to make any visitor's stay much more enjoyable.

The entrance to Clacton Pier in the Edwardian era. Both sides would eventually become different versions of the Blue Lagoon.

One of his first enterprises was to transform the old wooden building to the left of The Pier entrance which, before the Great War, had housed a few shops and a photographic studio. When he took over, this building, like much of the rest of The Pier, was showing definite signs of the neglect it had suffered during the War years.

He immediately transformed this building into the Blue Lagoon Coffee Lounge advertising it as "coffee specialists" and soon after into an American themed lounge with an "American soda fountain" where you could also obtain cream teas and cream ices.

The left side of The Pier entrance as it was just after the First World War when Ernest Kingsman bought The Pier. On the left, work is just starting on converting the buildings at the front to the Blue Lagoon Lounge.

This new American Coffee Lounge proved very successful and Kingsman soon extended the building to the rear making room for a tea rooms, a restaurant and a lounge where the soda fountain was moved. To the right of the building, there was a ticket office for The Pier Pavilion, while to the rear of that there was a cloak room. A new ornamental globe was placed above the rear extension. This was illuminated at night to attract visitors in the evening and extend the hours The Pier was open, while small trees lined the entrance to add to the whole attraction of the place.

In 1923, Kingsman employed a small orchestra to play background music in the lounge. The orchestra chosen was Teddy Dobbs' Brooklyn Orchestra.

Teddy Dobbs was destined to become a major figure in Clacton Pier's history. He was born in 1894 and acquired his interest in music while at school in Luton, where he was a drummer in the school band.

The building has been extended out the back in readiness for the opening of the Blue Lagoon Lounge.

After leaving school he went to work in the Vauxhall factory in Luton. When the First World War broke out, he joined the 5th Bedfordshires as a drummer boy but, because he was a skilled engineer, was recalled to his work at the Vauxhall factory.

In 1917, he again joined up, this time with the Royal Navy, serving on HMS New Zealand where he formed a band on the ship, becoming its conductor.

In 1921, he received his first professional musical appointment, becoming a drummer in the orchestra of a Southend theatre. After this his progress was rapid. He went on a world tour on the RMS Mauritania as a member of the band, later joining the band of the RMS Majestic, going on to tour America. When this engagement ended, Teddy formed his own band, the Teddy Dobbs' Brooklyn Dance Band and, took the band to London, where they played at many notable restaurants and venues, including the Trocadero.

In 1922, his daughter caught whooping cough and their doctor advised a spell of convalescence at the seaside, so the family came to Clacton for a short break. It was while in Clacton that Teddy Dobbs noticed the work going on at the front of The Pier and the new Blue Lagoon Lounge and said to his wife, *"I would love to put a band in that place."* And so, after discussions with Ernest Kingsman, that's exactly what he did and, in 1923, Kingsman was able to announce a new attraction at the Blue Lagoon.

As the Blue Lagoon Coffee Lounge continued to increase in popularity, an entrance porch was added to the front, and, by 1927, yet another extension was added to the rear, this time to house a small dance hall.

The Blue Lagoon Lounge opens as "Coffee Specialists".

The new dance hall was promoted as "*Dancing over the Sea*" and "*Healthy Happiness*". It was also promoted in newspaper advertisements as "*Dancing in Dreamland, with a myriad of lights, wonderfully coloured*" and as "*Waltzing in Wonderland*". Naturally, Teddy Dobbs was in charge of the dancing, changing the name of his band to Teddy Dobbs and his Blue Lagoons.

With the compulsory purchase of the land belonging to Clacton Council to the left of The Pier

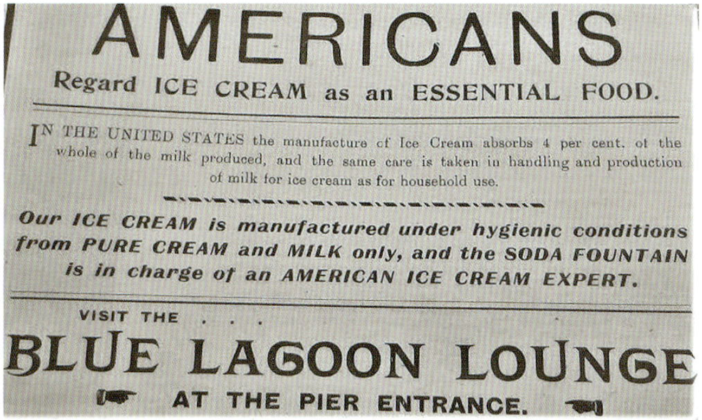

Ernest Kingsman modelled the Blue Lagoon Lounge in an American style as can be seen from the flyer advertising the lounge.

The new American style Blue Lagoon Lounge.

entrance in 1930, Kingsman drew up plans to further enlarge and improve the Blue Lagoon Lounge and Dance Hall as they had both become such popular attractions, and to build a brand new restaurant to the right of The Pier entrance.

In the end, however, Kingsman decided that he would scrap the idea for a restaurant and instead design a completely new and up-to-date Blue Lagoon covering an area of 12,000 square feet on the right, with an 18 ins deep spring dance floor large enough to cater for 750 couples, as well as a bar and tea rooms. This new building necessitated the widening of The Pier platform and it being joined up to the rear with the projecting platform on which the Ocean Theatre was located.

Outside, the new Blue Lagoon featured a stunning modern art deco design and construction, consisting of a steel frame with green marble panels, and, for the windows and doors, stylish glazing bars. Four towers topped the roof with truncated pyramids, and a lighted lantern completed by flag staffs. A bold illuminated 'Blue Lagoon' sign on a framework above the whole facade completed the new building.

Kingsman soon extended the Blue Lagoon to the rear even further to include an enlarged tea rooms and other visitor facilities.

By 1927, it had been extended still more to include a small dance hall.

This image shows the globe that was added to the building and illuminated to attract visitors in the evening as well as the new trees that lined the entrance.

Inside, the dance hall itself was arranged in the form of a sweeping architrave which covered the whole of the floor area. The colour scheme was pea green and white. The trellised ceiling was adorned with artificial roses and sweet peas interspersed with a myriad of tiny coloured lights. The hall contained tables and chairs for those wishing to partake of the refreshments or just sitting out a dance, with, in one corner, an alcove with concealed lighting which accommodated Teddy Dobbs and his Band on a small bandstand. The painting on the wall behind depicted a stave of music.

The original Blue Lagoon in its last full year of operation, 1933.

From the continuous windows, passers-by on The Pier could be seen, while the other side looked out on to the beach and the sea. At the far end was a mirrored wall which gave the hall an impression of enormous length, in effect doubling the area.

In addition, the building featured new revolutionary neon lighting which could be dimmed to get a constant cyclorama of colour, giving the effect of a series of rainbows. Ernest Kingsman announced this was the first installation of its type in the country and, possibly, the world. As well as these modern installations, there was a nod to tradition as some oak decorative work taken from the old Adelphi Theatre in London was incorporated into the new dance hall.

The swan song of the old Blue Lagoon came at Easter, 1934, after which It was then closed for good.

Two months later, on Whit Monday, fourteen rockets were fired into the sky to announce the official opening ceremony of the new Blue Lagoon Empire Dance Hall. The ceremony itself was performed by Local M.P. and Minister for Transport, Sir John Pybus M.P. In his opening speech, Sir John congratulated Mr and Mrs Kingsman and his good friend, Barney, on such a wonderful piece of work. "*Clacton is considered to be a town of progress,*" he said, *"and those who have watched its progress have to thank the Kingsman family from the bottom of their hearts. With the same management, the same atmosphere, and Mr Teddy Dobbs providing entertainment, I feel sure they will have many more happy evenings."*

With the opening speeches out of the way, Teddy Dobbs and his band struck up with "Ring Up the Curtain" and, in a matter of seconds, the dance floor was invaded by a throng of dancers all proud and eager to be there on its first official night.

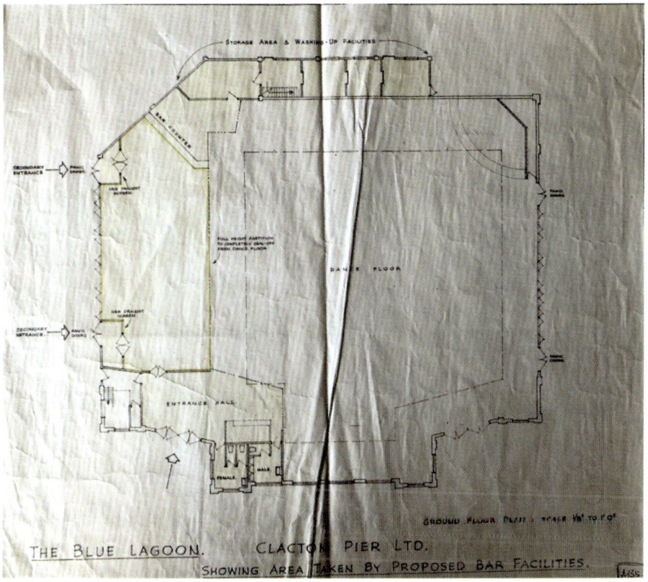

The plans for the new Blue Lagoon.

With the new Blue Lagoon now officially open, Teddy Dobbs and his Blue Lagoons played every day from 3.30pm, and again from 8pm. To begin with, The Pier announced a special offer on the admission price lasting from Whitsun to 30 June to "Test the new Empire floor".

Described as the largest Dance Hall over the sea, the new Blue Lagoon was an impressive addition, not only to The Pier, but to Clacton-on-Sea itself. In the evenings especially, approaching The Pier to go dancing at the Blue Lagoon and seeing it lit up was quite a magical experience and one that drew visitors to Clacton from all over the country as 1934 turned out to be a boom year for the resort.

Work started on the new Blue Lagoon in 1933 and took just six months to be completed.

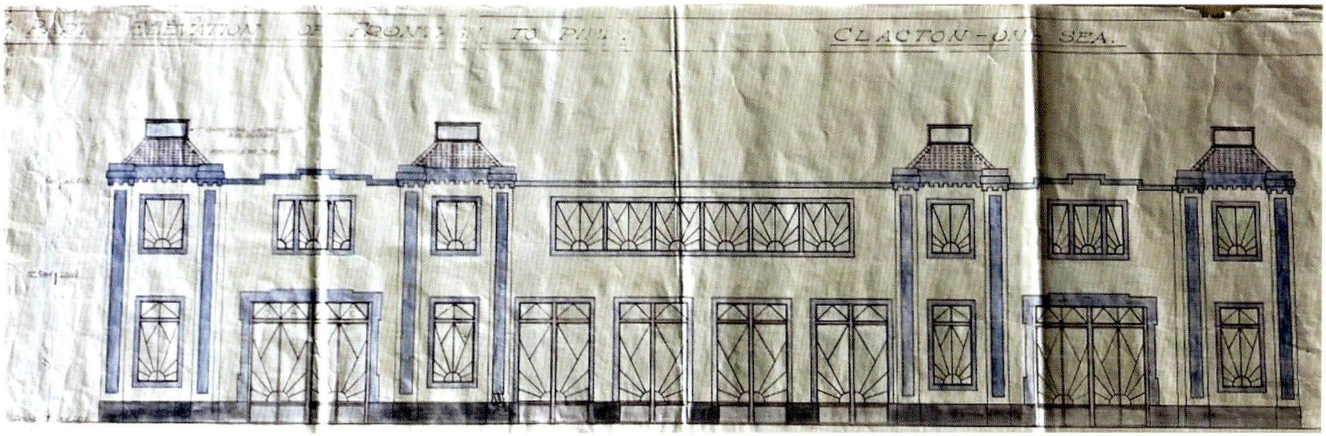

The architect's artist's impression of the frontage showing the sheer artistry of the magnificent modern art deco design and its stunning windows.

Sir John Pybus M.P. getting ready for the opening ceremony. He is towards the centre of the photo looking towards the camera. To the right standing near the band looking at Sir John is Ernest Kingsman.

The next major addition to the Blue Lagoon came at Whitsun 1937 when a new organ was added. A leading organist of the time, Donald Thorne, well-known for his radio broadcasts and for his appearances on the Granada Cinema circuit, was engaged for the inaugural concert.

A flyer advertising the special offer to "Test the new Blue Lagoon Empire Floor".

Following the opening concert, John Francis was appointed as the resident organist. Mysteriously, in July of that year, the 26 year-old Mr Francis went missing. After performing at the Blue Lagoon on 17 July, he never returned to his lodgings in Wellesley Road, nor even to his home in North Wales. What happened to him remains a mystery, but, after his disappearance, the very popular Sunday organ recitals were performed each week by guest artists.

As with everything else, the Blue Lagoon ceased operations on the outbreak of War. It was, however, the first attraction on The Pier to re-open after the War, holding its first dance on 7 July, 1945 in aid of the local Home Guard Benevolent Association. Special trains were laid on to bring visitors from Walton, Frinton and Kirby and return them later. The refreshment area, now known as The Café, opened the following day. After six years of War, Clacton was desperately in need of something to cheer up both the residents and visitors and Teddy Dobbs and his Band were back to provide that entertainment.

The entrance to the new Blue Lagoon Dance Hall shortly after its opening.

The new Blue Lagoon in all its glory.

Dancing at the Blue Lagoon to Teddy Dobbs remained one of the most popular pastimes in Clacton throughout the immediate Post-War period and on into the 1950s. But, following the 1959 season, Teddy Dobbs decided it was time to retire. He was now 64 years old and had been the band leader at the Blue Lagoon for just under 40 years, where he had delighted audiences, both young and old, who had come to dance or just to use the tea rooms/café and listen to his band.

His career wasn't just confined to the Blue Lagoon however as he had become a household name through his association with the BBC, his frequent radio broadcasts, including a number broadcast live from the Blue Lagoon, and his many records. He also wrote many songs, including one, specially written for his adopted home town, called "Sunny Clacton".

Following his departure, Phil Rich and his Orchestra took over as the resident dance band. But, as the 1960s wore on, with less holidaymakers and musical tastes changing, the numbers fell. Phil Rich left the Blue Lagoon at the end of the 1963 season and in 1964, different bands played on different days of the week with traditional ballroom dancing evenings becoming interspersed with modern dancing and guest pop groups as Barney Kingsman attempted to make the venue more attractive to youngsters.

The frontage of The Pier in the mid-1930s, showing the new Blue Lagoon but before the original Blue Lagoon was demolished to make way for the circus and indoor amusement centre.

The interior, showing the Empire Dance Floor and the refreshments area.

Teddy Dobbs and his Band on the small stage in front of the wall depicting a stave of music.

On 28 March 1964, Easter Saturday, one of the biggest names in pop at the time, Freddie and the Dreamers, appeared. Sadly, that evening was to herald the start of the infamous Mods & Rockers weekend, though the trouble started well after the concert finished as the 1,200 strong audience enjoyed the concert and left peacefully.

One teenager in particular, Suzette Mizon, remembers the concert well. *"It was on Easter Saturday 28th March that I headed off to the Blue Lagoon to watch and enjoy sixties pop band, Freddie and the Dreamers, who attracted an audience of 1,000 plus screaming teenagers myself included. It was a great evening and, although Freddie was small in stature, boy could he jump and leap across the stage.*

I remember how relieved my parents were when I arrived home safe and sound. Mum asked me if I screamed at Freddie, my answer was 'no of course not.' Just a little white lie which I thought I had got away with, until the following week when the Clacton Gazette came out. Again I was asked, 'Did you scream at Freddie.' 'No,' said I.

Laughing, my mum held up the paper with the Gazette's photo and said, 'I believe that is my daughter in the front row mouth open wide and screaming at Freddie.' 'Well mum, that is what us teenagers do,' I said, 'and sorry for telling an untruth.' My mum, bless her, ordered that photo from the Clacton Gazette which took pride of place on our mantle shelf, which was often spoken about with family and friends."

Freddie had even younger fans as Christine Stafford recalls, *"I met Freddie when he came to the stage door. He gave me a packet of fruit pastilles and a signed photo! I was only eight."*

Although nobody, except perhaps Barney Kingsman, knew it at the time, the final dance evening of 1964, held on Saturday 19 September, was to prove to be the Blue Lagoon's last as, in January 1965, Barney Kingsman announced that

"Dancing in Dreamland" and "Waltzing in Wonderland"!

Many couples took to the floor to try out "Dreamland" and "Wonderland". [Photo: Andy Dobbs]

The new Blue Lagoon organ installed in 1937.

the Dance Hall and café were to be turned into a ten-pin bowling alley, complete with "*licensed bar and catering facilities*". And so, 40 years of ballroom dancing on Clacton Pier came to an end.

As it happens, it didn't become a bowling alley at that time, but, after a complete renovation, part of the building re-opened in 1967 as the fully licensed New Lagoon Bar and was advertised in the Ocean Theatre programmes as "*adjacent to the theatre*" and the place to go for an interval drink.

Further big changes were to take place in that area over the next 50 years, but, as far as the Blue Lagoon itself went, that was the final chapter of a story that had seen many changes, including the construction of the largest dance hall over the sea anywhere in the United Kingdom and the first building in the world to use neon lighting. But, more importantly, an institution that had brought pleasure and delight to millions of holidaymakers and residents alike over its more than 40 years existence in various guises that had helped to make Clacton-on-Sea one of the leading seaside resorts in the country.

The Blue Lagoon just after the Second World War, still as popular as ever. The refreshment area was now referred to as simply the Café.

The Blue Lagoon lit up at night in the early 1960s. Note the number of people stood outside just gazing in through the large windows.

Teddy Dobbs, band leader at both the old and new Blue Lagoons from 1923 to 1959.

The sheet music to "Sunny Clacton", Clacton-on-Sea's anthem, written by Teddy Dobbs.

A 1961 poster for the Blue Lagoon showing Phil Rich and his Orchestra as the new resident band.

Freddie and the Dreamers, Easter Saturday, 1964. This is the photo that was published in the East Essex Gazette that Suzette Mizon didn't want her mother to see! Suzette is the girl in the centre wearing the white blouse with big black spots.

After the Blue Lagoon Dance Hall had closed and part of the building revamped as the new Lagoon Bar with the entrance now at the rear of the building.

The advert in the East Essex Gazette for the last-ever dance at the Blue Lagoon, although no-one knew it at the time.

An advert for the "New Lagoon Bar" in the Ocean Theatre programme for 1967 "Ocean Show".

Chapter Thirteen

Skeeball and the "Remarkable Lady"

The game of Skeeball inside the Crystal Casino.

Skeeball was invented in New Jersey in 1908 and spread quickly in America. After the First World War it found its way to this country and was one of the very first amusements Ernest Kingsman placed on Clacton Pier. At first it was played in a small hall on the left of The Pier, but later, in 1928, it was moved in to the main amusement arcade, the Crystal Casino.

The game was played by inserting money into a slot at the foot of the Skeeball machine which would then release nine balls. Each machine had an inclined ramp, approximately 10 feet long, up which the player rolled the balls one at a time. A sudden increase in incline at the end of the ramp launched the ball above the ramp towards a series of rings that directed the balls into holes of varying point values, with the smallest and hardest to reach giving the most points.

To entice people to play the game, big prizes were awarded to those gaining the highest scores. Kingsman felt he was fairly safe from having to spend too much money on prizes as it wasn't an easy game to master.

However, Skeeball quickly became something of a craze in Clacton and because, unlike holidaymakers, Clacton residents were able to practice all year round and not just during their one week's holiday, some Clactonians became very adept at the game with some of the best winning the top prizes week after week. It is said that a number of people actually furnished their homes with the prizes they won.

In fact, so adept did some Clacton residents become that Mrs Frank Malby, who, along with her husband, owned an electrical shop in High Street, won the All England Cup in 1930 at Olympia. She naturally won many prizes on The Pier as well, including a £45 Ariel motor bike.

The Clacton Graphic announced when she had won that it was "*a remarkable achievement for a lady.*"

Although the game still has a large following in America with players competing in leagues, it gradually died out in Clacton and Britain during the 1930s.

Skeeball was prominently advertised at the front of The Pier throughout the 1920s.

Mrs Malby, who won the All England Cup, with the £45 Ariel motorbike she won on The Pier.

THE
Crystal Casino
Amuses and Shelters.
Latest Games and Novelties.
SKEEBALL
A FASCINATING AND INTERESTING SPORT.
Really Useful Prizes

LADIES SCORES	- -	170 and over
GENTLEMEN	- -	220 „
BOYS (under 12)	- -	200 „
OUT OF A POSSIBLE		450.

Raleigh Bicycles. Handsome 8-day Clocks
Valuable canteens of cutlery, etc.,
AND
EVERY DAY
a £1 Note, with 2nd & 3rd, & Ladies' Special Prize, for Highest Scores
Nine Balls Sixpence. "It's Good Fun, Anyhow!"

Some of the prizes to be won in 1927.

Chapter Fourteen

Clown Bertram, not forgetting Filbert!

There is no doubt that best loved performer ever to appear on Clacton Pier was Clown Bertram who staged a Summer Season every year from 1922 to 1939.

Bertram had been a children's entertainer in London, but, in 1921, he came down to Clacton to appear in Summer Season at the Palm Hall in the Central Hotel under his real name of Bert E. Harvey as a member of the "Centrals Concert Company". (The Central Hotel was on the corner of West Avenue and Pier Avenue).

He returned the following Spring on spec, hoping to find a spot in one of the Summer Seasons taking place at various venues around Clacton. Unfortunately, he discovered that all the summer shows had already been booked and there was no room for another act.

Disconsolately, he walked along The Pier, pondering what to do next, when it suddenly occurred to him that this was actually the ideal place to set up a children's entertainment. Ernest Kingsman had only just bought Clacton Pier and there wasn't much in the way of entertainment available apart from The Pier Pavilion, which was really for adults. Consequently, he went along to Ernest Kingsman's office and told him firstly, that what he needed was a children's entertainer and secondly, he was just the man for the job.

As Kingsman was on the look-out for new entertainments that would bring in the customers, he decided to give this confident young man a chance so he agreed to give him a week's trial and sent instructions for a small open-air platform to be set up near the Pavilion for him to perform on with a carpet in front for the children to sit on.

A portrait of Clown Bertram.

The next afternoon, Kingsman was in his office when he was suddenly disturbed by a lot of laughter and cheering, so he came out of his office to investigate. As he walked towards The Pier Head, the noise got louder and louder and, when he arrived, he saw dozens of children sitting on the carpet with a thousand people standing behind them, all, children and adults alike, shrieking with laughter. He immediately offered Bertram a contract for the season at a far higher rate of pay than Bertram was originally going to ask for so he accepted on the spot.

Initially, for that first year, Bertram continued to appear on just an open platform. But he was

Clown Bertram appearing under his real name, Bert E Harvey, at the Central Hotel in 1921.

proving to be so popular that Kingsman invited him back for the following season and built him a small stage with a large carpet for the children to sit on and deck chairs at the back for the mums and dads. In these early days he performed the whole show himself with just a little help from his wife, Ruby, known to the children as Auntie Ruby. He would sing a few songs accompanying himself on the banjo and other novelty instruments - he could play at least 12 different instruments. Reciting his own versions of nursery rhymes was another staple part of his act. These are two examples:

"Mary had a little Dog
She called it Ragamuffin,
A motor car cut off its tail
And now it wags its nuffin'"

and

"Under a spreading chestnut tree
The blacksmith played his fiddle
The chestnuts fell upon his head
And parted his hair in the middle."

He also performed some conjuring tricks using a number of tricks he had invented himself, including his own anti-gravity wand, the changing die, the fairy tree and Disabell, a charming effect with a bell, later marketed by some of the country's leading magic dealers.

He presented chapeaugraphy, a novelty act in which a ring-shaped piece of felt is manipulated to look like various types of hats such as a pirate hat, a Russian fur hat and even Mickey Mouse ears, and Troublewit, a similar form of entertainment but with pleated paper which he used to form various items, such as hats, fans and umbrellas.

But the most eagerly looked forward to part of his act was holding a riotously funny conversation with his ventriloquist dummy, the irrepressible Filbert. And throughout the whole show he would clown about with quick fire gags, ad-libs and slapstick comedy.

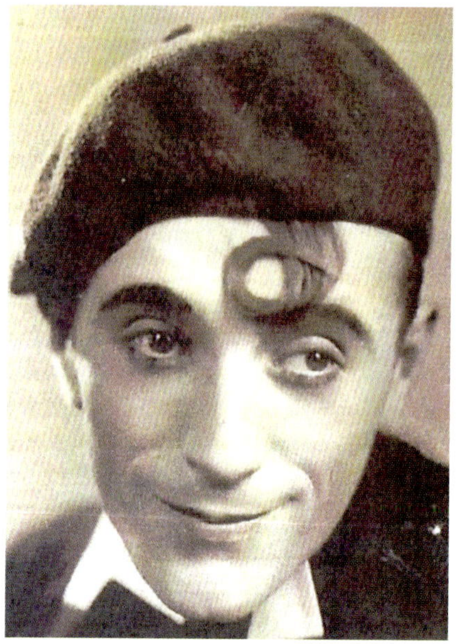

A young Clown Bertram at the time he approached Ernest Kingsman for a job.

Bertram with Filbert in his first season on Clacton Pier, 1922.

As the audiences got even larger, he began to introduce competitions to involve the children more. As well as the more straightforward talent competitions such as singing and dancing etc., these included balloon blowing, skipping, who could make the funniest noise and who could give the funniest answer to questions such as, "What do you want to do when you grow up?"

During these different activities, he or Ruby would play specific well-rehearsed music to accompany whatever he or the children were doing. So although there was a definite spontaneity about it all, it was set against a bedrock of a very well planned and finely rehearsed background.

With the children being drawn more or less at random from the audience, Bertram had no idea how good - or bad - they would be and indeed, some were just awful, though, on the other hand, some were absolutely brilliant. But however good they were, it all made for good fun and many's the time that even the adults laughed so much that tears rolled down their cheeks. This was, of course, due to Bertram himself. He never missed the opportunity for a gag or to exploit a situation that would produce laughs. Throughout his show, Bertram was noted for his quick witted ad-libs and spontaneity, which had the audience in stitches. His sharpness was his great strength and he played on it for all he was worth. Both young and old would cheer, clap, scream with laughter and everyone would get caught up in the incredible atmosphere created by this man.

Although he loved encouraging the youngsters and was able to use them as part of his act, Bertram's main fear was the epic poem as these could kill an audience stone dead. He once recalled how one young boy started to recite The Death of Nelson at half past three on a Wednesday afternoon and by six thirty on the Thursday, poor old Nelson was still on his way to Heaven. A bit of an exaggeration of course, but when a girl announced she was going to recite The Arab's Farewell to his Steed, an epic

Bertram with his wife, Ruby.

The "Changing Die", one of Bertram's magic tricks which he invented and made himself.

19th century poem written by Caroline Norton, he groaned inwardly. The little girl proudly stepped forward and said, "*The Arab's Farewell to his Steed. Ta ta gee gee!*" She won first prize.

Amongst the youngsters to win a prize on his show was Warren Mitchell, who won twice as a six year old dancer. He was so good that, after the second occasion, Clown Bertram said to him, "*Look, don't enter the competition because it's a bit unfair but I'll give you a prize if you'd like to come up and entertain.*" Mitchell thought that Hollywood was beckoning as he received his first "professional contract".

The way he handled the children and the genuine fun he made by his spontaneous quips, gags and clowning not only increased his popularity but brought more and more children and adults to his shows. And with so many standing trying to get a look at his shows, it was obvious he needed something better than a carpet and a few deck chairs, so Kingsman built him his own theatre, the Children's Theatre, near the end of The Pier, containing seats for 500 paying audience. It was always full, with queues forming hours before the performance was due to start.

Because he now had his own theatre, his performances were increased from an hour to a full show lasting 90 minutes. He performed twice a day, once in the afternoon and once in the evening. Queues for the second house would literally form as soon as the first house went in. With an extra half hour to fill he now employed some juvenile professional talent to support him. Generally aged between 14 and 17, they became known as his "Bright Young Things" and they would sing and dance and take part in comedy sketches. Some

"Look at me, son, I want a gottle o' gear and some gread and gutter."

Clown Bertram's Children's Theatre at the end of The Pier.

of them also had their own specialty acts such as contortionists, mind readers and ventriloquists and they became fully integrated into the act. With these new youngsters supporting Bertram, Ruby dropped out of the act, but continued to support him by making many of his props and costumes as she was an expert seamstress.

A number of these youngsters went on to forge careers of their own on the stage. One in particular, Hetty Braine , became very successful, going on to appear in revue, variety, pantomime and on the radio. Another youngster was the 14 year old, Dorice Smith, said to be the only child ventriloquist in Britain.

He also introduced a new element into his show, the Merry Midgets, small marionettes which he operated from a small Punch & Judy style booth on stage.

Occasionally, he invited well-known guest artistes on to his show. For example on one occasion the eighty year old Charles Coburn came on to sing his well-known song, Two Lovely Black Eyes. Others to make guest appearances on his show included George Robey, Wee Georgie Wood, Nellie Wallace and Stanley Holloway.

In an interview for Clacton Chronicle (journal of the Clacton & District Local History Society), Warren Mitchell said that their family holidays to Clacton actually revolved around getting ready to see his shows, so that, for example, meal times had to be planned meticulously to allow time to get in the queue. His family wasn't the only one as Clown Bertram's show became something of an institution and his name became synonymous with Clacton. No holiday was complete without at least two visits to his show during the week. His show was the theatrical highlight of a holiday in Clacton, eclipsing all the big stars who came to Clacton in the 1920s and 30s to appear in theatres like the Princes Theatre, Ocean Theatre and the West Cliff Theatre.

The Stage summed it up when it said in 1932, "*Of Clown Bertram's Children's Theatre, there is little more to be said than has been said already. Mr Bertram has become one of the institutions of Clacton, and to hear his audiences of kiddies singing in full-throated song is one of the joys of life. He has a notable insight into*

A typical queue of adults and children hoping to get in to see the show, stretching all the way down The Pier.

the child mind, and, perhaps as a consequence, he attracts a vast number of grown-ups. Indeed, it is not too much to say that Clown Bertram has become part of Clacton."

This "*vast number of grown-ups*" presented Bertram with a dilemma as the Clacton News reported in that same year, "*Bertram, the favourite of the Children's Theatre on The Pier, told a News reporter (confidentially), that he was in difficulties. And his trouble had arisen through adults - not children.*

"*So many adults come to the Theatre,*" he said, "*that I am often in difficulties as to whether I should give a show to please the children or the adults.*" He then went on to relay a story to emphasise this point, "*Johnny wanted to come to my theatre, but he was a shy little chap so he asked his father to come with him. Father scoffed at the idea, but when Johnny burst into tears he decided he must go and be bored. The next day, Johnny wanted to go for a walk, but father wanted to go back to the Children's Theatre and being 'boss of the house', there was no-one to stop him. And the stern parent was there every performance throughout their holiday.*"

Bertram performing with some children on the stage of the Children's Theatre.

A photo opportunity in front of the Children's Theatre.

In fact, so popular did he become that the Children's Theatre, even with its 500 seats, eventually proved far too small to accommodate the numbers wishing to get in to see his show and for the last couple of seasons before the War, Ernest Kingsman moved Bertram into the Jolly Roger, which he renamed the Jollity Theatre for him. This seated over 1,000 but there were still many times when the house was full and people had to be turned away.

Bertram's constant companion was, of course, Filbert. Bertram once recalled an incident with Filbert when he was reminiscing about the last show of the season. He said that on these occasions the theatre was always full and there was much excitement, applause and many tears. One year as they came to the finale when everyone took their bow, Filbert sat on a pedestal on the stage with his head proudly up looking out straight at the audience. The curtain came down, then went up again as they all stood in a line acknowledging the

Clown Bertram with three of his "Bright Young Things".

applause. As the curtain came down for the final time, Bertram breathed a sigh of relief and said to the company, "Well, that's that!" He then glanced at Filbert and saw his head had sagged forward on to his chest for all the world as though he was displaying human emotions and was both sad but relieved it was all over like everyone else. However, the explanation for his head falling forward was a bit more prosaic. It was simply that the elastic had snapped at the back of his head!

Because he was such a popular figure, Bertram also took part in many other events around the town. For example he used to play a prominent part in the Carnival each year, usually as the Court Jester to the Carnival King and Queen and also as King of the Kids. In 1925, his role as King of the Kids was featured on the front pages of the Daily Sketch and the Daily Mirror, which gained Clacton a lot of publicity. In fact Clown Bertram gained the town a lot of publicity over the years as most of the national newspapers gave excellent reviews of his shows on The Pier.

Sadly, along with everything else, his show came to a forced abrupt and final end when War broke out in 1939. During the War, Bertram toured the country, putting on shows to raise money for the War effort.

When the War was over, one of Bertram's first engagements was back on The Pier as, in the summer of 1945, he performed in front of 1,200 children at the Ocean Theatre. Ada Kingsman immediately offered him a contract to continue his shows as before, but Bertram felt unable to accept as he wasn't in the best of health, suffering from nervous exhaustion, and thought it would be too much of a strain to continue to put on two performances every day throughout the season. It is an astonishing fact that in his 18 seasons on The Pier before the War, he had not missed one single performance.

Nevertheless, he moved back to his home in Little Clacton, where he had moved to in 1922, and continued to appear locally in village halls, schools and small theatres around the area.

On stage with his "Bright Young Things".

Bertram performing his "Merry Midgets" act.

The Jolly Roger, renamed the Jollity Children's Theatre for Clown Bertram.

In 1951, he wrote a letter to the Live Letters page of the Daily Mirror. The appearance of his name sparked off such a correspondence that the editor of the Daily Mirror wrote to Bertram saying,

"As you will have seen I published your letter. The result of which has staggered me. I have had hundreds of letters from mothers and fathers now with children of their own, all couched in terms of the greatest affection and remembrance of the Children's Theatre. I have never known such a wealth of affection for a man whom they met perhaps only once or twice, or one remembered for the pleasure he has given. What grand work you must have done for children."

The editor of the Daily Mirror had discovered something that Clactonians and holidaymakers had known all along - Clown Bertram was someone very special and dear to the hearts of all who saw him.

His last performance was at the Weeley Village Hall in 1953. It was shortly after this, on 10th March 1953, that he died at the age of just 65.

CHILDREN WILL ENJOY CLOWN BERTRAM

the kiddies' pal, from Clacton Pier, who gives two Concerts on Saturday, April 20th, as follows: 10-30 a.m., Nacton Road Schools; 2-30 p.m., Stoke Junior Mixed School. Admission tickets, 2d. each, can be exchanged at the Concert for a bar of Co-operative chocolate, on sale at all branches

WIVES and MOTHERS OF MEN IN THE FORCES ARE INVITED

to attend our Special Afternoon Concert in the Co-op. Hall, on Thursday, April 25th, at 2-45 p.m. First-class Entertainment and Light Refreshments. Admission by ticket, obtainable at all branches, on production of suitable evidence

Clown Bertram advertising his War-Time Concerts. Note that the tickets cost 2d each, but they can be exchanged for a bar of Co-operative chocolate. All the money raised from these concerts went into the War effort.

Clacton carnival yesterday was bright, cheery and full of humour. The crowd that cheered the crowning of the Carnival King and his Queen.—(Daily Sketch.)

The crowning of the Clacton King and Queen.—(Daily Sketch.)

A page from The Daily Sketch reporting on the Clacton Pier Carnival. Clown Bertram, as the Court Jester, is in the centre of the lower image.

After the War, Bertram wrote a book on how to entertain children, in which he explained the secret of his success, including some of the jokes, songs and competitions he used and how to deal with hecklers using well-rehearsed, though seemingly impromptu, put-downs.

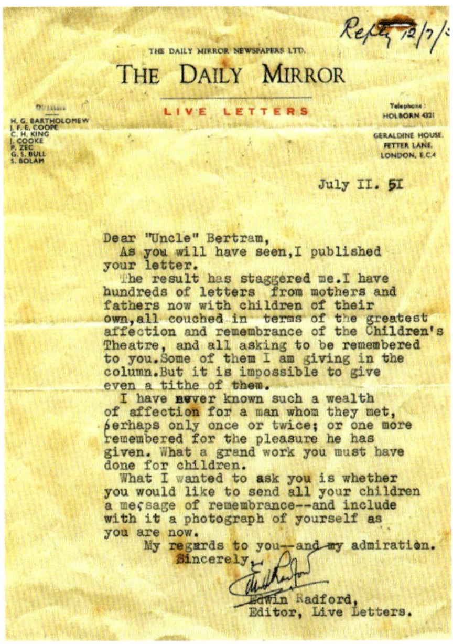

Reply 12/7/5

THE DAILY MIRROR NEWSPAPERS LTD.

THE DAILY MIRROR

LIVE LETTERS

Directors
H. G. BARTHOLOMEW
J. F. E. COOPE
C. H. KING
J. COOKE
P. ZEC
G. S. BULL
S. BOLAM

Telephone:
HOLBORN 4321

GERALDINE HOUSE,
FETTER LANE,
LONDON, E.C.4

July II. 51

Dear "Uncle" Bertram,

As you will have seen, I published your letter.

The result has staggered me. I have hundreds of letters from mothers and fathers now with children of their own, all couched in terms of the greatest affection and remembrance of the Children's Theatre, and all asking to be remembered to you. Some of them I am giving in the column. But it is impossible to give even a tithe of them.

I have never known such a wealth of affection for a man whom they met, perhaps only once or twice; or one more remembered for the pleasure he has given. What a grand work you must have done for children.

What I wanted to ask you is whether you would like to send all your children a message of remembrance--and include with it a photograph of yourself as you are now.

My regards to you--and my admiration.

Sincerely,

Edwin Radford,
Editor, Live Letters.

The letter the editor of the Daily Mirror Live Letters column sent to Clown Bertram expressing his admiration for the great affection in which he was held.

In 2015, the Clacton & District Local History Society were fortunate enough to be able to buy Filbert when he came up for auction in Colchester. During Clacton Pier's 150th Anniversary year, they were able to take him back to The Pier for the first time since 1945 for a ride on The Pier's latest attraction, the Elegant Wheel Experience.

Chapter Fifteen

Clacton Carnival "It all began here"

Clacton Carnival was the brainchild of Ernest Kingsman. In 1922, his first full year of ownership, Kingsman thought that a good way of bringing extra visitors to The Pier would be to hold a three day carnival with plenty of events going on. He quickly recognised that a three day carnival would provide great opportunities not just for The Pier but for Clacton as a whole and so he contacted both Clacton Council and the local Chamber of Commerce who seized on the idea wholeheartedly. A Carnival Committee was formed, which included Kingsman, Cllr C L Gregory, the Chairman of the Council, who was appointed Carnival President, plus other councillors and representatives of the Chamber of Commerce and individual business owners.

King Carnival's car ready to lead the procession.

The first meeting was held on 10 July at which a possible timetable of events for the Carnival was discussed. The meeting also heard that both the railway and the paddle steamer companies had agreed to lay on special services over the three days.

A further meeting was held the following week, at which the programme was finally agreed as well as the judges and the prizes to be made available for the various events.

The Carnival was held over three days starting on Wednesday 26 July, opening with a reception for "King Carnival" before the latter mounted his "Royal Car" (a Dion Lane) containing several appropriately attired courtiers, to lead the Grand Procession of decorated vehicles, including the town's lifeboat and crew and fire engine, motorcycles, cycles and something like 200 pedestrians in fancy dress, along with the band of the 104th Brigade Essex Yeomanry.

The first Carnival in 1922 as the procession rounds the corner from Station Road into Pier Avenue in front of Grimwade & Clarke's.

The procession started at High Street/Station Road corner. From there, it made its way down Station Road to Pallister Road, back up Electric Parade and Pier Avenue on to Old Road and Magdalen Green, right into Cambridge Road to Wellesley Road and Carnarvon Road before turning back into Station Road, then left into Rosemary Road, Church Road and St Paul's Road before coming back along Marine Parade to Tower Road where the procession terminated. The whole town centre was decorated for the occasion and thousands of visitors and residents lined the route.

Another view of the first Carnival in 1922; this time the Nursery Procession on The Pier.

Two prize winners in the "Children's Beauty Show".

The procession was followed by a "Battle of Confetti and Flowers" on The Pier and, in the evening, a Masked Ball in The Pier Pavilion, with one of the judges being Ada Kingsman.

On the second day, every event took place on The Pier and included a Nursery procession and competition, a children and babies' beauty show, another Battle of Confetti and Flowers and a Gala Performance by the White Coons in The Pier Pavilion followed by an impromptu dance.

The third and final day began with aquatic sports, swimming and diving competitions in the sea close to The Pier while a bathing costume parade took place on The Pier itself. These events were followed by sports events on The Pier including a ladies' egg and spoon race, a gentleman's' back-to-back race and a mixed three-legged race. Once again, a "Battle of Confetti and Flowers" took place with the final events in the three day Carnival being another gala performance by the White Coons and a dance, this time, billed as a "Planned Ball", in The Pier Pavilion, finishing at 1 a.m.

Everyone in the town agreed that the Carnival had been a huge success and, as soon as it was over, plans were begun for the following year's Carnival. It was even suggested that they hold two carnivals in 1923, though this never happened.

There was, however, one slight drawback which was reported at the final committee meeting of the year, when the Secretary, Mr B Ratcliffe, one of Ernest Kingsman's managers at The Pier, announced that the funds showed a deficit of £231. 14s 1½d. However, Kingsman said that he was very satisfied with the undoubted success of the Carnival and greatly appreciated the support it had received from the town. He further announced that he was prepared to make up the deficit himself.

From then until 1935, the Carnival continued to be held annually with much the same format, though the procession route was changed to allow for King Carnival and his entourage to finish up on The Pier, where he and his Queen were crowned.

In 1936, however, Clacton Council rebuilt the Band Pavilion with a stage and auditorium, which could also be used as a flat floor space and the Council decided to move the main carnival activities there, thus ending The Pier's association with the Carnival.

13 BRITISH CASUALTIES IN CHINESE RIVER FIGHT

Pip and Squeak Annual: Now Ready Price 6s.

Daily Mirror

SECOND INQUEST ON SHOT BOY

NEPTUNE RULES OVER THE LAST CARNIVAL OF THE SEASON AT CLACTON-ON-SEA

The Carnival gained a lot of publicity for Clacton as this Daily Mirror front page shows.

A 1920s view of the crowds waiting to see the Carnival.

The Carnival Procession along The Pier.

King and Queen Carnival with Jester, 1923. This year a new event was added to the programme, "The Dainty Ankles Competition".

The Procession reaches The Pier Pavilion with plenty of people on the balcony getting a good view.

King Carnival approaches The Pier to be crowned.

King Carnival, his Queen and Courtiers take a quick tour of the Laguna Belle before continuing their procession.

King and Queen Carnival being crowned surrounded by performers from the Ocean Theatre.

After the Rambla open air stage was built in 1932, their coronation took place there.

Mr Bernard Hudson and Miss Phyllis Ferguson, 1923 King and Queen Carnival.

Chapter Sixteen

The Laguna Belle

The Laguna Belle was built as the Southend Belle by William Denny & Brothers of Dumbarton for the London, Woolwich and Clacton-on-Sea Steamboat Co.'s Belle Steamer fleet, entering service on the London to Clacton and Harwich route in May 1896. In August of that year it became the first of the Belle Steamer to visit Great Yarmouth.

It continued to operate on the East Coast route as well as the Kent route to Margate until the First World War broke out, when it was requisitioned by The Admiralty as a minesweeper, based firstly at Harwich, moving to Liverpool in late 1917.

In March 1919, it was returned to Tilbury for conversion back to peacetime duties. It was purchased by the Kingsman Family in 1921 as part of the deal to buy Clacton Pier and was quickly sold off to the PSM Syndicate in 1922.

On the demise of the PSM Syndicate in 1929, she was sold back to Mr Kingsman, who used her to run a summer service from London to Clacton for seven seasons (1929 to 1935).

In 1936, she was sold again, this time to the General Steam Navigation Company, who continued to operate her on the London to Clacton route and to other resorts on the East Coast.

When World War II broke out, she was once again requisitioned for War-time duties as a minesweeper and sent to Dover. In 1942, she was redesignated as an anti-aircraft vessel and then as an accommodation ship in 1943.

She never again resumed peace time leisure duties and was broken up in The Netherlands in October 1946.

The Laguna Belle on its first voyage under the ownership of the Kingsman Family.

Captain Fred Smith (left) with Ernest Kingsman on board the maiden voyage.

Advertising the Laguna Bell by poster.

The Laguna Belle.

In the newspaper.

The Laguna Belle approaching Clacton Pier in 1933.

And by loudspeaker van.

Chapter Seventeen

The Ocean Theatre

Towards the end of 1927, plans were drawn up for a new theatre under the provisional title of "Winter Garden Pavilion". Ernest Kingsman had decided it was time for a brand new up-to-date theatre on The Pier. The Pavilion at the end (by now renamed Pier Theatre) was still doing well, but it was getting old and he felt that what was needed was a sparkling new venue for modern variety shows and other spectaculars nearer to the entrance of The Pier.

In January 1928 these plans were registered with the Board of Trade and building got underway. Just five months later, on 2 June 1928, seven rockets (one for each of the seasons that the Kingsman Family had owned Clacton Pier) were fired into the sky to herald the arrival of the Ocean Theatre as the Winter Garden Pavilion had now been christened.

This new theatre boasted a stage 42 feet wide and an auditorium with a capacity of 1,200 in tip-up seats. In reviewing the facilities, "The Stage", the Theatre trade journal, noted its *"comfort and airiness that will appeal to visitors."* Notwithstanding The Stage's review, there was one downside to the design of the auditorium and that was the fact the auditorium was wider than it was from stage to rear wall, meaning visibility from the sides was somewhat restricted.

One interesting feature of the Ocean Theatre was that it had shutters along the two side walls. On nice days, these shutters were left fully open for two reasons. The first was to freshen up the air inside the theatre, and second, so that people could look in and perhaps be enticed into buying tickets for

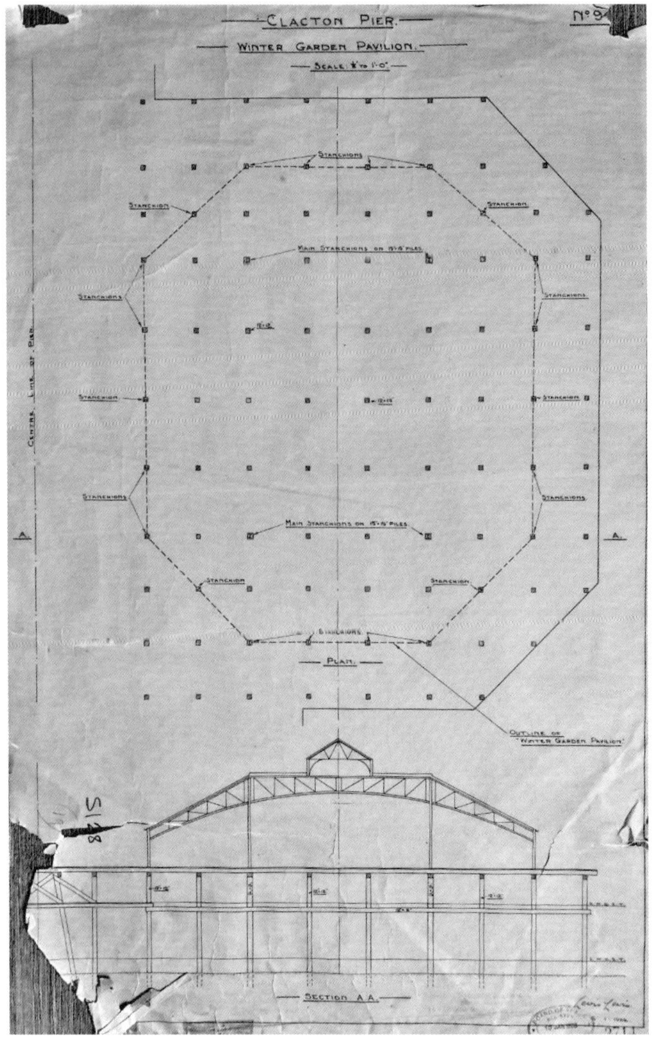

The structural plans for the Winter Garden Pavilion as registered with the Board of Trade in January 1928.

Building work on the new Ocean Theatre and reinforcing the decking nearing completion in 1928.

The Ocean Theatre now open to the public, c.1930, with the entrance at the shore end.

the evening show. During the shows themselves, the shutters were pulled down to cut out the noise of the amusements and rides outside, though not always very successfully, especially after the Steel Stella roller coaster was built nearby in 1937 as Ernie Wise recalled in a letter sent to the author in 1992: *"When you came to a tag line,"* he said, *"the roller coaster used to go by and nobody heard it."* The shutters as well as the sliding roof, another interesting feature of the Ocean Theatre, were often opened during the interval, weather permitting, to let fresh air in.

The first show to be staged was Stephenson's Excelsior Stage Circus. Amongst the acts on show were The Riding Aces, an equestrian act; Louise Medrano with her troupe of monkeys and dogs; a highwire dancer, Maisie Worth; novelty cyclists, Eddie Lotto and Partner; Funny Bobby and his giraffe; juggling comedian, Harry Platter; acrobats, The Three Royces and, of course, the clowns, Long Judd and Partner. The local paper described the show as a *"delightfully enjoyable circus"*.

The Circus ran every day except Sunday for four weeks. Each Sunday a "special" was staged, something for which the Ocean Theatre was to become very famous for over the course of its life and right from the beginning some of the top stars of Music Hall and Variety appeared, starting with Wee Georgie Wood and Albert Whelan.

After four weeks, the circus closed and was replaced by a Summer Variety Season called *Revels of 1928*, produced by Maurice Cowan and starring comedians Hal Bryan and Horace Lane with singers Marie Douglas and Elgar Villiers and specialty act, Bunny, who played the piano-accordion while his partner, Sunny, danced with "*an elfin-like grace*" to his music. The whole show was backed up by the dancers, the six Clacton Belles.

To begin the 1929 season, a show entitled, New Revels of 1929 was produced from June to Mid-July, starring Marriott Edgar. This show was moved to The Pier Theatre for the rest of the Summer. At the end of the season, Edgar went off to join the long-running London Revue, The Co-optimists, starring

A view of the Theatre looking across the Swimming Pool to the east side. Note, this is before the extension of The Pier that was joined to the Ocean Theatre extension, ready for the erection of the Steel Stella.

The Ocean Theatre stage.

Stanley Holloway and the following year wrote the famous monologue, "Albert and the Lion".

In July, Hal Bryan returned to star at the Ocean Theatre, returning in 1930. Maurice Cowan continued to produce the Summer Show until 1931. Following Cowan's retirement, Ada Kingsman herself took over the production of the 1932 season, called simply, "The Ocean Show of 1932". The show starred Gene Durham, but, more importantly, one of the other performers was a song and dance man called Frank Adey, who had begun his stage career in the 1920s.

Ada Kingsman was so impressed with Adey that she asked him if he would like to assist her in producing the 1933 show, renamed the Ocean Revue, the name it was to keep until 1966. Adey readily agreed. In 1934, although still officially shown as presenting the show, Ada handed over the production reins to Adey. Frank Adey was to continue in the role of producer until 1971 and was to become "Mr. Ocean Theatre".

In 1935, Clacton Magistrates' Court struck the Ocean Theatre what could have been a devastating blow when they refused it a licence to put on any shows on a Sunday that included *"jazz, patter songs or a compere"* under the provisions of the 1932 Sunday Entertainments Act following representations made to them by local churches and the Lord's Day Observance Society. Sunday was, of course, normally the day the Ocean put on its "big-name" specials, a big money-spinner for it and The Pier, so this was a real blow.

In a subsequent appeal against the Magistrates' decision, Ernest Kingsman stated that since Sunday concerts had been given in conformity with their decision, the fall in audience numbers was *"very marked"* with the theatre being only a quarter full and audiences of just 300 as against a normal capacity audience of 1,200. He said it was unfair just to restrict one type of music, namely jazz, when it was enjoyed by large numbers of people, more so

The auditorium in the 1920s.

than classical music. Clacton Pier was joined in the appeal by William Hinds, owner of the West Cliff Theatre, which had also been hit with the same restriction, who added that it was "*not a commercial proposition to give such entertainment as the Magistrates desired.*"

The appeal was dismissed as the magistrates said they were only following national guidance. Following the ruling, Ernest Kingsman took out a front page advert in the local paper saying, *"CLACTON PIER We very much regret that owing to recent proceedings there will be no SUNDAY MUSIC ON THE PIER".*

The matter caused a great deal of controversy in the town and the local papers were full of arguments for and against. It was also discussed in Clacton Council, where matters got decidedly heated with one councillor opining, *"Let them have all the filth they like on weekdays, but let them for goodness sake have a good wash on Sunday."* Another exchange almost led to blows as Councillor Shingfield said, *"Personally I am glad the bench has asked to cut out jazz – I hate the stuff!"* Councillor Elliott, who was also the solicitor acting on behalf of Clacton Pier in this case, replied, *"You hate it?"* Cllr Shingfield said, *"I hate it. Some people come here to do the work of clients instead of the work of the Council."* To which Cllr Elliott responded, *"I strongly object to that. If he wants to state that outside, I shall gladly accommodate him."*

It was to take over a year of discussions and appeals before the matter was finally settled and the Ocean Theatre was once again able to put on the concerts it wished for in the 1937 season, though by then, the big name concerts had disappeared and the Ocean Revue itself took place seven days a week.

The advert placed by The Pier on the front page of the local newspapers following the "No Jazz on Sunday" verdict.

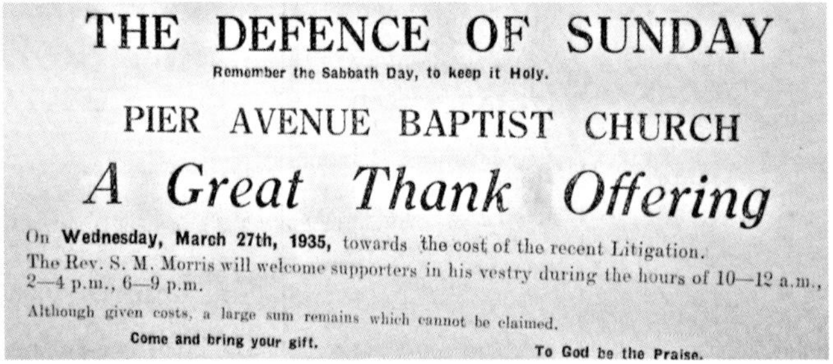

THE DEFENCE OF SUNDAY

Remember the Sabbath Day, to keep it Holy.

PIER AVENUE BAPTIST CHURCH

A Great Thank Offering

On **Wednesday, March 27th, 1935,** towards the cost of the recent Litigation. The Rev. S. M. Morris will welcome supporters in his vestry during the hours of 10—12 a.m., 2—4 p.m., 6—9 p.m.

Although given costs, a large sum remains which cannot be claimed.

Come and bring your gift. **To God be the Praise.**

The view from the other side. The Pier Avenue Baptist Church holds a thanks offering for the verdict.

In 1936, Frank Adey retired as a performer, continuing on exclusively in the role of producer while Bunny Doyle took over the starring role from Gene Durham. The show continued with a different star each year until 1939, when the Ocean Theatre closed on the outbreak of War.

The Theatre re-opened on 15 August 1945 with a show to celebrate VJ Day entitled *"A Midsummer Night's Scream – a Victory Revudeville"*. It was jointly staged by Ada Kingsman and Sergeant Jerome Bowick of the 16th Holding Regiment, Royal Artillery. The show was repeated the following night. Later in the year, a one-nighter was held, when local performer, Jack Chugg, staged a show called *"Stardust"* and then Clown Bertram re-appeared on The Pier for just one children's show matinee appearance.

1946 saw the full-scale return of both the Ocean Theatre and the Ocean Revue with Gene Durham reprising his role as star and compere. He continued until 1949. In 1947, Frank Adey signed up a young female singer by the name of Betty Martin. Not only was Betty to appear in every Ocean Revue until the last one in 1966, but she was also to become Frank's wife.

In 1950, Frank Adey took a chance on a young up-and-coming comedian who was beginning to make a name for himself on the wireless in shows such as Workers' Playtime and Variety Bandbox. His name was Tony Hancock and he proved to be an enormous success, bringing in full houses to practically every performance.

He used to open his act by coming on to the stage, looking to the stage manager's corner and saying, *"I won't be out here long, put the kettle on. Oh, I see you have, it suits you!"*

From there, Hancock moved on to radio's top-rated sit-com of the day, Educating Archie, where he gained national recognition and the rest, as they say, is history.

In 1951, Hancock's place as star of the Ocean Revue was taken by local comedian, Wally Dunn. In fact, Frank Adey had seen Wally perform at New Brighton and was suitably impressed, so he and Betty arranged to interview Wally for the role of lead comedian in the 1951 Ocean Revue. The only question asked at the interview was, *"Do you play cricket?"* When Wally replied that he did, Frank gave him the job on the spot.

Wally was a fast talking wise-cracking comedian in the Max Miller mould, even to the extent of wearing a flowery suit like his hero. His catch phrase was, *"Silly but happy."* He remained as star of the Ocean Revue for five years until 1955.

By the mid 1950s, Frank Adey's Ocean Revue had earned itself a national reputation as one of the very best Summer Seasons in the country and was drawing in full houses night after night. So much so, that, in 1954, Ada and Barney Kingsman had plans drawn up that would increase the Ocean Theatre's capacity.

The Ocean Theatre in the 1950s.

The plans and architectural drawings show the intention was to build an impressive new entrance with a first floor above. Although some of the initial structural work was completed, including steel work and pile and beam work under The Pier to support the weight, it was eventually abandoned as it was felt The Pier would not in fact support the weight of the extension after all.

Over the next few years, several plans to modernise the Theatre were drawn up, but it wasn't until 1961 that one of these new plans was actually partially implemented when a major change to the theatre's construction was made as new aluminium wall cladding was installed in place of the old weatherboard structure. It was felt this would brighten up the building making it a dominant feature of The Pier, both day and night. A new foyer and box office was also built.

This work was intended to be the first part of a bigger £100,000 scheme that would also improve the interior of the theatre, firstly by building a higher stage and headroom to allow, for the first time, full size scenery flyways and a new lighting gallery and secondly, to improve the auditorium as it was intended to ramp it and re-align the 1,200 seats. But, as in 1955, the second stage of the plan was never put into operation.

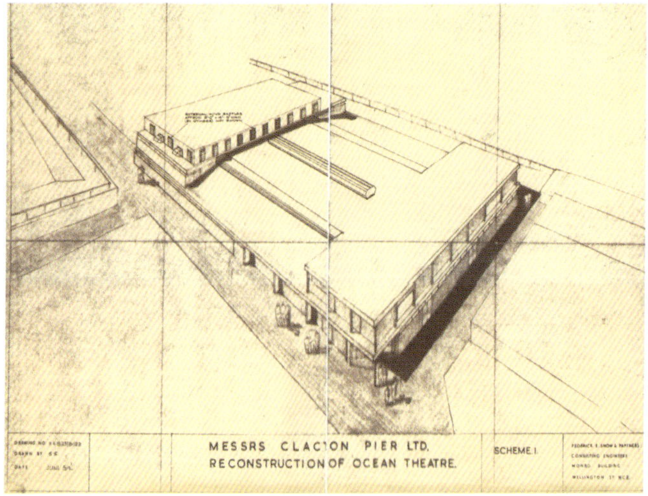

Plans for the proposed extension to the Ocean Theatre in 1954.

An artist's impression of what the new Ocean Theatre would look like, 1954.

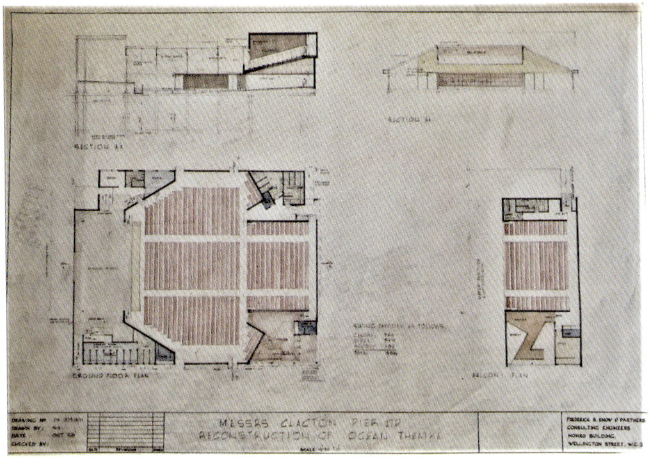

One of the many plans that were drawn up for improvements in the late 1950s and early 1960s. This one is dated 1958.

The late 1950s and early 1960s saw Frank Adey taking a chance on some young up-and-coming comedians who had not yet quite made the big time but who, partly through his support and guidance, were to become star names such as Billy Dainty, Felix Bowness and Ted Rogers, culminating in another young comedian by the name of Roy Hudd who starred for two years, 1964 and 1965. Many years later when asked who were the greatest influences early in his career, Roy said, *"One of my guides and mentors was a very special bloke indeed, Frank Adey."*

The following year, saw a more established lead, Don Smoothey, star in the last-ever Ocean Revue as, from 1967, the name of the Summer Season was changed to the Ocean Show. Frank Adey was still the producer with his wife, Betty, now taking on the role of stage manager. With the change of Pier ownership in 1971, the name of the show was changed to Showtime.

In common with the rest of the attractions on Clacton Pier, the Ocean Theatre was suffering from falling attendances so the new owner, Michael Goss, decided on an all-or-nothing policy and from 1972, staged Summer Seasons headlining the very top names in British show business hoping that this would win back the crowds.

Consequently, 1972 saw Dick Emery starring in The Dick Emery Show, though his place was taken for the last week of the run by Freddie & The Dreamers. Because these shows came with their own production companies, Frank Adey and Betty Martin's services were no longer required and both retired from direct involvement with the shows. Adey was appointed as Clacton Pier's Entertainment Manager and so still retained oversight of the Ocean Theatre along with his other responsibilities.

As well as Dick Emery's summer season, the Ocean Theatre also played host to more top names in a series of one-off Sunday concerts. In 1972, these included Bob Monkhouse, Leslie Crowther, Frank Ifield, Mike & Bernie Winters and Clive Dunn.

To maximise the use of the Ocean Theatre and hopefully to increase its revenue, Goss and Adey introduced children's shows twice a day in the morning and afternoon. The most popular of these were, "Mr Magic Man", Len Blease, and the clowns, Rolo and Shandy.

In 1973, five of the stars of the popular television programme, The Comedians, starred in the Summer Season, but, by then, the Ocean Theatre was really struggling to draw in the crowds. At one time, The Comedians complained they had more people on stage than in the audience!

Jim Bowen, in his autobiography, *From a Bundle of Rags*, remembers it well. He had this to say about the numbers:

A poster for Len Blease's twice daily "Merlin's Magic Show".

"Looking out from the stage to the back of the auditorium, night after night, I used to be able to say, 'I've slept with more people than we've got in the audience tonight and I'm not even very good at it'...we all got accustomed to working to a large empty space and soon a whole row of full seats was something to be eagerly reported backstage as a cause for major excitement."

The two clowns, Rolo and Shandy, advertising their show in 1974.

The Pier Entrance in 1973 advertising The Comedians Summer Season.

The 15 year old Julie Andrews tops the bill in a Sunday Concert at the Ocean Theatre in 1951.

A poster for a 1975 Sunday Concert starring Morecambe and Wise.

One person who did go and see the show was well-known local Clacton entertainer, Reg Young, one half of the comedy duo, the Young Brothers. Reg recalled that the night he was there, Jim Bowen was heckled by an audience member, who shouted out, *"Get off! The stuff you're using is terrible."* Jim Bowen replied, *"I'm paid to do 20 minutes and 20 minutes I'm bloody well going to do!"*

In spite of the falling audience numbers, Michael Goss continued with his policy of putting on big name shows for both the Summer Seasons and the Sunday Concerts with Harry Worth, Leslie Crowther and Arthur Askey and Dickie Henderson starring in the Summer Seasons and Morecambe & Wise, Larry Grayson and Hughie Green amongst many others in the Sunday Concerts.

All the stars now appearing at the Ocean Theatre were household names thanks mainly to their appearances on television and it was hoped this would guarantee large audiences. Sadly, it didn't work out that way and after the 1977 season starring Craig Douglas, The Pier finally pulled the plug on the Ocean Theatre and it closed for ever, initially being converted to a ghost train and later to an amusement arcade.

closure of The Ocean Theatre, from its ... with four theatres, The Pier now had none. A practical symbol of the decline of Clacton-on-Sea as a seaside resort and its knock-on effect on Clacton Pier.

There was one small postscript to the demise of the Ocean Theatre, when, on 12 March 1978, a special benefit concert was held at Clacton's Salon Theatre (formerly the Odeon Cinema) for Frank Adey to thank him for all his years of dedication to the Ocean Theatre. A number of well-known names, who owed much of their early stage experience to Frank's support and encouragement, took part, including Roy Hudd, Billy Dainty, Wally Dunn, John Hanson, Gordon and Bunny Jay and David and Tony Webb.

The sad end for the Ocean Theatre is summed up in this poster for the last-ever season, 1977, starring Craig Douglas.

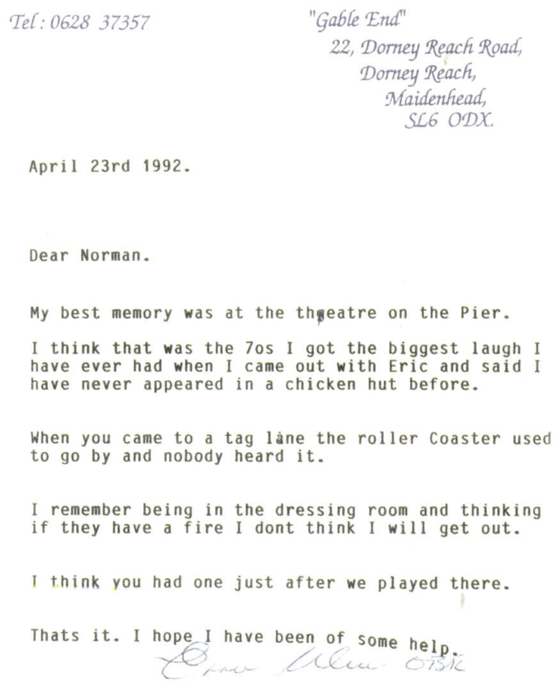

Tel: 0628 37357

"Gable End"
22, Dorney Reach Road,
Dorney Reach,
Maidenhead,
SL6 ODX.

April 23rd 1992.

Dear Norman.

My best memory was at the thgeatre on the Pier.

I think that was the 7os I got the biggest laugh I have ever had when I came out with Eric and said I have never appeared in a chicken hut before.

When you came to a tag lane the roller Coaster used to go by and nobody heard it.

I remember being in the dressing room and thinking if they have a fire I dont think I will get out.

I think you had one just after we played there.

Thats it. I hope I have been of some help.

Ernie Wise OBE

A letter to the author from Ernie Wise dated 1992, recalling his memories of the Ocean Theatre.

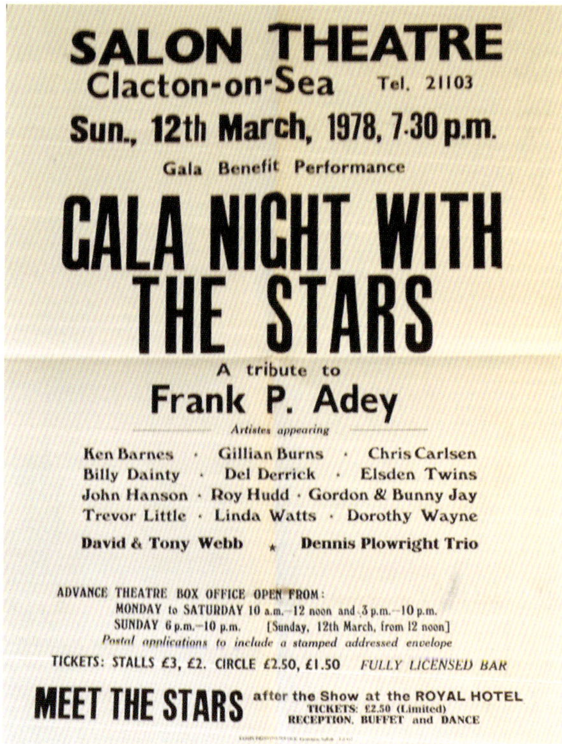

The poster for Frank Adey's Benefit Concert, held at the Salon Theatre on 12 March 1978.

Summer Seasons at the Ocean Theatre

Year	Show	Starring
1928	Revels of 1928	Hal Bryan, Horace Lane
1929	Surpassing Show	Hugh Renee
1930	Surpassing Show	Hal Bryan
1931	Surpassing Show	Ken Douglas
1932	Ocean Show	Gene Durham, Frank Adey

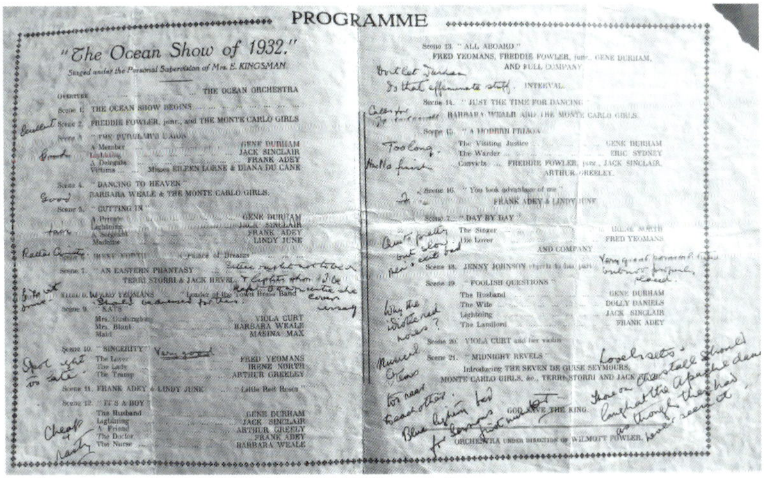

PROGRAMME

"The Ocean Show of 1932."

Staged under the Personal Supervision of Mrs. E. KINGSMAN

OVERTURE ... THE OCEAN ORCHESTRA

Scene 1. THE OCEAN SHOW BEGINS ...

Scene 2. FREDDIE FOWLER, junr., and THE MONTE CARLO GIRLS

Scene 3. ...
A Member ... GENE DURHAM
Lightning ... JACK SINCLAIR
A Delegate ... FRANK ADEY
Victims ... Misses EILEEN LORNE & DIANA DU CANE

Scene 4. "DANCING TO HEAVEN"
BARBARA WEALE & THE MONTE CARLO GIRLS.

Scene 5. "CUTTING IN"
... GENE DURHAM
Lightning ... JACK SINCLAIR
A Sergeant ... FRANK ADEY
Madame ... LINDY JUNE

Scene 6. ... "Palace of Dreams" ...

Scene 7. "AN EASTERN PHANTASY"
TERRI STORRI & JACK REVEL

Scene 8. FRED YEOMANS "Leader of the Town Brass Band"

Scene 9. "KATS"
Mrs. ... VIOLA CURT
Mrs. Blunt ... BARBARA WEALE
Maid ... MASINA MAX

Scene 10. "SINCERITY"
The Lover ... FRED YEOMANS
The Lady ... IRENE NORTH
The Tramp ... ARTHUR GREELEY

Scene 11. FRANK ADEY & LINDY JUNE ... "Little Red Roses"

Scene 12. "IT'S A BOY"
The Husband ... GENE DURHAM
Lightning ... JACK SINCLAIR
A Friend ... ARTHUR GREELY
The Doctor ... FRANK ADEY
The Nurse ... BARBARA WEALE

Scene 13. "ALL ABOARD"
FRED YEOMANS, FREDDIE FOWLER, junr., GENE DURHAM, AND FULL COMPANY

INTERVAL.

Scene 14. "JUST THE TIME FOR DANCING"
BARBARA WEALE AND THE MONTE CARLO GIRLS.

Scene 15. "A MODERN PRISON"
The Visiting Justice ... GENE DURHAM
The Warder ... ERIC SYDNEY
Convicts ... FREDDIE FOWLER, junr., JACK SINCLAIR, ARTHUR GREELEY.

Scene 16. "You took advantage of me"
FRANK ADEY & LINDY JUNE

Scene 17. "DAY BY DAY"
The Singer ... IRENE NORTH
The Lover ... FRED YEOMANS
AND COMPANY

Scene 18. JENNY JOHNSON ...

Scene 19. "FOOLISH QUESTIONS"
The Husband ... GENE DURHAM
The Wife ... DOLLY DANIELS
Lightning ... JACK SINCLAIR
The Landlord ... FRANK ADEY

Scene 20. VIOLA CURT and her violin

Scene 21. "MIDNIGHT REVELS"
Introducing THE SEVEN DE GUISE SEYMOURS, MONTE CARLO GIRLS, &c., TERRI STORRI AND JACK REVEL

GOD SAVE THE KING.

ORCHESTRA UNDER DIRECTION OF WILMOTT FOWLER.

The proposed 1932 programme with Frank Adey's hand written notes following a rehearsal. He obviously wasn't impressed with some of the acts, e.g. Scene 12 was "cheap & nasty"; scene 13: "Don't let Gene Durham do that effeminate stuff"; Scene 19: "Why the idiotic red noses?" Mind you, it wasn't all bad as Scene 2 was "Excellent" and scenes 3 and 4 "Good".

Year	Show	Starring
1933	Ocean Revue	Gene Durham, Macari & His Serenaders, Frank Adey
1934	Ocean Revue	Gene Durham, Lindy June, Frank Adey
1935	Ocean Revue	Gene Durham, Lindy June, Frank Adey
1936	Ocean Revue	Bunny Doyle, Sam Linfield & Co.

Gene Durham, star of the Ocean Theatre Summer Season from 1932 to 1935 and again from 1946 to 1949.

Frank Adey in his "song & dance" days before taking over as producer of the Ocean Revue.

1937	Ocean Revue	Scott Sanders, Emile Zigano and His Anglo-French Band
1938	Ocean Revue	Jackson Owen, Saxon Davis, May Goring Thomas
1939	Ocean Revue	Gus Chevalier, May Goring Thomas, Farleigh Price
1946	Ocean Revue	Gene Durham, Gate Eastley
1947	Ocean Revue	Gene Durham, Betty Martin
1948	Ocean Revue	Gene Durham, Gordon Norville, Betty Martin
1949	Ocean Revue	Gene Durham, Gordon Norville, Betty Martin

Bunny Doyle, star of the 1936 Ocean Revue.

The Pamela Devis Dancers supported the Summer Show from 1973-1976. They are seen here on The Pier in 1973.

Betty Martin, Frank Adey's wife, who appeared in 20 successive Ocean Revues from 1947-1966 before becoming the stage manager.

1950	Ocean Revue	Tony Hancock, Gordon Norville, Betty Martin
1951	Ocean Revue	Wally Dunn, Gordon Norville, Betty Martin
1952	Ocean Revue	Wally Dunn, Gordon Norville, Betty Martin
1953	Ocean Revue	Wally Dunn, Authors & Swinson, Betty Martin
1954	Ocean Revue	Wally Dunn, Betty Martin
1955	Ocean Revue	Wally Dunn, Gordon Norville, Betty Martin
1956	Ocean Revue	Billy Dainty, Gordon Norville, Betty Martin
1957	Ocean Revue	Felix Bowness, Gordon Norville, Betty Martin
1958	Ocean Revue	Tony Hughes. Arthur Sumner, Betty Martin
1959	Ocean Revue	Tony Hughes, Arthur Sumner, Betty Martin, The Edorics
1960	Ocean Revue	Tony Hughes, Arthur Sumner, Betty Martin, The Edorics
1961	Ocean Revue	Gordon & Bunny Jay, Betty Martin, The Edorics
1962	Ocean Revue	Gordon & Bunny Jay, Betty Martin, The Edorics
1963	Ocean Revue	Ted Rogers, Tommy Elliott, Paul Fox, Betty Martin
1964	Ocean Revue	Roy Hudd, Anna Harriman, Betty Martin
1965	Ocean Revue	Roy Hudd, Les Giross, Van Buren & Greta, Betty Martin
1966	Ocean Revue	Don Smoothey, Peter Crago, Betty Martin

Local Comedian, Wally Dunn, seen here in the Ocean Theatre, starred in the Ocean Revue for five years from 1951-1955.

A publicity photo for the 1965 Ocean Revue showing Roy Hudd being levitated by illusionist Fred Van Buren.

Frank Adey at the time of his retirement as producer of the Summer Season.

The Comedians on stage, showing Russ Abbott, Sammy Thomas, Pat Mooney, Jimmy Marshall and Jim Bowen.

The poster for the 1974 season, starring Harry Worth.

1967	The Ocean Show	Billy Burden, Johnny Pace, Bruce Allen
1968	The Ocean Show	Billy Burden, Johnny (Legs) Burton, Gilmore & Terry
1969	The Ocean Show	Felix Bowness, Emerson & Jayne, Gilmore & Terry
1970	The Ocean Show	Ronnie Collis, Valentino, Pat Hatton & Gloria
1971	Showtime	Brian Burdon, Clive Bennett, Rainbow's End
1972	Dick Emery Show	Dick Emery, Eve Boswell, Bert Weedon

1973	The Comedians	Jimmy Marshall, Jim Bowen, Russ Abbott, Pat Mooney, Sammy Thomas
1974	Here's Harry	Harry Worth, Peter Goodwright, Dai Francis
1975	Crowther's in Town	Leslie Crowther, The Karlins, Johnny Vyvyan
1976	Showtime '76	Arthur Askey & Dickie Henderson, Roger Stevenson
1977	Holiday Spectacular	Craig Douglas, Gordon Peters, Karen Kaye

Leslie Crowther, with Johnny Vyvyan and the Karlins in a publicity photo at the foot of the Cresta Run advertising the 1975 season.

Arthur Askey and Dickie Henderson with one of the Pamela Devis Dancers in a publicity photo advertising the 1976 season.

Chapter Eighteen

Clacton's Wonder Swimming Pool

Following Ernest Kingsman's successful bid to compulsorily purchase Council land at the front and side of The Pier in 1930, one of his first and arguably the most ambitious projects to make use of this new area was the building of an open-air swimming pool, the first to be built on a pier anywhere in the world.

But he wasn't interested in just any old swimming pool, Kingsman wanted it to be amongst the very best in the country, a building that would not merely be an attraction for holiday-makers, though that was certainly a major reason behind building the pool, but he also wanted it to be capable of hosting regional, national and even international events.

Consequently, the pool was 55 yards in length with a width of 20 yards. The fixed high diving boards were 16 feet 3 inches and 9 feet 9 inches, with a spring board also at 9 feet 9 inches plus another spring board at deck level, all of which met the needs for international competition.

The depth of the water varied between 3 feet and 6 feet with a 9 feet deep area in front of the diving boards. To encourage children and the everyday visitors, 60% of the swimming area was below 4 feet 6 inches.

The whole swimming pool with surrounding changing rooms and audience viewing area, amounting to an overall area of 165 feet by 60 feet, was constructed throughout of reinforced concrete standing on piles 25 feet above the sea-bed.

Building the "New Wonder Swimming Pool" is well underway. It took just nine weeks to build the pool from start to completion.

The water was pumped into the swimming pool through a chamber housed between the deep end and the Blue Lagoon Dance Hall at the rate of 20,000-30,000 gallons of water an hour, ensuring the provision of a continuous supply of fresh sea water.

The design and construction of the pool was carried out by leading British reinforced concrete specialists, Bierrum & Partners of Victoria Street, London, and was ready to open in time for the 1932 season.

The "Pier Wonder Swimming Pool", as it was called, was officially opened on 2 July 1932 by local M.P. and Minister for Transport, Mr. John Pybus, C.B.E., M.P., along with speeches by Ernest, Ada and

Barney Kingsman. Many local Councillors were in attendance as well as the High Sheriff of Essex, Brigadier General Kenneth J. Kincaid-Smith, and other local dignitaries. As soon as the speeches were finished, the water fountain that stood at one end of the pool was illuminated red, and the pool itself in luminous green. This heralded the start of an "aquatic gala", kicked off by veteran diver, the 74 year old George Webb, diving into the pool off the top board to carry out the official baptism.

A number of water events then took place including a *Balloon Race* for Ladies only, a mixed *Hidden Clothes Race, Musical Lifebuoys* for gentlemen only, *Cock Fighting* and a comedy water polo match put on by that year's Ocean Revue performers. In addition there was also a diving display by W S T Burns, one of Great Britain's representatives at the 1928 Olympic Games while throughout the day, Teddy Dobbs' Blue Lagoon Band played music.

Swimming Pool

Prices of Admission

Swimming Ticket : 6d.

Tickets taken at Pier Entrance include Pier Toll.

Costumes and Towels may be obtained at small charge

Hot and Cold Showers

Separate Lock-ups Provided for Swimmers' Clothes

Spectators' Enclosure : 2d.

A Fully Equipped Cafe

will be at the service of Patrons.

Refreshments at Popular Prices

BANDS WILL PROVIDE MUSIC ALL DAY

Clacton's Wonder

Swimming Pool

Souvenir Programme

GRAND OPENING

SATURDAY, JULY 2nd, 1932

The programme for the grand opening of the Wonder Swimming Pool, 2 July 1932.

A large crowd gathers for the opening speeches.

To finish off the day there was a grand fireworks display which the local paper described as "*a magnificent spectacle enjoyed not only by the people at the Pool but by thousands along the front.*" There was one unrehearsed incident however and that was when a flying spark set fire prematurely to the fireworks that were due to finish the display with a colourful set piece exhibiting the words "God Save The King!"

Nevertheless, it was a magnificent occasion that cemented Clacton Pier's place at the very centre of Clacton-on-Sea's official, cultural and business life.

Once opened to the public, the "New Wonder Swimming Pool" became a major draw for visitors, whether swimming, diving or just sitting in the stands to watch big events. The Clacton Swimming Club made it their home base for swimming and water polo matches against other clubs and for their own championships.

Because its dimensions and facilities adhered to international standards, many world class special events were organised, drawing in thousands of spectators. For example, as soon as the following year, 1933, the National Salt Water Championships were held there. This was the first time the national championship of any sport had been held in Clacton. The Southern Counties Championship was also held there that year which included a diving display by the European champion, Austria's Josef Staudinger, and a Water Polo league match between Clacton and Chelmsford.

In the following year, 1934, the men's 880 yards British Championship was held, while Essex took on the full Hungarian national team in a water polo international.

For the rest of the 1930s, the swimming pool continued in the same vein, with local swimming galas and championships organised by Clacton Swimming Club and other local clubs, such as the Police Swimming Club, as well as regional championships, including the Essex County Championships. To top all of this, the swimming pool also showcased the world's elite in special

Ernest Kingsman getting the official opening of the Swimming Pool underway.

Ada Kingsman, surrounded by Ernest and Barney, presents a gold watch to Mr C.D.H. Haynes, the resident engineer and general foreman of Messrs Bierrum and Partners who built the pool. Looking on behind are Brigadier-General K.J. Kincaid-Smith, John Pybus and Mrs L. M. Hill, the mayor of Harwich.

displays. In 1936, for example, a swimming and diving display was given by the Japanese Olympic team as well as diving displays by Olympic Gold Medallists, Canadian, Pete Desjardins, and American, Harold "Dutch" Smith.

There were also cabaret type shows put on by visiting artists such as the Eugene Mermaids, led by Channel swimmer, Sunny Lowry, who gave displays of swimming, diving and formation swimming.

So popular did the swimming pool become and so much in demand by local, regional and even national organisations that a new terrace had to be built to increase the seating capacity by 1,500 as well as making room for 600 changing cubicles. To accommodate this, 36 new concrete piles had to be driven into the sea-bed.

Those wishing to use the pool for swimming rather than watching were not forgotten. When there were no galas, internationals or shows, the pool was open to all. And, for the more competitive, swimming galas were arranged for visitors to take part in every Tuesday and Thursday.

One of the events at the special opening day gala was canoe tipping, which was a popular event at swimming galas in the 1930s.

The New Wonder Swimming Pool became one of the star attractions on The Pier and undoubtedly played a big part in enticing the ever-increasing number of visitors now flocking to Clacton-on-Sea.

As with all the other activities on The Pier, it all came to an abrupt end with the outbreak of the Second World War.

Although Clacton Pier was able to re-open in a very limited fashion in 1946, the swimming pool was not ready until Whit Saturday 1948, but once it re-opened it quickly regained its status as one of the leading attractions, not just on The Pier but in Clacton-on-Sea as a whole.

Into the 1950s, the regular galas and championships continued as well as weekly water polo matches, including international matches featuring the Great Britain team.

In addition, water variety shows were held weekly through the Summer Season with names such as Water Follies and Water Frolics. These included swimming and diving displays, comedy routines, underwater escape acts, Daredevil Diving from Ricky Dare, whose most famous feat was to dive from a special diving board 60 feet high into just five feet of water and, as it was the 1950s, the inevitable line-up of "The Glamorous Water-Lovelies" or "The Aqua Pin-Ups".

Although the swimming pool was a great attraction for holidaymakers, drawing in tens of thousands of visitors each year, just to use the pool themselves or to see the special galas and events that went on there, it also played an important part in the lives of Clacton residents as well, who were very fortunate to have a world class swimming pool on their doorstep.

For Clacton Swimming Club it was the ideal place for their headquarters and for all their inter-club matches and championships, including water polo. Local schools took advantage of it for their swimming lessons. Individuals too could sign up for coaching and lessons provided by expert tutors. In fact a special campaign was run during the 1950s called the Learn to Swim programme. In 1954, Hackney schoolgirl, seven year old Priscilla Best, had her first-ever swimming lesson in this programme. Six years later she became the British

A general view of the pool in the 1930s.

A close-up view of the diving boards.

100 yards junior swimming champion and was even tipped for the UK Olympic team that year in Rome, though in the end she just missed out.

Sadly, as already detailed in Chapter Five, the good times in Clacton and on Clacton Pier were gradually coming to an end as visitor numbers began to drop off in the 1960s. The announcement in 1964 that the swimming pool was to be closed caused uproar in Clacton. Many of the town's businesses were aware that the swimming pool was a major attraction and one which brought many visitors to Clacton, especially when there were regional and national swimming galas, not to mention the international water polo matches. The Clacton Swimming Club was devastated by the announcement and many local schools complained as they used the pool for their own galas and swimming lessons.

In the end Clacton Council itself was forced to step in and guaranteed to underwrite any losses made on the pool during the year enabling Barney Kingsman to agree to reopen the pool in 1965.

But this was only a temporary reprieve as, in 1968, Kingsman once again decided the swimming pool had to close. He said, "*It has lost money over the last three years despite all the Council's assistance, so we have decided we should shut it.*" Once again the town's businesspeople felt they could not allow this to happen and, this time, a consortium of the town's businesses stepped in to underwrite the costs.

However, it wasn't to last and one of the first acts taken by Michael Goss who took over The Pier in 1971 was to close the swimming pool and replace it with a Dolphinarium. And so, one of the major achievements and attractions of Clacton Pier, an Olympic Size swimming pool built over the sea, came to an end, leaving just memories behind.

That wasn't quite the end of the story though as, in 1985, following the removal of the last killer whale, Nemo, to Windsor Safari Park, Francis McGinty reinstated a smaller swimming pool called the Fun Lido on the site. This new lido contained three water chutes which spiralled down plunging those looking for a bit of an extra thrill to go with their swimming. The whole revamp cost £250,000.

But, with visitor numbers continuing to fall, this didn't last long and the area more or less became derelict apart from a small aquarium on the site which was eventually to become The Living Ocean.

A close-up view of the fountain.

The year after its opening, the pool was visited by the leader of the Labour Party, Mr George Lansbury, seen here to the right of Ernest Kingsman.

In its heyday, Clacton Pier Swimming Pool had played a major part not only in boosting Clacton as a seaside town but also as a first class facility that residents could use all the year round. And still today, Clactonians look back on The Pier swimming pool with great affection, though the coldness of the water also seems to be an abiding memory! Here are just a few of those reminiscences:

> Roy Begernie: *"We Went there on coaches from London Road School for PE/swimming lessons and learned to swim... then whole summers in the water or up on the sides in the sun! Jumping and diving from the boards took a while but I summoned up the courage in the end.... halcyon days."*

> Ann Headworth: *"I spent many happy years there as a member of Clacton Swimming Club and was honoured to be Ladies' Captain for a while. Great memories, most of all probably remembering how jolly cold that water was and cups of hot Bovril in the little cafe to thaw out."*

> Alan Radmall: *"At one stage there was a Cadbury's hot chocolate stand just outside the entrance/exit of the pool. The first stage of warming up after the very cold water."*

> Harry Francis: *"I have a memory of a Brylcreem machine in Clacton swimming pool on The Pier. My memory is of a wall mounted machine, you put in a penny, pushed a plunger and got a squirt of Brylcreem in your hand; disgusting sound but we all used Brylcreem in the 1950s. I said I would dive off the top board to show off but jumped instead.*

COMING SWIMMING AND OTHER EVENTS :

June 29. (Saturday) 3.30 at Pier Pool.
Gala Swimming Event & Water Polo
CLACTON v. LONDON FIRE BRIGADE S.C.

June 30. (Sunday) 4.30 p.m. at Pier Pool.
Water Polo Match
CLACTON S.C. v. HOUNDSFIELD S.C.

July 2. (Tuesday) 7 30 at Pier Pool.
Grand Gala
Swimming and Water Polo
Cambridge University v. Walthamstow S.C.

July 7. (Sunday) 4 30 at Pier Pool.
Inter Club Contest
Swimming Events and Water Polo Match
CLACTON S.C. v. K.E.B. S.C. LONDON

July 10. (Wednesday) 7 p.m. at Pier Pool.
Grand Gala
Visit of Pete Desjardins
World's Champion Diver Olympic Games 1928
also CLACTON v. IPSWICH, WATER POLO
Swimming Events, East Anglian Swimming League

July 13. (Saturday) 3.30 at Pier Pool.
Inter Club Gala
CLACTON v. OLD STORFORDIANS S.C.
Swimming Events and Water Polo.

July 20. (Saturday) Pier Pool.
Water Polo
Clacton v. Maldon N.E. Essex League

July 21. (Sunday) 4.30 at Pier Pool.
Water Polo Match
CLACTON S.C. v. LEANDER S.C. LONDON

July 27. (Saturday) 3 p.m. at Pier Pool.
Open Gala (Events Later)
S.C.A.S.A. Ladies 220 Championship,
Water Polo. CLACTON v. BRAINTREE
N.E. Essex League.

Aug. 7. Grand Gala, 7 30 Pier Pool.
Hillegersberg S.C. of Holland
Details Later.

(Wednesday) 8 p.m. at Pier Pool.
Water Polo Match
CLACTON v. CHELMSFORD
Final of the Lewis Cup.

Aug. 19. (Monday) 7.30 at Pier Pool.
Water Polo Match N.E. Essex League.
Swimming Events. East Anglian Swimming League
CLACTON v. COLCHESTER

Aug. 21. At 7 30 at Pier Pool.
Water Polo Match
CLACTON S.C. v. R.A.F. MARTLESHAM

Aug 24. (Saturday) 3.30 Pier Pool.
Grand Gala
Zwemvereeniging Het. v.
of Holland Details Later

Aug. 31. (Saturday) 3. p.m. at Pier Pool.
Open Gala (Events Later)

The programme for the Summer of 1935, showing the wide variety of events that took place.

An advert for 1936 showing the quality of the attractions on offer.

A signed photograph to Barney Kingsman of Pete Desjardins in action.

Channel Swimmer, Sunny Lowry, leader of the Eugene Mermaids, who gave special displays which included stunt dives with titles such as Australian Splash, Charlie's Aunt and Dead Man's Drop.

This is one of the Eugene Mermaids stunt dives.

An advert for the pool from 1936.

A leaflet showing some of the events on offer in 1938, including the Police Championship Gala.

Clacton Pier's Wonder Swimming Pool was a very popular place before the War.

The Police Gala in full swing. Notice that many of them are still wearing their helmets! The Police Galas continued well into the 1960s. Nigel Nicholas remembers the Police Galas in the 1960s. He said they 'would fool around on the boards in their uniforms, then fall in in all sorts of poses! I remember the Met. Police water polo team were especially "tough", and many could stand on the floor of the pool, especially even up to the 6ft. end'.

The 1950s continued to see the Swimming Pool home to International and National events, such as this International Gala involving a Dutch Club in 1951.

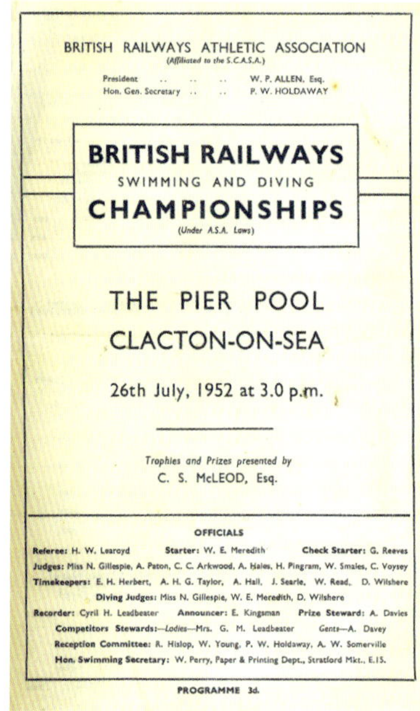

And the British Railways National Swimming and Diving Championships in 1952.

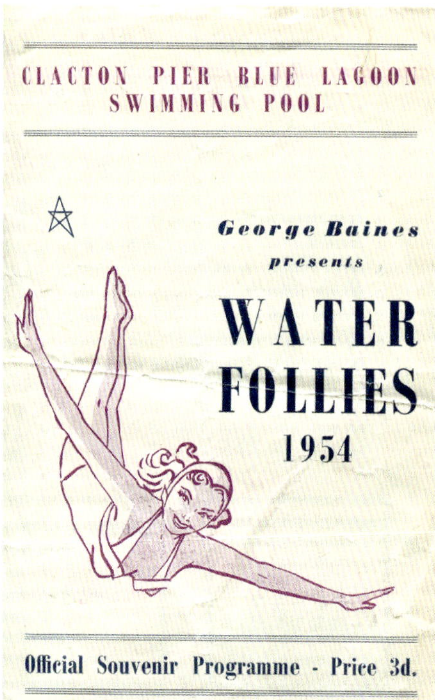

The Mid 1950s saw an annual water variety season. In 1954 it was Water Follies.

While the following year saw Water Frolics.

The Variety shows included comedy acts such as this one, "Demolition Limited" performed by the "Ministry of Twerps".

The 1955 Clacton Swimming Club Water Polo Team, who played their matches at the pool every Sunday, l-r, rear: Merry W.E. Meredith, Hugh Arnot, Peter Berry, John Ransome, Brian Graver, Peter Mallows, front Brian Taylor, Ken Dart, Peter Beales, Nick Hodges.

A swimming lesson taking place in the pool in 1954.

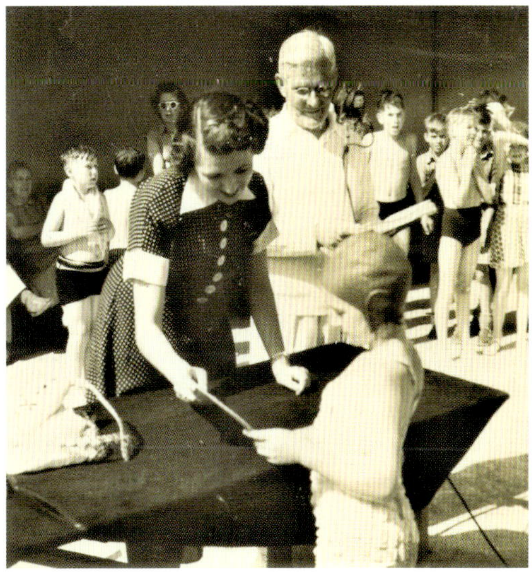

Priscilla Best receiving her certificate for completing the Learn to Swim course.

A general view of the swimming pool in the 1950s.

An advert for the swimming pool from The Pier's 1960 brochure.

CLOSURE OF PIER POOL 'A GREAT BLOW TO SWIMMING'

BOMBSHELL, but not a death blow! That was the reaction of chairman Eddie Herbert and his Clacton Swimming Club colleagues to the news that the Pier Pool, centre of competitive activity since 1932, would not be available in 1969. And the reason? Because despite financial assistance from Clacton Council the pool continues to lose money and as a result is to be closed next summer.

* * *

The East Essex Gazette reporting the closure of the swimming pool in 1968. Fortunately, it did manage to survive a bit longer.

The second incarnation of the swimming pool under Francis McGinty, complete with water chutes.

The Pier entrance in August 1987 showing the large advertisement for the Lido and Water Slides.

The final days of the swimming pool, abandoned and awaiting re-development.

Chapter Nineteen

Come to The Circus

The first circus to be staged on Clacton Pier was Stephenson's Excelsior Stage Circus which opened the Ocean Theatre in 1928. But the first permanent home for a circus came in 1936 following the widening of The Pier entrance and removal of the Blue Lagoon Dance Hall to the right hand side of The Pier.

A large four pole marquee was erected in its place to house Chapman's Old English Circus and Zoo, owned and run by another formidable Ada, this time Ada Mary Chapman. The zoo included lions, tigers and elephants, which also appeared in the circus. In fact, the elephants gave Clacton a new attraction as holidaymakers used to turn out especially to see the elephants take their morning dip in the sea before appearing in the circus shows.

The circus also featured the "unrideable mule", a troupe of "Circusettes" and the clowns, the Austins.

At the beginning of the 1937 season, although originally still advertised as the Old English Circus, Miss Chapman changed the name of her circus to the Royal Bengal Circus, though it didn't seem to make much difference to the acts on offer with Jan Doksansky and his elephants still a major attraction along with Harry Schmidt and his sea lions and Harder Jonsson and his "comedy black bears".

At the end of that season, Ernest Kingsman planned a whole new under cover extension on the left hand side of The Pier, which was to include a new circus ring seating 1,040 spectators.

The Old English Circus sets up in a marquee on the site of the original Blue Lagoon Dance Hall, after the latter was demolished.

One young boy who went to see the Royal Bengal Circus in its new home in 1938 was David Harris. He later recalled having *"vivid memories of the Hermans' rolla-bolla act; the Flying Potters on the trampoline; a riding act by Bobby and Tommy Roberts and lady juggler, Roxea Royal."* He added, *"The clown act included the swallowing the candle routine and I thought the subsequent emergence of the candle in the backside of the clown's trousers was hilarious. My mother was not so amused and gave me a clip round the ear."*

Other acts to appear that year were Miss Louise's "amazing and antique" dogs and monkeys; the Trio Volair, a trapeze act; June Night, a contortionist billed as "The Flexible Wonder" and a new bear act, a group of Himalayan black bears presented by Senor Carloff.

Unfortunately, there did seem to be a number of mishaps involving the animals during the season. For example, an 11 year-old boy was clawed by one of the bears during a performance and had to be rushed to hospital with a nasty gash in his calf.

The Royal Bengal Circus and Zoo continued in much the same vein in 1939 – even including the accidents. On one occasion, a monkey escaped from the zoo and leapt off The Pier on to the beach landing in the lap of a small boy, who, fortunately, was not hurt. The monkey itself remained free until the following day when it was seen still on Clacton beach and recaptured.

It wasn't just young boys who fell victim to the animals as, on another occasion, the lion tamer, Sidney Howes, was clawed by a young lioness, causing a gash in his leg about two Inches long.

But, accidents apart, the Circus proved to be a great success and regularly drew in large crowds. Sadly, it all came to an end when the War broke out as the Circus did not return to The Pier immediately after the War.

Harder Jonsson and his comedy black bears. Note there is no barrier between the bears and the audience.

The 1936 Old English Circus Company.

In fact, it had to wait until 1982, when Francis McGinty staged Sally Chipperfield's Circus inside the Jolly Roger. This was advertised as "*The only circus in the world on a seaside pier*". It staged three one hour shows and one two hour show every day from 17 June to 4 September. Among the acts taking part were the Five Petrescu, acrobats; Tom Junior, a juggler; the Giovanni Sisters on the low wire and the clowns, Jimmy and Jamie Scott. Also featured were a number of animal acts, including Sally's Poodles, an exotic group of camel, llama and zebra; Dexter and Ankole cattle, six tigers, two leopards, two black panthers and, of course, an elephant act.

Francis McGinty himself even appeared once when he went inside the tigers' cage for a charity event, raising £1,000 for the South Atlantic Appeal.

Sally Chipperfield's Circus was a one-off and the circus did not return to Clacton Pier until 2017, when Billy and Elliot Ball staged Circus Fantasia, with three shows daily, again in the Jolly Roger. The producers were Matthew Wingate and Anya Stefanyuk. Matthew Wingate said it was a

Sneaking a look inside!

completely new experience for him and the Circus as they had always appeared in a big top before, so appearing in an indoor arena was a challenge he was looking forward to.

A brand new brightly-coloured fascia was erected at the front of the Jolly Roger. Inside, the old theatre had been converted into a circus ring with sections of the 1982 seating at each side of the ring and seven tiers of brand new tip-up seating also installed, facing the ring.

The circus was a fast-moving affair with a whole range of exciting and spectacular performances following each other in quick succession without any breaks for announcements. And, for the first time in a Clacton Pier circus, there were no animal acts.

Circus Fantasia became an instant success and returned in 2018 and 2019. Amongst the many acts that appeared over those three years were a death-defying springboard act from the Hungarian State Circus; Miss Xsenia, who performed on the low wire; fast action from the four-strong Africa United with their hoop diving, limbo and acrobatics; Professor Wacko, who had appeared on Britain's Got Talent in 2015, with his trampoline act, Miss Anya on the silks and Jidimis, who provided an amazing act of magic and illusion.

There was also the musical dancing water fountains which featured more than 2,000 litres of coloured dancing waters and, as always, the clown. This time, Philip Walker, known as "Phillipo". He used to stand outside before the show enticing customers in and perform the initial warm up, encouraging the audience to react to his "clap", "cheer" and "boo"

The elephants drawing the crowds to the beach.

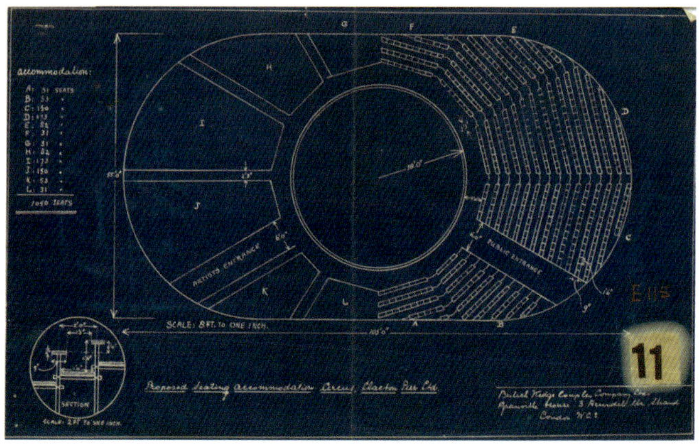

The blueprint for the new indoor circus ring (1938).

cards, using his giant mobile phone. He also performed various acts during the show including a demonstration of unicycling with a young volunteer from the audience on his shoulders and juggling.

Sadly, Circus Fantasia did not return in 2020, bringing to an end the last circus to appear on Clacton Pier.

The new permanent home for the circus being built ready for the 1938 season.

Entrance to the Royal Bengal Circus and Zoo.

The Giovanni Sisters' low wire act in Sally Chipperfield's Circus, 1982. [Photo: Anthony Allston]

Francis McGinty (right) looking a bit apprehensive as he enters the tigers' cage to raise money for charity.

Poster for Circus Fantasia in 2019.

Four very popular Circus Fantasia acts.
1. Philipo with his giant mobile phone.

2. Miss Anya on the silks.

3. The acrobatic team, Africa United.

4. Professor Wacko with his spinning plates.

Chapter Twenty

"If you want a little cheering" The Rambla Concert Party

Clacton-on-Sea had a long tradition of open air concert parties dating back to the 1890s setting up on the beach and on any patches of waste ground they could find around the town itself. The earliest was probably l'Art Minstrels who arrived in 1892. They were followed by groups such as Jack Holland's Concert Party, Braide & Partridge's Minstrels, The Yorkshire Pierrots and the London Concert Company.

As indoor theatres began to grow up in the late 1890s and the early 1900s, these Concert Parties either died out altogether or moved indoors. The London Concert Company for example built a theatre on the West Cliff Gardens, a theatre still open today as the West Cliff Theatre.

One other group was the White Coons, a name we would certainly see as inappropriate these days, who moved into The Pier Pavilion in 1909.

By the 1920s, although some of these concert parties continued in their new theatre homes, the days of the outdoor concert party was over and there were none left in Clacton.

In 1932, with the ever-growing crowds swarming on to The Pier looking for new attractions, Ernest Kingsman hit on the idea of reviving these once popular open-air concert parties and built an outdoor arena next to The Pier Theatre, just beyond the Lifeboat House, with a small stage and alfresco deck chair seating for 200 in front.

He engaged a 31 year old cabaret performer, Rex Deering, to form a company to be called the Rambla Concert Party, frequently referred to as just The Ramblas.

The first season saw 14 artistes taking part in two shows weekdays only, 11:00 a.m. and 3 p.m. Each show lasted about 90 minutes and cost the audience 2d each. As well as producing the show, Deering also took part as one of the players. Others in that first company included the lead comedian,

THE RAMBLAS

(*Under the direction of Rex Deering*).

AT PIER HEAD. Daily at 11 and 3 o clock. Sundays, One Performance Only, at 3.30.

A–Dorothea Harrison
1 Tom Thumb's Drum
2 Getting Sentimental
3 Was That the Human Thing to Do
4 Evening in Caroline
5 Keeping Out of Mischief
6 We'll be Together Again
7 Extra

B–Billy May
1 Snap your fingers, Clap your hands
2 I wanna go home
3 Taking my father's Tea
4 The Boxer
5 I'll have to ask my mother
6 Bertha, the barmaid of the old Brown Bear.
7 Extra

C–Rex Deering
1 Shipmates o' Mine
2 The Trumpeter
3 A Fool and his Follies
4 Lullaby of the Leaves
5 When the Sergeant Major's on Parade
6 For You
7 Extra

D–Tiny Tim Riley
1 Me
2 Blue-eyed Blonde
3 Falling in Love
4 In a little Bungalow
5 My Man
6 She's got that little Something
7 Extra

E–Sheila Crocker Betty George Queenie Walsh in Speciality Dances.

F–The Sunshine Revellers
(Under the Direction of Ernest S. Heather and including Jimmy Barron, Billy Eddas, Geo. Call, Leon West and Tony Wills).
1 Martial Moments
2 Faust Selection
3 Chu Chin Chow, Selection
4 Lustpiel Overture
5 Morning, Noon and Night
6 Indian Love Lyrics
7 Rhapsodic Rose
8 Sailing on the Robert E. Lee
9 Just Friends
10 Whistling Waltz
11 I Know You're Lying
12 Kiss by Kiss
13 You
14 Just Humming Along
15 Somebody Loves You
16 Dream Sweetheart
17 Live, Laugh and Love
18 Lovable
19 I Thank You, Mr. Moon
20 Good Night Vienna
21 Extra

G–Production Items
1 Happy-go-Lucky Days
2 The Three Scamps
3 The Three Jays
4 Beating the Band
5 The Conjurors
6 Parliamentary Speech
7 The Bookmaker
8 Love versus Jazz
9 Buying a Pub
10 Americanisms
11 Charades
12 Musical Wooing
13 Musical Motorist
14 Theatrical Agency
15 Why am I Sad
16 Russian Drama
17 Cherchez la Femme
18 Wanted a Baby
19 Recitations
20 Extra

A Rambla Concert Party programme from their first season, 1932, showing what a typical show consisted of.

Rex Deering, the Ramblas first producer, 1932-1938. Long after leaving the Ramblas, Rex Deering played many roles in television dramas including the Jury Foreman in Crown Court, the Police Sergeant in Crossroads and Bob Eckersley, the Mayor of Weatherfield, in Coronation Street.

Billy May and Dorothea Harrison, the main singer as well as another comedian, Wee George Riley, and the Sunshine Revellers Band under the direction of Ernest S Heather.

The show was a big hit with the public, particularly Billy May, who became a firm favourite with holidaymakers and Clacton residents alike. Deering, May and Harrison all returned the following year, 1933, with a "new" comedian called Tiny Tim Riley, though it is highly likely this was the previous year's Wee George Riley under a different name.

The show was again staged at 11:00 a.m. and 3 p.m., only this year, the advertisements added, "*If wet – performances will be in the Ocean Theatre.*"

1934 saw the three leads return again with yet another new comedian called Sonny Riley. I think we can guess who he was! For the first time, the show was also staged in the evenings in the Jolly Roger Theatre under the title, "The Jolly Revellers". Also for the first time an open-air Sunday show was added at 3:30 p.m.

Deering and May returned in 1935 but a new singer, Madge Villiers, took the place of Dorothea Harrison. There was also a comedian just called Sonny this year as well as a local musician, Fred Walker.

In spite of the fact that the price of admission had gone up to 3d, the show was continuing to draw in large crowds with the local paper, the Clacton Graphic, waxing lyrical about it:

> *Attractions strong from start to end,*
> *To laughter and bright spirits tend –*
> *A jolly, gay enchanting show.*
> *Is there to oust dull care and woe,*
> *So if you want a little cheering*
> *See a production by Rex Deering.*

Rex Deering and Billy May continued to produce and appear in the shows until 1938. In 1939, their places as producer and lead comedian were taken

Billy May, principal comedian with the company, 1932-1938. Billy May was a firm favourite with the audiences.

The Rambla Concert Party and audience, 1936.

The Ramblas on stage in the 1930s.

by one man, Gordon Henson, who was destined to play a major role in The Ramblas after the War.

Henson had formed his own concert party before the First World War called the Barnstormers. During the War, his group were the first entertainers to be sent out to entertain the troops. He spent six years touring the Middle East, visiting 20 countries. On returning, he spent most of his summers touring the seaside summer shows, appearing in the Ocean Revue in 1937.

The Rambla Concert Party did not return immediately after the War and had to wait until 1950, when Gordon Henson got together a new company which included Joan Pendleton, a well-known comedienne, who had had an extensive career in Summer Shows around the country.

The shows began in June and continued the tradition of two outdoors performance per day at 11:00 a.m. and 3:00 p.m. The main difference to pre-War days was that the price of admission had gone up to 6d. Though it has to be said that not everyone paid to see the show as Roger Kennell remembers: *"The open area was surrounded by tall canvas screens fixed to metal uprights. The gap between the edge of the canvas and the stanchion was enough for me as a small boy, to watch some of the show through this gap."*

In all there were five different shows which changed for each performance, so each cycle took 2½ days to complete. In mid-July, the evening show in the Jolly Roger returned, only this time it was called Show Time. There were two different programmes which changed weekly.

Once the Jolly Roger shows started, Gordon Henson always used to finish the Ramblas' shows by thanking the audience and reminding them that the programme changed with each performance and then saying, *"We are here every weekday at 11 and 3, and in the evening, we put on our dinner jackets and play Show Time in the theatre upstairs* (pointing to the Jolly Roger). *If you liked the show tell your friends, if you didn't, tell your enemies!"*

The Ramblas' continued to perform under Gordon Henson's direction and in much the same format for the next 15 years. That is the show would start with a musical introduction and dance number, followed by comedy sketches, songs by the solo singer, the specialty act, magician, juggler, ventriloquist, depending on who it happened to be that year, solo comedy acts and a rousing finale.

There was a rapid turn-over of cast members, with very few staying for more than one year. The only other performer, apart from Henson, who stayed for any length of time was glamorous and vivacious light comedienne, Claire Ruane, who began with the Ramblas in 1956 and appeared every year until 1964 apart from two, 1959 and 1963.

Claire had actually first appeared on Clacton Pier as far back as 1930 in a Sunday Concert in the Ocean Theatre. She was later to go on to appear in a number of television shows including the Benny Hill Show, Larry Grayson and the Marty Feldman Comedy Machine.

Taking the reverse view – looking out to the audience from the stage.

The Ramblas on stage, 1935.

PIER HEAD

COMMENCING 6th JUNE

RAMBLA CONCERT PARTY

Daily

11 a.m. to 12.30 p.m. (Sundays Excepted) 3 p.m. to 4.30 p.m.

ADMISSION INCLUDING DECK CHAIR

6d.

IF WET OR COLD — IN THE JOLLY ROGER THEATRE

Vide Press :

The Rambla Concert Party continues, as it has for so many years now, to provide entertainment at what must be quite unequalled value for money. Is there anywhere else in Britain which provides a pierrot-type show and a deck chair in the sun for sixpence a head ?—*The Stage*, 1959.

A 1960 leaflet advertising the Rambla Concert Party which included a nice complimentary review from The Stage, the theatrical trade paper.

The end for The Ramblas' came at the end of the 1964 season. Clacton Pier was running into financial difficulties and Barney Kingsman was looking to make some cuts. By then, outdoor concert parties had become very much a thing of the past and, in fact, the Ramblas was the last to operate anywhere in the United Kingdom on a regular basis. So, the end when it came was not a complete surprise, but a sad day nevertheless.

A post-War advertising board for the Ramblas, showing the price had gone up to 6d.

The Ramblas Concert Party in 1961. Gordon Henson is on the left and Claire Ruane in the centre.

JOLLY ROGER THEATRE

MRS. E. KINGSMAN
presents
"SHOWTIME"
Devised and Produced by GORDON HENSON

PROGRAMME No. 1

PART ONE

1. SHOWTIME — THE COMPANY SAYS "HELLO"
2. PRESENTS — THE COMPANY
3. GUESS WHAT — THE COMPANY
4. SINGING FOR YOU — SHIRLEY GREEN
5. DEAR CLAIRE — GORDON & CLAIRE
6. STEPPING OUT — CHRIS MELVILLE
7. A DOGGY STORY
   - ARTHUR ... ... GORDON HENSON
   - ANNIE ... ... CLAIRE RUANE
   - VICAR ... ... JOHN FREDERICO
   - MOTHER-IN-LAW ... ... CHRIS MELVILLE
8. THE MAGIC MAN — JOHNNY HART
9. OLD TIME MUSIC HALL "AT ENORMOUS EXPENSE" — THE COMPANY

INTERVAL

PROGRAMME No. 1

PART TWO

10. FOUR BOYS AND A PIANO
11. LOTS OF HONEY — GORDON, JOHN & ALAN
12. OUR IRRESISTIBLE COMEDIENNE — CLAIRE RUANE
13. SONGS YOU LOVE — ALAN MACK
14. THE Z RAY
    - DOCTOR ... ... JOHN FREDERICO
    - NURSE ... ... CHRIS MELVILLE
    - LOVER ... ... GORDON HENSON
    - 1st PATIENT ... ... CLAIRE RUANE
    - 2nd PATIENT ... ... ALAN MACK
    - 3rd PATIENT ... ... HAROLD BURBAGE
    - 4th PATIENT ... ... SHIRLEY GREEN
15. VIBRAHARP VIRTUOSO — JOHN FREDERICO
16. JOLAES PUPPETS with DENNIS THE MENACE
17. AT THE ELECTRONIC ORGAN — HAROLD BURBAGE
18. HE'S AT IT AGAIN — GORDON HENSON
19. GO-TIME FOR SHOWTIME — THE COMPANY

GOD SAVE THE QUEEN

Scenery Painted by: DAVID CHAPPELL
Wardrobe Supervisor: DORIS SUMNER

The Management reserve the right to alter or omit any item or artiste

Programme no.1 from the 1961 season. That year the specialty act was Jolaes Puppets.

The Ramblas final year, 1964, with, once again, Gordon Henson on the left and Claire Ruane in the centre. By the time of their final year, Gordon Henson had been associated with the Ramblas for a quarter of a century.

Chapter Twenty One: The Kingsman Family

Ernest Kingsman

Ernest and Ada Kingsman.

Ernest Kingsman was born in Newington, South London, in 1870. He originally trained as an architect but, by the turn of the century, had tuned his hand to property development specialising in the leisure industry and by the time of the Great War, owned a number of hotels in East Anglia. This led him to buy a large tract of coastland near Lowestoft with the idea of building a racecourse to tie in with the Yarmouth races, making a kind of "Suffolk Fortnight." However, the local churches objected and it was never built.

Too old to be called up for military service during the War, he nevertheless volunteered to serve with the British Red Cross in France, but his managerial abilities were quickly recognised and he was appointed by the British Army to look after the welfare of wounded and former soldiers. His involvement in this work and with the YMCA and how this led him and his family to own Clacton Pier is detailed at the beginning of Chapter Three.

Throughout his whole life and particularly once he took on Clacton Pier, he was a man of vision and forethought with a never ending stream of ideas. Although many of his ideas were to turn Clacton Pier into a world-beating amusement and entertainment centre, not all his ideas came to fruition. Two of his biggest fell by the wayside.

The first came in 1925, when he proposed a new pavilion for The Pier. This was designed to completely transform the front of The Pier and create a multi-purpose building stretching 200 feet along The Pier. On the ground floor this was to include at the front a new "Continental Café" and at the rear a "Palais de Dance" to replace the Blue Lagoon, both designed to give a continental flavour, while above there was to be a reading and writing room together with balconies for promenading.

His other proposed project was not on The Pier but designed for the centre of Clacton itself. In 1937 he designed a modern holiday/hotel camp to accommodate 5,200 visitors, comprising of ten 520 room hotels, each with their own kitchens, tennis courts and gardens with common theatres, dance halls, swimming pools and sports facilities including tennis courts, bowling greens, gymnasiums, miniature golf courses and billiards and snooker rooms. Its precise proposed location in Clacton was never revealed and, of course, it never got built; Butlin's opening the following year instead.

Ernest and Barney Kingsman, both wearing the trademark Kingsman beret.

One of Ernest's plans which did come to fruition was his idea of building a home for himself and his family on The Pier itself. As part of his improvements to the frontage in 1938 he had built an extension of glass bricks that stretched right above the turnstiles and nearly across the whole breadth of The Pier to include his new home. His 5 rooms faced inland so he could watch the visitors arriving.

One end his gallery overlooked the ballroom where in the mornings, the show-girls practised their routines whilst at the other end his flat overlooked his circus.

Sadly, there wasn't much room for Mr Kingsman's favourite Dutch oil paintings of farmyard poultry but he did manage to hang two on the wall in his office.

During the Summer, he lived with his family in this flat, but spent the winter in the family villa in Villefranche in the South of France.

He was a great supporter of local organisations, in particular sports clubs and donated many trophies which bore his name. His other great passion was supporting Clacton Hospital. Two events in particular, a dance in the Blue Lagoon and a fireworks display, were held annually with all the proceeds going to the hospital. Each year they raised something in excess of £25 (getting on for £2,000 in today's money). He also donated an ambulance to the Clacton-on-Sea St John Ambulance Division out of his own money.

Ernest sadly died on 6 November 1942 while staying at the Royal Forest Hotel in Chingford and was buried in the Kingsman family grave in Norwood, South London.

Ada Kingsman

Ada Kingsman's role in turning an almost derelict pier into one of the leading amusement and entertainment centres in the whole of the United Kingdom and with it making Clacton-on-Sea itself one of the most visited seaside resorts in the country, worthy of comparison with places like Blackpool and Brighton, is often played down but she really deserves an equal place in Clacton Pier's history along with Ernest.

Ada was born in 1869 in Holloway, London. In 1895, she married a farmer, Edward Garnham, in Surrey. In the 1911 census, Ada is shown as the manageress of the Grand Hotel in Penmaenmawr, North Wales, where "widower" Ernest Kingsman and his son, Herbert, are also shown to be staying. Ernest is

Ernest's proposed new Pavilion on The Pier (1925).

described as an architect. Sadly, Edward Garnham died in 1914,

In 1917, Ada and Ernest married and from then on Ada became involved with all Ernest's business ventures. When Ernest, Ada and Herbert came to Clacton they brought with them, Ada's niece, Hilda, who was treated as an adopted daughter and took an active part in the management of The Pier.

Ada's role in managing Clacton Pier cannot be overestimated. Although there is no doubt that Ernest was the ideas man but he needed Ada, who was a very astute businesswoman, to turn them into reality. In fact, at least three of the major innovations on The Pier were Ada's "babies".

The first was the Laguna Belle, which she ran almost as her own personal project. She would often take a trip on it to make sure everything was as it should be. On one occasion she decided to sample the food being served up on board and sat down at one of the tables in the dining room. She was horrified to see the table cloth was stained, so she called the waiter over to complain and demanded he lay a new tablecloth. The waiter was very offhand with her and dismissed her complaint, saying, "*Who do you think you are, the owner?*" Ada replied, "*As a matter of fact I am and you're fired!*"

Another of her special projects was the Ocean Theatre, which she ran as her own and took careful interest in the acts to make sure there was no bad language or innuendo which could offend family audiences. If a comedian overstepped the mark, they'd receive one warning and any more they'd be sacked whoever they were.

The third was the Blue Lagoon, which as far as she was concerned was for ballroom dancing. She certainly did not approve of the 1930s fad of Jitterbugging and had a notice put up in the Blue Lagoon ballroom saying "No Jitterbugging" and she told the band leader, Teddy Dobbs, that if he saw anyone jitterbugging, he was to stop the music and warn the couple with expulsion from the floor and

Ernest Kingsman with his car at the front of The Pier.

Ernest (left) taking a ride on the dodgems with Pier manager, Leonard Tomlinson, who later married Hilda Bowerman.

resume playing slow music. She was also known to get down on her hands and knees to scrub the floors herself.

She was also not afraid of anyone, whoever they were. For example, when John Pybus, the local M.P. and Minister for Transport, came to open the swimming pool, she thought his speech was going on too long, so she leaned across to him and said, "*Can you hurry up, we've got a swimming gala to get through.*"

Another famous personality to fall foul of her tongue was Billy Butlin. In the 1920s and 30s, some of the rides were let out as concessions. One concessionaire was Billy Butlin. At the time, before he opened his holiday camps, Billy Butlin was a well-known fairground operator in his own right. When he took on some of the rides at The Pier, he decided to dress the staff operating his rides in his red and white uniform (like the later redcoats). Ada was not impressed. She told him that they were not his rides; they were The Pier's and he was just being allowed to operate them and told him to remove the uniforms. Butlin meekly complied. It has been said that Ada Kingsman was the only person ever to get the better of Billy Butlin!

In 1950, the well-known actor, Ian Carmichael, produced a show called Lagoon Follies at the Jolly Roger. In his autobiography, he had this to say about Ada:

"[Clacton Pier] was the property of an indomitable, elderly power-house of a lady called Mrs Kingsman. Her son was her henchman and adjutant but, make no mistake, Mrs Kingsman was the one in charge and the sight of her small dowdy figure – which was to be seen daily, walking stick in hand, hobbling up and down her domain – disguised the authority of an admiral bestriding the bridge of his battleship.

"When we opened Lagoon Follies, she sought me out on the morning of our first night to enquire exactly what time our curtain would come down. Her concern was not for us or anything to do with the show, it was purely so that she could issue concise instructions to her son which would ensure

The Pier Entrance after the extensive 1938 building works showing the Kingsmans' flat going across the entrance.

An architect's drawing of one of the hotels for Ernest's proposed new holiday camp in Clacton.

that the public lavatories would not be locked up until 20 minutes after the theatre had been emptied. She was a remarkable lady."

In spite of her formidable and no-nonsense presence, she was in private a very compassionate and generous woman. She involved herself in many of Clacton's charities. She was president of the local branch of the Soldiers', Sailors' and Airmen's Families Association, Clacton Swimming Club and Clacton Sea Angling Club and strongly connected with the St John Ambulance and the Lifeboat.

Ada remained a director of Clacton Pier until her death at her home in St Paul's Road, Clacton, on 29 July 1963 at the grand old age of 95.

Barney Kingman

Ernest Kingsman's son, Herbert Ernest (known to everyone as Barney) was born on 9 January 1901. His mother was Ada Caroline Dean, who died when Barney was just seven years old. He was appointed a director of Clacton Pier in 1922 along with his father and adopted mother.

Just like his parents, he played a very active part in all The Pier's activities and, when Ernest died in 1942, stepped up to become the public face of Clacton Pier. After the War, he became a very well-known Clacton personality never seen out in public without his beret on.

Like both his father and step-mother, he was very active in local charities, including the RNLI, Clacton Operatic Society and Clacton Sea Angling Club. At one time he was also president of Clacton Swimming Club, Clacton Amateur Dramatic Society and St John Ambulance.

But his real passion outside The Pier was for his cars. He was a founder member of the Clacton Motor Car and Motorcycle Club in the early 1920s. His pride and joy was his 1924 Rocket Schneider. During the Second World War it was kept in the Kingsman's villa in the South of France. A German officer billeted there would not allow anyone to touch it. Barney still had the car in the 1970s when it still passed its M.O.T. every year.

He also had a Mercedes. In the winter, he used to whizz up and down The Pier as fast as he could, doing a 180° turn at the end. For some reason he also used to like reversing it along the front of The Pier, on one occasion smashing into the front and

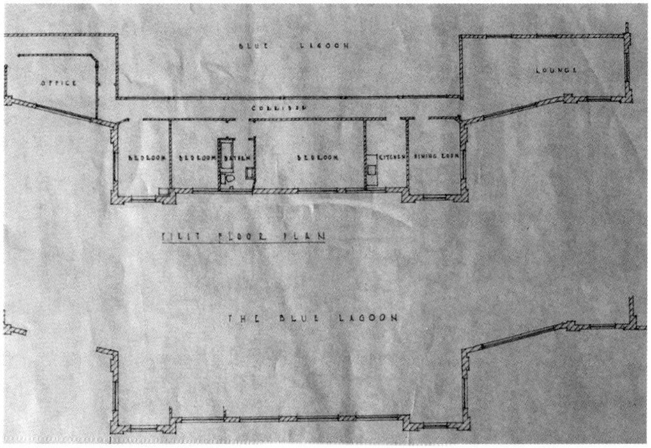

A plan of the Kingsmans' flat above the Blue Lagoon.

bringing the glass frontage down on top of him and his car.

He also used to go out to the car park at the front of The Pier dressed in his shirt sleeves, making sure the cars were parked properly. Visitors used to think he was the car park attendant. Sometimes while he was there he might notice that the traffic lights at the top of Pier Gap had packed up. On those occasions he would go up to Marine Parade and direct the traffic.

Barney continued to lead an active life after retirement from The Pier. His last public engagement as President of Clacton St John Ambulance coming only three months before his death at his home in St Paul's Road at the age of 76.

Hilda Bowerman

Hilda Bowerman was Ada's niece, the daughter of her brother, James. Hilda lived with the Kingsmans for many years and became to all intents and purposes their adopted daughter, even to the extent of changing her name to Hilda Ivy Kingsman.

In 1946, Hilda married Leonard Tomlinson, a senior manager at The Pier.

When Ada died, she left 50% of her shares in Clacton Pier to Barney and 50% to Hilda, so Hilda and Barney became joint owners of Clacton Pier.

Hilda was very much a behind-the-scenes director concerned with the financial side of the operation, though she could often be seen in the kiosk in the Ocean Theatre, selling sweets, chocolates and ice creams before each performance.

She died in 1990 at the age of 85.

Susan and Peter Kingsman

Susan and Peter were Barney's two children, both born in the 1940s. They have many good memories of being brought up in a home actually on Clacton Pier. Here are a few of those memories:

Susan: *"All our birthday parties were held in the Blue Lagoon; sometimes, grandmother [Ada] would arrange for the Carnival Queen to visit. After tea*

Ada leading the passengers off the Laguna Belle's maiden voyage.

The "No Jitterbugging" sign that Ada had posted on the Blue Lagoon Dance Hall.

we might go and see the Rambla Concert Party, in reserved seats of course!

At other times, Mum would take us to meet Dad for afternoon tea in the Blue Lagoon. Sometimes, a World Champion ballroom dancer would be giving demonstrations there and Dad would ask him to give me a whirl round the floor. It was divine.

I used to enter the Fancy Dress competitions held in the Blue Lagoon. It was a bit unfair really because we used to go and borrow costumes from that year's Ocean Revue. They were wonderful costumes but a bit uncomfortable. I usually won! Peter only entered once. That year we went as Claire Ruane and Gordon Henson, the two stars of the Rambla Concert Party.

Another thing I can remember is watching Freddie & The Dreamers performing in the Blue Lagoon from our flat. That must have been in 1964.

During the winter, Peter and I used to have the place pretty much to ourselves apart from the workmen as that was when The Pier went through its annual maintenance and decoration with all the decking under The Pier being replaced. I used to love skating on the skating rink Dad had built on The Pier."

Peter: *"Sue and I used to spend a lot of time in the Swimming Pool. In fact, much of our growing up was done there. When I passed my swimming exams, Dad paid for a coachload of my school friends to a party on The Pier.*

I can remember the year the Ramblas closed [1964], I went up to help sort out all the costumes and bring them back from the Jolly Roger.

The one thing I didn't like was the Steel Stella. I took a ride on it once, went green and never went back again!

But all in all, I loved growing up on Clacton Pier. It was great and I feel Sue and I had a very privileged upbringing as everything centred around The Pier. What youngster wouldn't have loved that sort of life?"

Ada ready to "pounce" on John Pybus C.B.E., M.P., for going on too long!

Ada Kingsman at 80 in 1950.

Barney Kingsman with Canadian Olympic champion, Pete Dejardins by the swimming pool in 1936.

Barney Kingsman in his beloved 1924 Rocket Schneider.

Hilda Bowerman on the balcony of the Kingsmans' villa in Villefranche with Ada and Ernest Kingsman.

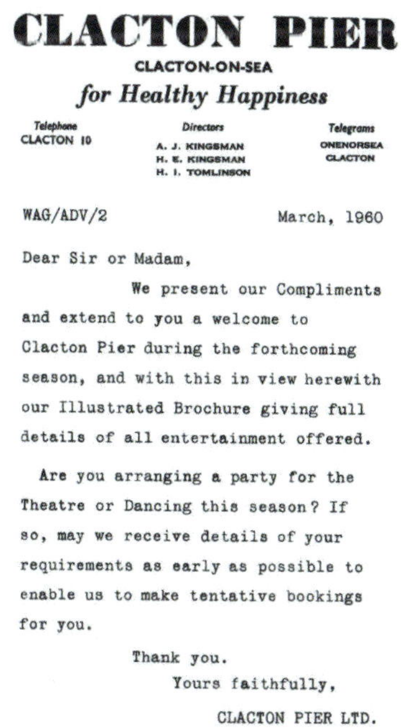

CLACTON PIER

CLACTON-ON-SEA

for Healthy Happiness

Telephone	Directors	Telegrams
CLACTON 10	A. J. KINGSMAN H. E. KINGSMAN H. I. TOMLINSON	ONENORSEA CLACTON

WAG/ADV/2 March, 1960

Dear Sir or Madam,

We present our Compliments and extend to you a welcome to Clacton Pier during the forthcoming season, and with this in view herewith our Illustrated Brochure giving full details of all entertainment offered.

Are you arranging a party for the Theatre or Dancing this season? If so, may we receive details of your requirements as early as possible to enable us to make tentative bookings for you.

Thank you.

Yours faithfully,

CLACTON PIER LTD.

Clacton Pier headed notepaper from 1960 showing Ada, Barney and Hilda as the three directors.

Chapter Twenty Two

North Sea World, the Dolphinarium and Aquarium

There is evidence of sea lion shows being held on The Pier as far back as the 1920s and certainly they were included in the Circus and Zoo that were held on The Pier in the late 1930s, but it wasn't until 1971 that a Dolphinarium was established.

It was created by Reg Bloom, an old school friend of Michael Goss, who had spent his whole life working with animals going back to the 1940s when he was living in East Africa catching, collecting and transporting mammals, birds and reptiles back to zoos in Europe and America. After marrying Margaret in 1948, the pair of them were responsible for pioneering techniques for the care and husbandry of wild animals brought into human care.

Some ten years later, they returned to England, where Reg entered the Zoo world as the Curator of Chester Zoo, later becoming a full partner in the building and opening of Twycross Zoo before opening Windsor Safari Park for the Smart family. As a result of all this, Reg became involved in bringing many of the first dolphins and killer whales to this country.

Reg Bloom shakes hands with one of his charges.

Having converted the swimming pool to take sea mammals, Goss and Bloom arranged to bring over two dolphins, Bubble and Squeak, from America, but their shipment was delayed and so the honour of the first dolphin to "*educate and entertain*" the public on Clacton Pier went to Maria, who was imported from Malta. She arrived with two sea lions, Adolph and Sallar.

An early advert for the Dolphinarium showing the title, North Sea World Training School.

At first it was just a training facility going by the name of "North Sea World Training School" which allowed people to watch. But, as Reg Bloom later explained, "*The people kept coming in and we suddenly realised lots of people were waiting in great queues to come in. So we decided to put on proper training shows and charged half a crown. It was a great success and we did very well.*" Maria gave five public performances a day each lasting 45 minutes, with Reg and his assistant, Paulette.

Towards the end of that first season, Bubble and Squeak finally arrived. So now, with the three dolphins and two sea lions proving to be very popular, a decision was made to keep North Sea World open during the winter as an aquarium. Consequently, in October 1971, workmen set about covering the heated area of the pool. Following on from that, new building took place over the winter to create a Dolphinarium in what had been the deep end of the swimming pool.

Everything was now ready for the opening of the Dolphinarium at the start of the 1972 Summer

Paulette with Maria in 1971.

Bubble and Squeak with Reg Bloom.

Season, allowing the dolphins and sea lions to show what they had learnt, in proper shows. In between shows, Reg and Paulette continued to teach them tricks and keep them active but Reg admitted the dolphins taught them as much as they taught the dolphins!

Reg told Martin Allen in an interview some time later that "*Squeak was a little terror and on training would play up and not do as she was told some of the time as she always wanted to do things her own way, trying different ways of doing things. She loved playing football in the pool.*"

In 1973, North Sea World gained a new attraction, when six Humbolt penguins were introduced with a special pool being built for them. A bit later on, some of the penguins took part in a TV advert of the time.

Over the years, more sea lions were added included Anna, Kojak, Marcus, Bimbo and Barney. Anna was noted for being able to balance a ball on a pole on her nose, so much so that, in April 1975, she appeared on television's talent show, Opportunity Knocks.

There was more good news for the marine life in the Dolphinarium in 1975 when it was announced in May that Squeak was pregnant.

The first two sealions on The Pier, Adolf and Sallar, doing a bit of promotional work for the Goss Family who owned a scales company.

A bad storm in January 1978 caused a lot of damage to the Dolphinarium and all the animals had to be evacuated. Nevertheless, it was ready to open for the 1978 season. But there was some very sad news in August that year, when it was announced that Bubble had died after swallowing a child's toy windmill that had been thrown into the pool. For some time afterwards, Squeak was too ill to perform as she was pining after her partner. A vet thought she might even die as she was not eating either.

To try and help the situation, Reg Bloom brought in a new companion for her, a killer whale called Suzi Wong. At first, it seemed to make little difference

A Pier poster advertising the fact that the Dolphinarium was open all year round.

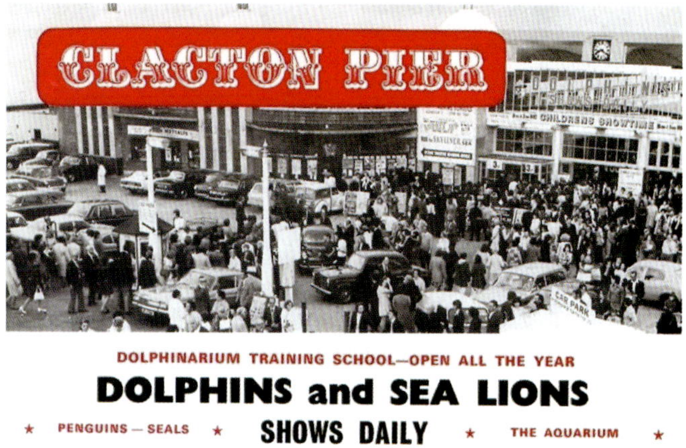

The Dolphinarium became the star attraction on The Pier. This is an advertising poster dated 1973.

to Squeak, but, after a while, she perked up a bit and started eating and was able to take part in the shows again.

Another bad storm hit The Pier in January 1979. Once again all the sea life had to be evacuated, with Suzi Wong and the dolphins being removed to other parks, never to return to The Pier. This time the damage had been even more severe and the Dolphinarium was not ready to open again until 1981.

When Francis McGinty and his consortium took over The Pier, Reg Bloom was still in charge of the Dolphinarium and the shows.

By then, there was also an aquarium, run by David Mallet, located in what was the former Ladies' changing rooms for the swimming pool. The walk through was just black walls with the fish tanks inset into the wall.

However, the biggest change to the Dolphinarium came in 1981, when three killer whales were introduced to the pool. On lease from International American Exchange, an American firm of animal brokers, who had saved them from an Icelandic

And this shows the prominence given to it at the front of The Pier in 1976.

cull, they were flown in in November to get them acclimatised ready for the 1982 season. The lease stipulated that they would remain on The Pier for two years, as it was felt that, by then, they would have grown too big for the pool.

McGinty announced a competition for children to name the whales with free day passes to The Pier as a prize for those choosing the winning names.

The Dolphinarium was also perfect for photo opportunities for the Ocean Theatre's visiting stars. This photograph shows Rod Hull with Emu meeting Reg Bloom and one of the dolphins.

Sadly, just one week later, the smallest of the whales died. McGinty explained that, *"The whales were playing and rushing around but the large one was too boisterous with the small one. It was a one-in-a-million accident."*

It wasn't just The Pier as Clacton itself advertised the Dolphinarium as one of its main attractions. This is the front cover of a Tendring Guide Book from 1975.

The death of this killer whale on Clacton Pier however landed The Pier in the centre of a big controversy as the international conservation organisation, Greenpeace, launched an immediate campaign to "Free The Clacton Two", organising newspaper campaigns, petitions and even a march through Clacton. They argued that *"from the day that three wild killer whales arrived at Clacton they were sentenced to spend the rest of their lives in an artificial and alien environment, imprisoned*

And, of course, many Clacton postcards were issued featuring the dolphins.

The first six Humbolt penguins attracting an audience of children.

in a disused swimming pool." On behalf of The Pier, Francis McGinty argued that if they hadn't agreed to buy these three killer whales they would already be dead as they were saved from the Icelandic cull.

While this was going on, the two remaining whales were named Nemo and Neptune and remained in the Dolphinarium. However, 18 months later, Neptune died of peritonitis, giving fresh impetus to the Greenpeace protest now renamed "Free The Clacton One" and they campaigned to raise enough money to buy Nemo, so he could be returned to the sea.

By the beginning of Summer 1985, it was three and a half years after Nemo's arrival rather than the two years originally agreed and Francis McGinty was getting very concerned that Nemo was growing far too big for the pool and on 14 June, it was reported that negotiations were well underway to move Nemo to Windsor Safari Park, to a pool that was much larger than the one on Clacton Pier.

Eventually, the great day came and Nemo was due to be transported to Windsor on 21 June. However there was a slight hitch as part of the crane used to lift Nemo out of the pool crashed through the boards near The Pier Entrance and it took some considerable time to be able to free the crane and move it out of the way, so it wasn't actually until the following day, 22 June, that Nemo finally left Clacton Pier for his new home in Windsor Safari Park. His trainer, Peter Bloom, Reg's son, went with him and stayed for a few days to help him settle into his new surroundings.

With the departure of Nemo, the Dolphinarium was converted back into a swimming pool, with just a small area remaining for the sea lion shows.

Meanwhile, the aquarium had been given a major face lift which, although it kept the original water tanks, was transformed into the wooden interior of a sunken galleon. Mostly done with cement art (rockart) creating false timber ships ribs between the tanks, with new lighting and soundtrack to create the feeling you were in a shipwreck under the sea.

The first killer whale, Suzi Wong, playing in the pool.

Some of the 1978 storm damage to the Dolphinarium.

After the Fun Lido was closed a new aquarium was built on the open deck at the diving board end. The main steel work of the building used a number of the old water slides' structural columns for the vertical supports with the main lattice roof trusses being from the Jolly Roger's first floor after they were removed to accommodate the Circus.

When this was completed the old aquarium was turned into a storage and kitchen area for the Sea Lion shows that had by now moved up to the shallow end of the pool.

The three killer whales who arrived in 1981, Nemo, Neptune and one unnamed.

A rock cave entrance was also added with a new rock art façade to add a bit of a themed interest. This brought the entrance up into the main thoroughfare of The Pier rather than through the old entrance which was tucked down the back (the old exit to the swimming pool).

With the whole area being given this further face-lift it was renamed "The Living Ocean". The advertisement for it exhorted people to

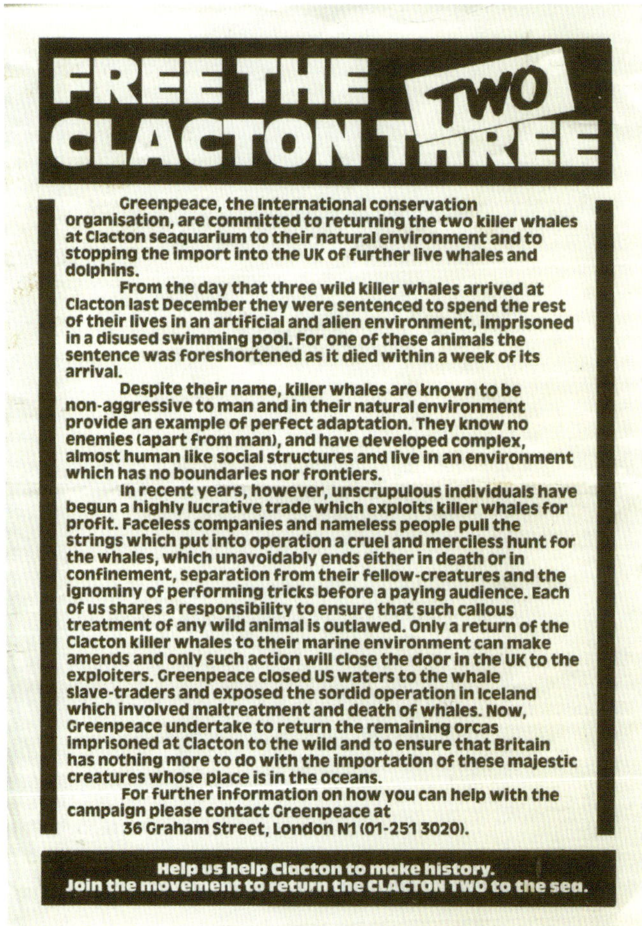

FREE THE CLACTON ~~THREE~~ TWO

Greenpeace, the International conservation organisation, are committed to returning the two killer whales at Clacton seaquarium to their natural environment and to stopping the import into the UK of further live whales and dolphins.

From the day that three wild killer whales arrived at Clacton last December they were sentenced to spend the rest of their lives in an artificial and alien environment, imprisoned in a disused swimming pool. For one of these animals the sentence was foreshortened as it died within a week of its arrival.

Despite their name, killer whales are known to be non-aggressive to man and in their natural environment provide an example of perfect adaptation. They know no enemies (apart from man), and have developed complex, almost human like social structures and live in an environment which has no boundaries nor frontiers.

In recent years, however, unscrupulous individuals have begun a highly lucrative trade which exploits killer whales for profit. Faceless companies and nameless people pull the strings which put into operation a cruel and merciless hunt for the whales, which unavoidably ends either in death or in confinement, separation from their fellow-creatures and the ignominy of performing tricks before a paying audience. Each of us shares a responsibility to ensure that such callous treatment of any wild animal is outlawed. Only a return of the Clacton killer whales to their marine environment can make amends and only such action will close the door in the UK to the exploiters. Greenpeace closed US waters to the whale slave-traders and exposed the sordid operation in Iceland which involved maltreatment and death of whales. Now, Greenpeace undertake to return the remaining orcas imprisoned at Clacton to the wild and to ensure that Britain has nothing more to do with the importation of these majestic creatures whose place is in the oceans.

For further information on how you can help with the campaign please contact Greenpeace at
36 Graham Street, London N1 (01-251 3020).

Help us help Clacton to make history.
Join the movement to return the CLACTON TWO to the sea.

The Greenpeace leaflet campaigning to "Free The Clacton Two".

Peter Bloom with Nemo shortly before his removal from The Pier.

"Come with us on a journey through time back to the creation of Earth onward to the land of dinosaurs through the Tree of Life until the present day.

Then journey to the bottom of the Ocean to the Sea-Lab with only a sheet of glass between you and the perils of the deep.

Watch the ballet of huge rays glide past you. Are there sharks lurking in wait?

Emerging from the Sea-Lab enter the Aquarium section, and browse amongst the different aquaria with the tide pool rhythmically washing the beach or the touch pool where you can really get to know the fish. Be amused and amazed by the antics of the Sea Lions."

The Living Ocean remained until 1995 as did the sea lions. Following the 1995 season, the new Pier owners, the Harrisons, leased the Aquarium to Joe Larter, a well-known name in the East Anglia leisure industry as the developer of Pleasurewood

Nemo being made ready for transportation to Windsor Safari Park.

Hills amongst a number of other enterprises. Larter immediately improved the entrance area and the tanks ready to relaunch The Living Ocean as Seaquarium. In 1997, a new "Live Reptile Safari" feature was added. In 2002, it was announced that a new Tropical Fish Aquarium would be located in the Seaquarium.

When present owners, Billy and Elliot Ball, took over in 2009 they kept the Seaquarium, announcing in 2015 that they had made *"huge improvements to enhance visibility and the quality of the fish tanks"* as well as making progress in *"theming the environment."*

At the time of writing the Seaquarium is still a major attraction on Clacton Pier which, as well as being a tourist attraction, also lays on educational visits for schools and environmental groups.

Inside the Aquarium.

Two sealions taking part in a show on their stage.

A poster advertising the sealion shows.

The former sealion stage in 1995 just after their live shows came to an end and demolition of the area began.

Joe Larter acquires the lease to the Aquarium and renames it Seaquarium. L-r: Joe Larter, Ted Harrison, Rob Hicks, the new manager of Sequarium.

Steve Mallett, pictured at the entrance to the new Reptile Safari after Joe Larter had added the fibreglass reptile on the roof.

A leaflet advertising the new Seaquarium.

Beginning the work of refurbishing the Seaquarium.

The entrance to the Seaquarium in 2010 after Billy and Eliot Ball had taken over. [Photo: Anthony Allston]

The Ball Brothers announce "Exciting Plans" for the development of the Seaquarium.

Chapter Twenty Three: The night the Steel Stella caught fire

At 9 p.m. on 4 August 1973, Pat Mooney was performing his solo spot during that evening's showing of The Comedians at the Ocean Theatre to an audience of approximately 300, when a pier worker ran on to the stage, grabbed the microphone from Pat Mooney's hands and calmly announced, *"Don't panic, The Pier's on fire!"*

In his autobiography, Comedian Jim Bowen describes what happened next, *"The whole audience replied as one, 'Aaaaaagh!'. The man in green overalls said, 'There's no need to rush. Please don't rush. Don't fight to get out. Please stay calm, ladies and gentlemen.' But it was too late because 1,200 limbs were already flying in every direction.... Jimmy Marshall, who had just bought a new car, was first out of the stage door with the words, 'Where's my Bentley!?' and he moved along The Pier very purposefully in order to rescue his vehicle."*

Jim added, ruefully, *"We were sick because we had missed the opportunity to work to a proper audience* [this had been their biggest audience all season] *and there was absolutely no chance of getting them back in the theatre. If only we could have led them out in an orderly fashion and then marched them back when the all-clear was given, perhaps even picked up a few more on the way. As it was, we had little choice but to watch our potentially record-breaking audience queue up to get a refund."*

Jim Bowen mentions the fact that the audience were *"flying out in every direction"*, but others

The beginnings of the Steel Stella in 1937.

The Steel Stella in its heyday.

remember it differently. David Woods said, *"I noticed comedian Jim Bowen standing at the back helping the usherettes show people out. It was all done so quietly. There was no sign of panic"* In all approximately 3,000 people were evacuated from

The iconic view of the Steel Stella from the beach and prom

The Pier before the Clacton, Frinton and Weeley fire services turned up to put the fire out.

The following day, the Sunday Mirror, in its front page article, reported that *"Jimmy [Marshall] and colleagues Jim Bowen and Pat Mooney, with dancers in mauve hot-pants and knee-length boots, helped old women and children from the theatre as holiday-makers and staff threw buckets of water over the blazing roller coaster."*

As for the Steel Stella itself, Martin Allen explains what happened on his dolphin-art.co.uk website: *"Pier worker Neal Rowland scrambled up in vain in an attempt to contain the fire. Pier staff quickly got the people off as it was just loading up for the next ride, they then alerted The Pier manager, Joe Rose, to call the fire brigade. Quick-thinking staff got on to the roof of the Ocean Theatre to damp it down to prevent the fire from spreading as there was a lot of sparks and hot ash blowing about.*

"Neal and his workmate, Andrew Jardine, helped run the hoses across the theatre roof as the fire engines had to stay in the car park at the front of The Pier in case the weight of them went through The Pier boards. Unfortunately, the fire hoses couldn't reach the heart of the fire in the engine room so all they could do was dampen the ride and surrounding area down to stop it spreading to the rest of The Pier.

"Pier staff had formed a bucket chain from the dolphinarium to the fire, their fire fighting attempts were seen as playtime by the dolphins as they dipped the buckets in for water, Bubble and Squeak even

The fire in full swing. Neal Rowland can just be seen on the right scrambling up in a vain attempt to contain the fire.

playfully grabbed some of the buckets and swam off with them. A number of the buckets were recovered from the bottom of the pool the next morning. All the staff involved that night got a free meal in the canteen as a thank you for saving the rest of The Pier from going up in flames. Two gangs of staff were formed shortly after, armed with chainsaws and spanners to make the roller coaster area safe."

Sunday Mirror
5p August 5 1973 No. 537
ANOTHER HOLIDAY FIRE
CLACTON PIER DRAMA

How the news of the fire was reported in the national press the following day.

The fire naturally was a great spectacle that could be seen all around Clacton and many people came down to The Pier to get a closer look from Marine Parade with the Venetian Bridge being a particularly well sought after vantage point. One person who stopped to witness the fire was Michael O'Grady, who said, *"I was out for a walk and saw flames coming from the switchback, which is about half way along The Pier. The flames were about 20 feet high."* Even those who had been in the Ocean Theatre and on The Pier stayed around to have a look.

The burnt-out gate house.

Some of the damage to the structure.

FRIDAY, DECEMBER 14 1973 4p

GOING... GOING... GONE

STEEL STELLA, that screamy attraction that has drawn thousands of holidaymakers onto Clacton pier each season went out with a bang last week when demolition men pulled down the last section of the fire-damaged structure.

For 36 years the roller ride has given thrills to youngsters — and the dads. But on August 4 an electrical fault started a fire in the top section and though the damage was limited it spelled the end of Steel Stella.

The holiday maker of 1974 will be offered new thrills which should be taking shape in the New Year. Planning permission had been given before the fire to dismantle the ride and erect brand new rides.

All the wood salvaged from Steel Stella has been given away as firewood — and many a local resident will look into his fire this Christmas and see a landmark go up in smoke.

Photos: ROY MULLEN

The final demolition of the Steel Stella as reported in the East Essex Gazette on 14 December 1973.

Reg Young, who was at the show that night with his family, remembers going up to the Prom after evacuation and staying on to watch.

Afterwards, Michael Goss praised the public for their swift and orderly exit as well as The Pier staff, saying, *"There is no doubt that The Pier firefighting staff prevented what might have been a serious fire."*

It was later discovered that the fire had been caused by an electrical fault in the junction box on the west side gate house that housed the electrical machinery and was fanned by a good stiff westerly breeze. Although the structure that held up the track was made of steel scaffolding poles, the track itself was made primarily of wood so the fire quickly took hold. An Essex Fire Brigade official commented, *"A section of the railway track was severely damaged by fire. No-one was injured."*

The task of dismantling what was left of the Steel Stella began in November 1973 and was completed in December, so that no trace of The Pier's former crowning glory remained. The wood from the Steel Stella was placed outside the entrance of The Pier and offered as firewood free to the public. Jon Salisbury remembers that his dad *"made several trips to collect pieces, which we used to replace our collapsing garden fence. It survived until the bottom of the garden was sold to a developer in the early 2000s."*

Chapter Twenty Four

A Day in the Life of a Summer Pier Worker

Robert Gunthorpe worked on Clacton Pier for three seasons in the early 1990s. Here he gives an insight into what life was like for the ride staff at that time.

The outside of the Jolly Roger restaurant.

"Ride staff would arrive at work about an hour before The Pier opened to the public. We'd spend the first half an hour mopping down all the rides and public areas, clearing away any rubbish into dustbin bags. After that we would all head up to the Jolly Roger restaurant for breakfast and a cup of tea. All the food and drink outlets on The Pier had a reduced price for staff, plus you could 'get it on tick' which invariably made a painful dent in your pay-packet at the end of the week.

Just before opening time we'd all walk down to the front office and consult the ride sheet which would be pinned to a notice board: it would tell you what ride you'd be working that day. Once you knew your ride you'd collect your ticket box from the ticket office and head to your ride. You'd do a quick safety test which for most rides involved starting the ride, doing an emergency stop and then resetting it. Then you'd be ready to meet the public.

The days would pass pretty quickly at the height of summer as the stream of holidaymakers was relentless until around an hour before closing. You dealt with a LOT of people. Rainy days were the worst, especially if you were working on a ride all on your own, sat in a (cold) wooden box for hours with nothing much happening.

At the end of the day 'last rides' would be called over the tannoy and if no one was on your ride that meant switching it off and making your way to the front of The Pier with your ticket box. After that it was often a quick trip to a local pub with the other ride staff or home.

Go Gator

Without a shadow of a doubt, Go Gator was the very worst ride to work on. Universally hated by ride staff (and even a lot of the customers), working on it felt like a punishment.

It was the first ride name that you'd look at on the ride sheet for that day and pray your name was not written next to it. If you saw your name next to Go Gator your heart sank because you knew the pain you were in for. Your ride staff brethren would 'sympathetically' clap you on the back like a condemned man, laughing and chanting "Go-ch-go, ch-ch-ch-ch, Go-Gator!"

Being outside, Go Gator was always either too hot or too wet but with no real shelter or seating. You had to stand all day long on a narrow platform; It was a very noisy ride too. The customer access platform was a shiny metal floor that banged and crashed like so many cymbals as people got on and off and it reflected the sun and heat into your eyes all day long.

Aimed at younger children, it was surprisingly fast and a bit too 'lurchy' for many who would often end up in floods of tears. You could usually tell just by looking at the kids (and their overenthusiastic parents) which ones were going to cry or be sick or attempt to stand up while the ride was moving. The biggest red flag was parents (usually Dads) who would insist: "Oh he'll be alright!"

Imagine working on that having been at Oscars the night before..."

Some of the rides Robert would have worked on in the area vacated by the Whirlwind Including in the foreground, the 'Big Jets' and the figure of eight coaster 'Sprinter'. Behind the 'Big Jets' is the 'Red Barons' and behind that is the 'Helicopters'. On the left, the steps to the 'Speedway' can just be made out. In the background, on the site of the old Ocean Theatre and Ghost safari is 'Harrison's Kiddies Corner', which consisted of coin operated children's rides.

The dreaded Go Gator!

Chapter Twenty Five

"Lasers visible for miles" Memories of Oscars

One of Clacton Pier's biggest successes in recent years was undoubtedly Oscars, the nightclub near the entrance. Opened in the Summer of 1983, it lasted for 16 years and played host to some of the top DJs, bands and solo artists.

Amongst those who appeared there were Blur, The Prodigy, Boy George, Shades of Rhythm, Matt Lucas, Steve Wright, Micky Finn, Fabio and, of course, Oscars' very own Busta Brooker.

It was voted amongst the top three nightclubs in Britain for several years running by Radio 1 listeners.

Once inside, Oscars was a dark, sweaty and extremely loud affair with artists like Slipmatt and Ratpack playing jungle and hardcore. Some might call it intimidating. The bass bins would rattle the air in your chest and blow the sweat off your skin.

On these pages are some memories of Oscars in words and pictures finishing with an image of Blur performing live on 17 September 1995.

Oscars was a pretty big deal on the dance music scene back in the day. Big acts like The Prodigy played there and people would come from all over the country. The queues would sometimes stretch up the hill under the Venetian Bridge.

Sometimes Oscars would be open all night until 6am. I once vividly remember stepping outside (topless) into the cool summer morning air with sweat rising like steam off my skin.

It was a formative experience for most people that braved it. Robert Gunthorpe

I loved Friday nights there. There was always a top rave DJ in the house back in the 90s. Andy Sage

I was at the very last night of Oscars when Ratpack performed. Also used to go to Baby Oscars on a Thursday night (under 16s) late eighties/early nineties. Good times. Nicola Jane Jones

They used to have rather nice moulded pint glasses when they first opened. They disappeared so quickly that they couldn't keep up with demand as they were being taken as soon as they were filled. Nick Beales

I missed The Prodigy and Shades of Rhythm as was only 14 in 91/92 but we used to go to under 18 Oscars on a Thursday night. Or 'Kiddies Oscars' as we called it. First time I heard 'Your Love' by The Prodigy was in there, on the springy dance floor. Ian McKeown

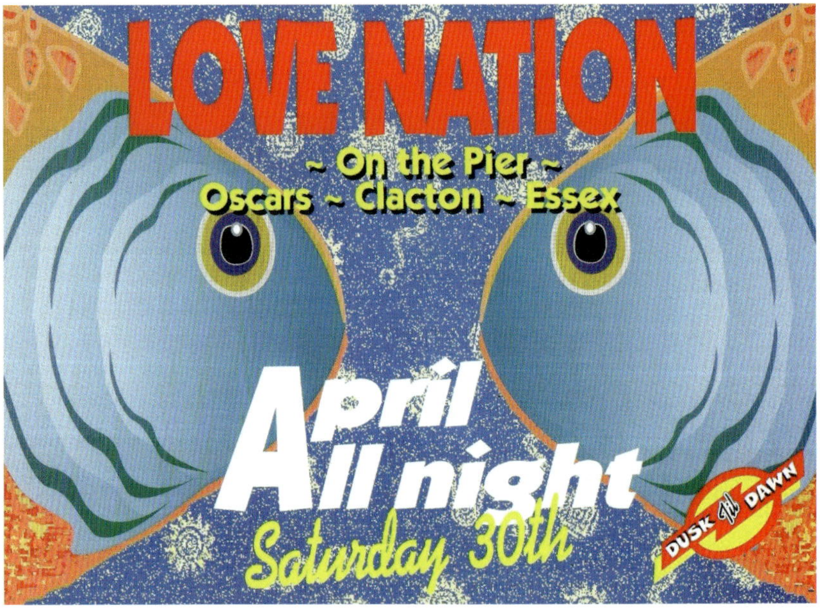

The most famous [nightclub] in Clacton was the original 1980s Oscars with the lasers outside that were visible for miles. Andrew Polson

I worked in Oscars when it first opened as a waitress then a glass collector. My mum, Carol Wood, worked on the bar and my grandmother's best friend, Dot, cooked the hot food. Busta was the first DJ and most of the doormen were lovely and made sure I was always safe working. Jacs O'leary-Papworth

I definitely miss the Oscars days. I started going to Oscars in the 1980s when I worked at the poolside diner for Sylvie and Francis McGinty, and when it changed from the soul nights to the rave scene in the late 80s/early 90s. Pippa Hook

I remember Oscars from 1984, fancy dress on Boxing Night, Cockney Pride and champagne bar. Great times. Then going to the all-nighters in the mid 90s. Michelle Hickson

I remember going to see radio DJ, Steve Wright, and on another occasion being photographed by somebody from the Clacton Gazette while dancing and the photo being plastered on the centre page in an article about local night clubs. Eddie Sheffield.

I think I spent most my time doing the Running Man on the stage or on the bouncy spot. Sometimes I'd just camp in front of a speaker and lose myself in the music I remember Red Stripe being served, greatest beer ever. Oh, Oscars, I miss you so much. Best vibes ever!!!! Mathew Seymour

And the final word:

If you can remember anything from those nights you probably weren't there!
Marcus Free

The last night of Oscars before it was turned into a Ghost Train was 11 September 1999. Epidemik were the promoters (Grant and Sean it was back in those days but it's just Grant now). The last DJ to play in the main arena was Ray Keith. I know because I was the last but one DJ to play that night.
Rob Guymer

Chapter Twenty Six

The Ball Family

Billy and Elliot's grandfather, William Alfred Ball (Billy), moved to Clacton with his wife, Ivy, and two children, Monya and Billy jnr, in 1946. They had family who were connected with Billy Butlin and so had gained the opportunity to rent some space to operate their fairground games, a small arcade and a children's ride on the Butlin's Camp in the town.

Alfred Ball (great great grandfather of Billy and Elliot) is pictured on the left in top hat and tails, and his son William Ball 1st is pictured on the right steps in three piece suit.

The family's heritage went back several generations in the fairground industry as travelling showmen, a term used for the community of people who were born into the fairground way of life. Showmen are the people who generally own the rides and attractions at a fairground and the whole family usually play their part in the family business.

Billy Snr's grandfather and father, Alfred and William Ball, had travelled the country with various forms of entertainment including the Joywheel, an early type of ride; the New Lyceum Show complete with dancers and music from a fairground organ; his famous Bioscope, an early form of cinema and a Boxing Booth, where he and his employees would fight for prize money. In fact, Alf was at one time a champion bare knuckle fighter and even had a pet lion that he would take into the ring and playfight with. Ivy's family had similar roots in the industry and so it is perhaps easy to see that this is an industry that is very much in the blood.

With the couple having moved to Clacton for the summer season they were able to give their children a regular education with summer spent in school in Clacton and then Winters back in Enfield when the holiday camp was closed. Billy Butlin often offered business opportunities to showpeople, and so provided space opposite the park for the numerous living wagons that were home to the show families. Today this land is occupied by the Marina Court flats development.

The Harrisons and the Balls. Top left Ted Harrison, Top Right Mable Harrison, bottom left Ivy Ball, bottom right Billy Ball Snr.

It was while the Balls were at Butlin's that Billy Snr became friends with Ted Harrison Snr and the close relationship between the families continues from 1946 right through to the present day. It is strange to think that both families would eventually end up with periods of ownership of the famous pier only a short walk away.

By 1954, the Balls had bought a home in the town and settled in the area permanently. This allowed Billy Snr to look for new business opportunities. In the same year he did a deal with the O'Dell family to set up an amusement offering at their Seawick Holiday Park in St Osyth. The family operated their amusement, bingo and rides business at Seawick for over 60 years before consolidating their operation to focus on The Pier. As his son, Billy Jnr, came of age he further embellished and added to the operation at Seawick and also purchased and developed similar amusement facilities in Jaywick, Walton, Ipswich and, more recently, Pier Avenue, Clacton.

The Balls always had an interest in Clacton Pier and the current generation, Billy and Elliot, were no exception, they went there as children and always enjoyed their visits. Although not all visits were for fun, sometimes it was for business when their dad bought and sold rides with pier owners. They also had extended family that had business interests in The Pier in the 80s and early 90s and would spend time with their parents, visiting friends and family who worked there. Billy can remember being outside in a pushchair with his dad at a very young age and having a photo with one of the seafront monkeys!

Billy and his dad with The Pier Billy was later to own in the background.

The children's carousel owned and operated by the Ball family at the Clacton Butlin's camp.

The industry was Billy's main pastime as a boy and he spent many hours with his father, going along with him to work whenever possible and it was the main topic of discussion at the meal table. With so many friends and family in the same industry and with the same roots it was hard not to be interested.

Elliot, who was three years his junior, was really into sport and was often to be found in the garden with a ball, whether it was football, golf or tennis. Although he too was expected to help in the family business and spent many summer holidays looking after the small coin operated cars mainly at the family's Seawick site.

The brothers are the first to admit that the Harrisons did them a great favour in helping them when they bought The Pier off them. It was financially a tall order, but the two families worked together to make it happen, and in the end it led to the best outcome for both sides.

"From there we relied on the reputations that both our grandfathers and father had in the industry. We were fortunate to be able to strike deals with our suppliers, who thankfully had confidence in us and gave 12 months free credit on new arcade equipment to get things up and running," said Elliot.

"Without those we may never have had the success that we have enjoyed over the past 13 years. There is a huge thanks owed to the Harrisons', financiers and suppliers that we had been dealing with for three generations.

Following the purchase, the brothers were able to bring their ideas and passion to the table, along with sheer hard work and graft. They also had the extensive family experience to draw on. Billy said, *"The industry is in our blood and although taking on The Pier was a massive step up it was a challenge that we relished."*

The purchase was really a natural progression from their existing business. Their knowledge of amusement arcades, which are often a main contributor of income for a seaside pier, meant they understood the first rung of the ladder well. As far as the rides went, their mother Lynn's family had been in the business at Codona's in Aberdeen since the 1970s, and, for many generations before, on the fairground circuit as one of Scotland's best-known operators.

"We have been lucky to have had lots of experience around and about us to call on, we even have relations who owned piers, such as dad's first cousin, Stanley Threadwell, who is succeeded by his family in the business" added Billy. *"It is wonderful to share a common interest and to be able to share information relevant to The Pier."*

The brothers were dealt a major blow in 2012 when their father, William Ball 3rd, passed away. However, it also provided a motivation. Throughout his illness the brothers wanted to achieve as much as possible while he was still alive. To them, it was all about a family legacy which they wanted to maintain and embellish.

Sadly, during that winter of 2021, Billy and Elliot's mother, Lynn, also passed away while visiting relatives in Scotland.

Lynn had always been there, supporting first her husband and then her boys in whatever they did. She had shown a keen interest in the family business all her life and was always there with plenty of encouragement and reassurance.

"We often popped round for a meal she had made for us when we were up against it and she helped us maintain our sanity through the difficult times," said Billy and Elliot.

"Mum was often on The Pier working in various departments and did so right up until she died. She was a real character, was known by all the staff and turned up with treats to force feed them, whether they liked it or not!

"She provided another pair of eyes and ears for us when she was there and just like dad, is sorely missed."

Billy and Elliot are very proud of Clacton Pier's long history. They feel very fortunate to have the opportunity of being The Pier's current custodians. With only around 50 piers left in the UK they see it as both an honour and huge responsibility. They feel piers are a British institution that must be preserved for future generations to enjoy.

"We are always looking to invoke the past with a modern twist," said Billy. *"The number of piers has halved over the past 100 years and there are good reasons why the ones that survive are still here and that's diversity from other offerings in the modern world. It's a technological world and we embrace that, but our attractions have never been more*

The mini-jets at the Balls' Seawick Park concession, later sold by Billy jr. to The Pier in the early 1980s.

prevalent. It is more important than ever that families and friends can spend quality time together to get away from the distractions of modern life".

"Our pier offers a good clean and active day out, families interact together, make great memories away from screens, smart phones and social media. We truly believe a day at The Pier positively helps with visitors' welfare and well-being.

"At the same time there has never been more competition for the secondary spend so you have to get the whole experience just right."

There were many ups and downs over their first 13 years and there was constantly the financial struggle they had always anticipated. Clacton Pier has never stood still – and it never will while Billy and Elliot have anything to do with it.

The brothers drive to continue to develop the business is very much in honour of their mum and dad and that will never diminish.